FROM MACON TO JACKSONVILLE

MORE CONVERSATIONS IN SOUTHERN ROCK

MUSIC AND THE AMERICAN SOUTH

Praise for From Macon to Jacksonville

Since I started reading Buffalo's latest book, I can't seem to get anything done. I can't put it down. *From Macon to Jacksonville* is full of life stories straight from the mouths of your favorite Southern Rockers.

—Paul Hornsby, producer and musician
at Muscadine Studios, Macon, Georgia

Once again, as in his critically acclaimed *Capricorn Rising*, Michael Buffalo Smith captures the true essence of Southern Rock in this new book, *From Macon to Jacksonville*. A great read!

—Willie Perkins, author and former
tour manager for The Allman Brothers Band

Michael Buffalo Smith has been a long-time friend, and I can say unequivocally that he has more knowledge of the history of Southern Rock than anyone I know.

—Chuck Leavell, pianist/keyboardist for
The Rolling Stones, The Allman
Brothers Band, and Sea Level

Michael Buffalo Smith is truly the "keeper of the flame!" He has always honored the great Southern way to play and has presented us players, writers, and fans in an honest (warts and all) loving and human way. I was so honored to have been chosen to grace the second ever hard-copy cover of *Gritz* magazine! Thanks Michael. As the late, great Gregg Allman always put it: "Don't forget to boogie, baby!"

—Bonnie Bramlett, songwriter/recording artist;
co-leader of Delaney & Bonnie & Friends

Michael Buffalo Smith writes of what he knows and what he loves; those who share in that love him.

—Henry Paul, singer/songwriter;
and member of Outlaws

Michael Buffalo Smith was a highly respected friend of my brother, Tommy Crain. He is a good man and a straight shooter.

—Billy Crain, songwriter/musician; and member
of the Henry Paul Band and Outlaws

Michael Buffalo Smith is one of the biggest Southern music followers and supporters. As a writer, musician, and publisher, he has dedicated his life to promoting this music. Michael was my favorite interviewer—one reason is because he has great knowledge of the subject. His two latest books are *From Macon to Jacksonville* and *Capricorn Rising*, and I highly recommend both if you have an interest in music from the South.

—Alan Walden, former manager of Lynyrd Skynyrd
and Outlaws; 2003 Inductee,
Georgia Music Hall of Fame

MERCER UNIVERSITY

MERCER UNIVERSITY PRESS

Endowed by

TOM WATSON BROWN

and

THE WATSON-BROWN FOUNDATION, INC.

FROM MACON TO JACKSONVILLE

MORE CONVERSATIONS IN SOUTHERN ROCK

Michael Buffalo Smith

MERCER UNIVERSITY PRESS | MACON, GEORGIA

2018

MUP/ P570

Published by Mercer University Press
1501 Mercer University Drive
Macon, Georgia 31207

9 8 7 6 5 4 3 2 1

Books published by Mercer University Press are printed on acid-free paper that meets the requirements of the American National Standard for Information Sciences—Permanence of Paper for Printed Library Materials.

Regarding photos: Every effort was made to recognize the original photographer of each image used herein. Because many of them were given to us for use in *GRITZ* or *Kudzoo* magazines, many are listed as "file photos." I want to thank everyone for the use of their images in helping to illustrate the interviews included.

Printed and bound in the United States.

This book is set in Adobe Caslon

ISBN 978-0-88146-668-3
Cataloging-in-Publication Data is available from the Library of Congress

In Loving Memory of Absent Friends…

Gregg Allman

Col. Bruce Hampton

Butch Trucks

Johnny Sandlin

Dave Hlubek

Our most recent losses within the family.

Special thanks to: God, my family, the gang at Mercer University Press, all of my interview subjects over the past twenty-five-plus years, Dave Shuping at Spartanburg Methodist College, Hilda Morrow, Greg Loescher (former editor of Goldmine magazine), Billy Bob Thornton, The Boxmasters, Paul Hornsby, Craig Stephens, Charlie Daniels, Billy Eli, Tom Coerver, James Calemine, Colleen Knights, Laura and Steve Flacy and Zack Tomco, Joey Parrish, Bruce Wall, Tom Clarke, Hal and Tonya Stewart, Rebyll, Scott Greene, The Allman Brothers Band Big House and Museum, Bob Nosbisch, Krazy Kenny Mullins, Tim Shook, Dr. Lori Malvern, Dr. Paul Ross, and Dr. Nick McLane.

And to my biggest influences: Hunter S. Thompson, Lester Bangs, Cameron Crowe, Larry Brown, Pat Conroy, and Stephen King.

And a huge thank you to every one of you who has supported my writing and is reading this now.

Contents

The Interviews

Foreword

I'm not sure that I could be considered an authority on the music and musicians contained in this book. I was born three months after the release of *Second Helping* by Lynyrd Skynyrd, so I wasn't there to experience the "hey day" of these bands firsthand. However, like many, I have devoured this music and the details about its creation and creators like an addict from my childhood years to this very day. I will assume everyone who reads this book understands exactly what I mean. This music was never intended to be casual listening. These bands made albums, not pop singles. They weren't flashy dressing prima donnas and they didn't seem to be concerned with following any musical trend. They most definitely set their own…

With this book, the great Michael Buffalo Smith focuses on the like-minded musicians and bands that followed in the wake of the Allman Brothers Band and Capricorn Records. From Jacksonville, Florida to Spartanburg, South Carolina, over to Nashville, Tennessee and just about everywhere in between, these artists worked with various record labels who started to recognize that there was something to these Southern bands making this amazing music.

I've been asked how I would define "Southern Rock" more times than I can count on both hands and feet. I dare say that is impossible to do. You could say it's guitar driven music, but look at Wet Willie, they had a fine guitarist in Rick Hirsch, but that band was obviously led by a harmonica and sax blowing soul man, Jimmy Hall. You could say it's all down home, back porch kind of music, but Blackfoot were heavier than some of the British heavy metal bands they toured with in the early 80s. You could say it's all big, loud swinging blues, but the Marshall Tucker Band and Charlie Daniels band could "out country" most country bands. You get the point, which is, each of those bands have their own fingerprint and the "box" that the industry decided to throw them all into. That box should've been a whole lot bigger…maybe the size of an ark. The only answer that I can ever come up with if pressed, is all these bands actually do seem to have one thing in common…musical freedom.

Enjoy.

Charlie Starr, Blackberry Smoke

Lynyrd Skynyrd, early promo photo.

Courtesy MCA Records

Gary Rossington on the Simple Man Cruise.

Photo by Julia LaRue

Artimus Pyle, 2017.

Photo by Tom Bell

Randall Hall (left) plays alongside Ed King in the Lynyrd Skynyrd Tribute band, 1987.

Courtesy Randall Hall

Ed King.

Gritz Magazine, *courtesy Ed King*

The Lynyrd Skynyrd Honkettes:
Cassie Gaines, Leslie Hawkins and Jo Jo Billingsley.

Courtesy MCA Records

Charlie Daniels jams at the Angelus event in Tampa, 2017.

Author's collection

Mike Estes.

Courtesy Mike Estes

Rickey Medlocke greets fan and photographer Tom Bell
on the Simple Man Cruise.

Photo by Julia LaRue

Donnie and Johnny Van Zant pose with photographer Julia LaRue.

Photo by Tom Bell

Dale Krantz burning up the stage with the Rossington Collins Band.

Gritz Magazine, *courtesy Dale Krantz Rossington*

Rickey Medlocke rocks with Lynyrd Skynyrd
on the Simple Man Cruise.

Photo by Julia LaRue

Blackfoot: Greg T. Walker, Charlie Hargrett,
Jakson Spires, and Rickey Medlocke.

Courtesy Atco Records Photo

Jakson "Thunderfoot' Spires.

Courtesy Jakson Spires

Greg T. Walker.

Photo by X. Caupenne

Dave Hlubek having fun with Doug Gray during Marshall Tucker's Late Night Jam on the Rock Legends Cruise

Photo by Tom Bell

Danny Joe Brown of Molly Hatchet.

Gritz Magazine, *courtesy Danny Joe Brown*

Molly Hatchet.

Courtesy Epic Record

Dave Hlubek taking a break with the author during one of his Molly Hatchet outdoor shows.

Author's collection

Molly Hatchet at Greenville Memorial Auditorium, South Carolina, 1980.

Photo by Lynn Armonaitis Photo

Don Barnes of 38 Special rips it up on his Gibson.

Photo by Isaac Rodriguez

Doc Holliday.

Courtesy Bruce Brookshire

Chris Hicks.

Photo by Jack Benas

Dennis Winters back in the day.

Photo by Tony Busco

John Galvin of Molly Hatchet, 2015.

Photo by Tom Bell

Henry Paul of The Outlaws
performing at the annual Angelus event in Tampa.

Author's collection

Willie Perkins (left) with Red Dog Campbell.

Courtesy Red Dog

Col. Bruce Hampton at the Allman Brothers Big House.

David Peck Photo, Maconga City Limits

The original Gov't Mule: Matt Abts,
Warren Haynes, and Allen Woody.

Photo by Kirk West

Charlie Starr of Blackberry Smoke.

Author's collection

Introduction

I had no way of knowing. These small events can happen in our lives that really don't seem like anything much at the time, but then they end up completely changing our world. Such was the case with me, back in 1972. I was a freshman at James F. Byrnes High School in Duncan, South Carolina, and one day I caught a group of guys gathered around one of those school phonographs, the kind that had the built-in speakers. The sound coming from that corner of the room reeled me in like a bass on a fishing line. I stood with the other guys, tapping my foot and doing the "head bob" to the beat of a song called "Whippin' Post." The album was called *At Fillmore East*, and the band was the Allman Brothers Band. I was caught, hook, line, and sinker.

Thus began my Southern-rock education. I had never seen a double-album where two of the four sides contained only a single song. I quickly learned the Southern rockers like to jam and many of their songs are way too long ever to be released as singles. It was all about the jam, the groove. It was the best of blues and rock blended with a bit of jazz and a whole lot of soul. It was my kind of music.

I would become a huge fan of Capricorn Records in Macon, Georgia, and all of the bands that were signed by that label. Those are the bands that were featured in the book prior to this one, *Capricorn Rising: Conversations in Southern Rock*.

Of course, at the same time all of this musical magic was transpiring in Macon, Florida was bursting at the seams with great Southern-rock bands. Led by the absolutely legendary Lynyrd Skynyrd, Florida gave us the Outlaws, Blackfoot, 38 Special, and Molly Hatchet, among many others. These are some of the artists covered in the book you now hold in your hands.

These interviews were conducted between 1998 and 2017. Close to 20 years' worth. We cherry-picked what we felt were the best interviews from those years. You'll notice a few artists that fall into the Macon, or Georgia, category as well, including a fun interview I had with the late Red Dog Campbell about life as perhaps the most popular "roadie" of all time. And there's one of several highly entertaining interviews I conducted with the late great Col. Bruce Hampton, and an interview with a man I consider to be the torchbearer of Southern rock, Charlie Starr of Blackberry Smoke.

I genuinely hope you enjoy the stories told by these great artists as much as I did. This is true Southern history. This is Southern rock. Now bring all my mules out here and kick 'em one time!

—Michael Buffalo Smith, Spartanburg, South Carolina

Gary Rossington

2003

Although they live right down the road in Atlanta, we somehow ended up speaking to Lynyrd Skynyrd's Gary and Dale Rossington from the road in Glasgow, Scotland, for our 2002 cover story in GRITZ *magazine. Go figure. The guys seemed to be missing home, especially the South, quite badly. They were touring in support of a new album,* Vicious Cycle.

Gary: Where are you at, Michael?

MBS: I'm in Greenville, South Carolina.

Yeah. Wow. I wish I was there. I'm over here in Glasgow, Scotland. It sure isn't America. I love America. We've been coming here since the seventies. The first time we came it was cool to be in England and all that because we were big Beatles fans, and all those other European groups, just like everybody our age at that time. When Beatlemania hit, England was cool, and to come over was great. But once you've done it, you know, you've done it. And America is so much better. You learn to appreciate things, even little things like ice. They don't put ice in their drinks here. And they don't have butter. They don't use condiments very much. You have to ask for every little thing. It's funny. We're all Southerners, and when we get tea, the glass is full of ice with some tea in it. Over here you ask for ice and they'll put one or two cubes in it. It's crazy. Still, it's a great place. We love it here. It's just different, you know?

All the reviews and fan comments on the Web regarding *Vicious Cycle* call it one of Skynyrd's best records in years. What do you feel makes this one so special?

I think on this particular album we just tried real hard. We took three years to do it. Not intentionally, but, we were touring and doing projects. We were always writing and working on it. As a matter of fact, Leon [Wilkeson] is on it. He had started the record with us, and after he passed away we decided we needed to use at least a couple of songs with Leon on 'em. Because it was *him*, and there's a million reasons to do it. We just redid "The Way" and "Lucky Man" and kept his bass parts and played to them. The writing was different. We wrote with a few different people to get a fresh feeling and have a little bit of a newness. We tried to make the songs more—I can't say "like Skynyrd," because we *are* Skynyrd—but just more our style. We tried real hard, and I think it shows.

"Red, White, and Blue" is getting played on radio a lot. How does that make you feel?

Oh, it's a great feeling. We haven't had a song on the charts in a long, long time. (Laughs) "Sweet Home Alabama" and all of those get played a lot on the classic rock stations, but we haven't had a *new* song played in a while. And the song, to me, is just about us and our fans. It's all about what's happening. It's been 30 years since our first album, and we're all getting more grey or white hair, we're all working, and most of our fans down South have a little bit of a redneck in 'em, whether they admit it or not. (Laughs) And a lot of them will admit it right out, too! But we just wanted to say we're proud to be Americans. After 9/11, everybody started writing about it, but the song is really about us, and our fans, you know.

You had Kid Rock on the album on a very different version of "Gimmie Back My Bullets." How did that happen?

We just ended up just being friends with him. Through the years, when we played with ZZ Top and some other bands, he'd come out. And we'd go to some of his shows when we were close enough. He ain't as crazy as everybody thinks. He puts on a little front there. And sitting in a hotel room with a guitar, we just sat around and played a bunch of old Merle Haggard tunes, and Hank, Jr., and Hank Williams, we played a lot of country tunes. We talked about old-style music and what it's all come around to, including rap. What he's doing. But he does it all. He does rap, rock, blah, blah. He just puts it all together in one song. He's a good guy. On that particular song, Rickey Medlocke just thought of a song that we could do that would have a little bit of a rap feel and a new kind of energy. Rickey put it together and sent it up to Kid Rock who has a studio at his house in Detroit. He just sang it a few times and sent it back to us to mix it. So, it's Johnny singing and Kid Rock. And at the very end, some of the ad-libs are Ronnie. So, it's Ronnie, Johnny, and Kid Rock on it. It's pretty cool, you know.

I have read on the Internet about a few people complaining about Kid being allowed to redo a classic like "Bullets," and I have said more than once, I may be wrong but I feel like if Ronnie were alive, he'd like Kid Rock.

Yeah, I know he would, because I knew Ronnie so well. Ronnie loved country music and Merle Haggard and stuff like that, and so does Kid Rock—he loves every kind of music. They would have gotten along and been friends, 'cause they are both just down-to-earth guys when it comes right down to it. Besides, Ronnie was a songwriter. He'd like for his songs to be heard. And the biggest compliment you can give a songwriter is to play his song, you know? I'm sure he'd be pleased with it.

Everyone was very concerned when we heard about your recent heart problems and surgery. How are you feeling now?

I appreciate that. I feel pretty good, but I'm a little weak. I don't have as much stamina as I did have. I kind of wear out easy. I'm sure in a few months I'll be healed up and be fine. But right now, I feel good, and the shows are going good, and the traveling is not too bad or hard like I thought it would be. Everything's working out real great. I had some great doctors there in Atlanta, great nurses. And I went to cardio rehab after the operation and they get you back in shape. It's pretty neat. I went there for a month. They say it usually takes six months to a year to get over open-heart surgery, but I feel really good, and I just thank the Lord every day for letting me live some more on this great planet, living and seeing things going on around me. It's great. I've got a little pond out in my backyard, and every time I catch a little fish, or see my daughters, or have a good meal, or watch the sun set out there on the lake, I just thank God for it. Every little thing you just appreciate, you know?

Boy, do I. Since you are in the middle of a European tour, I wanted to ask how you find the audiences over there, and are there any favorite places you like to visit while in Europe?

We come here every few years. I love Japan myself, but I love Scotland and Ireland. We were in Ireland yesterday. One of Dale's parents is from there, so she was real excited seeing her homeland and all. It's really pretty over here. It's great. We're touring with Deep Purple, and they're real big. They have a big following here.

Is Steve Morse still with them?

Steve is. He's great. We see him every day. He's not from here, of course. He's an ol' Southern boy. It's good to have an American around us with them guys, too. But it's going well, the shows are pretty much sold out, and you can already see the fans singing the words to the new songs. And nobody's walkin' out or leavin' when we start up on a new song, which is good. (Laughs) It's like American audiences, they just come to rock and roll. We played Germany at the beginning of the tour, and they can't understand you. Johnny would be standing there saying all his little things he says between songs, and they don't understand a word. It's funny. He'll realize that after about thirty seconds of talking, and he'll just say, "Oh, the hell with it, you can't understand me anyway." But if he says the name of the song, they'll cheer.

After thirty years, what would you say have been some of the high points in your career thus far?

To me, it was me and Allen and Ronnie had this dream to make it big, and we were gonna try to make it until we died. That dream came true for us. I remember us three talking about it on the way back from England the first time, "We did it," you know? That and playing with the Rolling Stones, and meeting Paul McCartney and John Lennon out in L.A. The people that you get to meet in this business that you never dreamed you'd meet. I met Jack Nicholson over in England at Knebworth, and we sat there in the dressing room and talked. Met a lot of big movie stars. A lot of people come to rock shows you wouldn't think would. Some of my favorite people are the athletes. Ryan Klesko and John Rocker and Randy Johnson—a lot of football and baseball players—Doug Flutey. They always have free passes because they play at all the big stadiums, and they're big shots in their towns. (Laughs) It's fun to meet them, because I'm a big football and baseball fan. I watch every game of football, and I'm a big Braves fan. I like to watch the teams that I know somebody on. Those have been my highlights, and also doing some charities where people thanked you, or you knew it really helped some people out. A lot of people come up and say how much a song meant when they played it at their brother's funeral, or some people just got married and they played "Free Bird" or something, and they get excited telling you about what the song means to them. Things like that.

"Free Bird" must be one of the most played songs in history. But a song like that just seems to always hold up.

I love playing it. It's kind of like an anthem these days. Everybody knows it and wants to hear it, but my feeling is everybody has a certain time in their life when they heard that song a lot. Something was going on that they remember, and they relate to it. People have said, "Man, we used to dance to 'Free Bird' in high school. That's how I met my wife." Everybody's got stories, there's good and bad stories about it. Not just "Free Bird," but certain other songs. And that's a great feeling to know a song touched somebody that way, a song that you wrote or helped write. Telling some kid to just be a "simple man," or telling him to just do the right things, and it's a great life, you know?

Everybody knows that Lynyrd Skynyrd has had quite a few deaths in the family, and I just want to get you to tell us the first thing that pops into your mind when I mention each of these individuals. Starting with Ronnie Van Zant.

First of all, he was like my best friend. We went bass fishing all the time together, and camping and doing things outside. We were teenagers doing things like that. I don't remember any of the bad things or any of the bullshit things or the business stuff. I remember playing live onstage with him. It was always great. He was a great guy and great fun to be with, and I miss him a lot.

How about Allen Collins?

Allen was crazy. You know how you have certain people in your life that you consider your best friend—well he was one, too. We were like the three musketeers at one time. And then we were the two musketeers. (Laughs) And now, I guess, the one. But he was crazy. I don't mean "crazy" crazy, but crazy for life. He loved life and loved doing anything he wanted to do, and would do it in a big flamboyant way. If he wanted to buy a car, he'd get the biggest and best, the most flashy and coolest car. He'd get the best. He was just a flashy kind of guy. When he played the guitar, he was exciting and flashy. He just had a lot of "rambunction" in him. I loved and miss him a lot, too. Both of them were great guys.

How about the brother and sister, Steve and Cassie Gaines?

They weren't around as long as the other guys because we had just met them a few years before, so I don't have as many stories. I just know they were great people, and they had a lot of stories themselves. Cassie Gaines was in the original cast of the musical *Hair*, which was the biggest play happening at the time. That was a big thing for her to have done. She was just so nice. She was like a big sister. She was a few years older than us, and kind of took care of us and helped us through little dumb things and little brotherly things. She'd sew a button on your coat or your shirt. She was just a great girl. And Steve—at that particular time, in bands, you buddy up with certain people at certain times for a while, and then you buddy up with another guy, and then another guy. At that time, I was buddying up with Steve a lot. He was a great, kind guy. Very natural, into nature. I loved and miss him a lot, too.

And most recently we lost Leon Wilkeson.

Yeah, Leon. He was just such a nice guy. So down to earth. Leon was just Leon. He did so many funny things. We used to call him "Leon Spillkerson," because he always spilled his coffee. Or his Coke or drink. He was always doing so many things at one time, it caused him to spill things. And every time he came in or out of a room something would get knocked over. He was so funny. Out on the road, one of us would hear something fall or something and we'd say, "There's Leon!" (Laughs) He used to always press the alarm or bell buttons on the elevator—they're emergency alarms really, you're not supposed to touch them—but every elevator he'd ever get into, he'd push those buttons. So, you could always tell Leon was coming by the bells ringing. Now, sometimes elevators would stop when you did that. He'd do that and we'd get mad at him. But he was just a great guy. He was amazing. I really miss him a lot. His loss is still fresh in our hearts, you know.

Definitely. I want to talk about guitars for a minute. Who influenced you most as a guitarist?

We were kind of British influenced, you know, by the Beatles and the Rolling Stones, Cream, the Yardbirds, the Animals—all that kind of scene came out, and that's what really got us. Then when I started really playing and trying to learn, it was Duane Allman. Duane and Jimi Hendrix, Eric Clapton—all the great blues cats. And Muddy Waters and B.B. King we started listening to a lot. We put all those together and kind of came up with our style. Allen and I would listen to those records and figure out leads and jam to them, get 'em in our head. All those guys were just so great. Of course, all the old British-invasion bands. Every one of those bands were our influences.

What are your favorite guitars? I know you play an SG.

Yeah, I play a Gibson SG. I always play it on "Free Bird." I always played the slide part on that and still do today. Basically, I play a Gibson Les Paul. And recently they gave me a special-edition signature model. They make it like mine, an old '59 reissue. They redid that, and they sell those. They did that for Duane [Allman], too, and a lot of other folks as well. They put out this one with my name on it, and it's a great honor, very humbling. I just love Gibson Les Pauls. That's what I love and what I play. Now, the one I was playing most, with all the hardware on it, weighed close to thirty pounds. Since this operation and trying to get back into shape and get my muscle strength back, they built me two guitars and they both weigh five pounds! They're Les Pauls, and they sound just like my old '59, but they only weigh five pounds. It's amazing, because I can't sit there and hold up a thirty-pound guitar for two hours each night in my condition right now. It's like holding an acoustic guitar, they're so light. You can just pick 'em up and sling 'em anywhere. (Laughs)

So many of us are big fans of both the Rossington Collins Band and the Rossington Band. One question I just have to ask is, do you have any plans to let Dale do some lead vocals sometime?

Well, our record company, Sanctuary, has asked Dale and I to do a blues album. She's still got her pipes. She's a wailing, screaming...*girl.* We call her something else, but I'm not gonna say that. (Laughs) She's a great singer, and everybody keeps asking us to do one, so I think after we finish this big long tour, we're gonna take a few weeks and just me and her go in and do some blues tunes we've been writing, and some laid-back pretty stuff—not Skynyrd stuff, of course—and some more Rossington Collins type tunes. So, yes, there will be a time, and it's coming soon. It won't replace Skynyrd, because Skynyrd is bigger than any of us, but it will be something we do in addition to Skynyrd. I love to hear her sing, and it'll be fun to do something other than Skynyrd. And blues guitar is my favorite to listen to anyway. I'll break out all my styles and models and take 'em into the studio and do 'em all. And I can't wait to hear her sing.

What are your immediate future plans with Lynyrd Skynyrd?

Well, actually we're just doin' what we do. We're doing this tour that lasts until Thanksgiving, and that's pretty much the whole year. And everybody's got family, so we usually take the holidays off to spend with our families. We're gone most of the rest of the year, so...so we're doing that, playing and paying tribute to the guys who are no longer with us. And every night when we play we still feel them onstage. The audience feels it, too, you can see it in their faces. I can feel Ronnie and Allen and Leon right there with me, and it's a heavy thing, a spiritual thing that happens every night. I love it. We're gonna keep doing that, pushing this *Vicious Cycle* record and showing them that we do new stuff, too. We're very, very proud of the old stuff and we'll never stop doing it, but we're proud of the new stuff, too. We're growing, and we still love to write songs. That and the blues album we talked about. We have two kids and we're gonna be grandparents, so that's really a biggie. (Laughs)

You're going to be a grandparent? That's great.

Yeah, Grandma and Grandpa Rossington. That's on our minds, too, so we've got a big year coming up. •

Ed King

1999

Ed King was one of the original members of Lynyrd Skynyrd, and when the group reunited at the 1987 Volunteer Jam, Ed once again joined forces with the surviving members of one of the South's best-loved rock-and-roll bands. In our 1999 interview, he expounded upon the legendary band, lead singer Ronnie Van Zant, the band reunion, and the article in SPIN *magazine that had many Skynyrd fans ready to spit nails.*

MBS: Ed, tell us a little about your pre-Lynyrd Skynyrd career, "Incense & Peppermints," and your other accomplishments.

Ed: I grew up in Southern California and the Strawberry Alarm Clock was my first real major band. I was 17. By November 1967, we had a #1 song with "Incense and Peppermints" and our picture on the cover of *Cash Box* magazine. We never had another hit and the band went bankrupt in late 1968. But it was on one of our last tours that I met Ronnie Van Zant and the Lynyrd Skynyrd band. They were our opening act for about three months of college dates we did in the South in 1970. Ronnie and I got along really well, and I told him if he ever needed another guitar player or bass player he should call me. And he did in 1972 when Leon Wilkeson quit the band.

By the way, even though the music to "Incense" was written by myself and Mark Weitz, the keyboard player, we were not given credit and never paid a dime for it. We were ripped off by managers and publishers and the like. Oh, well, we had a good time.

Sum up your days with the original Lynyrd Skynyrd band.

I played on the first three albums along with the *First and Last* album, which was actually the first album [that had been rejected by various record companies]. I was recruited to play bass on the first album, *Pronounced*, but during rehearsals, Leon came out to the rehearsal cabin. While there, the band played "Simple Man" with Leon on bass. I had never heard the song before. After hearing Leon play bass, I decided he should be the bass player. He's the best I've ever heard. To this day, I never write a bass part without asking myself, "What would Leon play?"

As a matter of fact, the last two songs we recorded, "Free Bird" and "Simple Man," contain my bass parts that are very far removed from all of the other bass parts on that album. Mainly because I had caught the vision from Leon of how the bass should be played for this band.

One night, after the first album was done but not released, Ronnie came to me. I was sitting on my bed playing my Stratocaster. He put his arm around me and said, "Ed, you're really the *worst* bass player I've ever played with." So, the next day Ronnie and Gary went out to this ice cream factory where Leon was working. They asked him to return to the band. Two days later, with Leon on bass, we wrote our first two songs with the new lineup, "Sweet Home Alabama" and "I Need You." Not bad for the first day.

I really enjoyed working with Al Kooper. I believe, had it not been for Al, no one would've heard of Skynyrd. He was the visionary behind the band and how it should be presented to the world. We didn't always agree with Al, but I certainly enjoyed his presence.

When we drove up to Atlanta to record "Simple Man," we played the song for Al in the studio. He hadn't heard it. He didn't care for it and said, "You're not putting that song on the album." Ronnie asked Al to step outside. He escorted Al to his Bentley and opened the car door. Al stepped in. Ronnie shut the door and stuck his head in through the open window. "When we're done recording it, we'll call you."

Al came back a few hours later, added the organ part, and it was a keeper. I don't think any band before or since, making its debut album, could get away with doing that to the record producer. There was a healthy respect happening there and that is a really funny story that reflects that.

There's a somewhat controversial article—at least among Skynyrd fans on the Web—in the April issue of *SPIN*. In it, the author mentions a time during the early '90s when Leon got his throat cut in his sleep, and some people blamed it on you. What's the story?

We had just finished playing a gig in Nashville. That night Leon walked on stage totally drunk and really screwed the gig up. We were all pretty annoyed. Seems that he had waited all day at the Nashville airport for his girlfriend Rhonda to fly in. She was five hours late and he had spent the entire day at the airport bar.

That night some of the guys flew back to Jax except me, Randall Hall, Leon, and Rhonda. Early in the morning I woke up—I had been sleeping in the lounge in the rear of the bus—and walked to the front to talk to the driver. On the way back to the rear I noticed Leon's arm dangling out of his bunk and some blood dripping from it. On further examination Leon's throat had been cut and he was laying there in a pool of blood with Rhonda. We went straight to a hospital and had him stitched up—what a mess. Never did get to the bottom of it. Leon said he'd stumbled and must have "cut" himself in the bus hallway. Hmmmmm.

His girlfriend had been a source of problems, like bringing a handgun on the road and holding Leon hostage in his hotel room, not letting any band members talk to Leon on the phone. And, at one point, she told us Leon couldn't tour with us anymore unless he got more money. That was in '93 when we had to hire a sub bass player for two legs of a tour because Leon had "quit." Later that year he beat Rhonda up and got sentenced to three months in prison. They *shaved his head*! Man, it was ugly. So, as soon as we reached Jax that day, the word started circulating that I had cut Leon's throat.

By the way, Rhonda [Leon's ex] somehow slashed Leon's wrist a year after this incident, and that left Leon with no feeling in his little finger and some damage to his ring finger on his right hand, the one he uses to fret with. It's a reporter's job to write about what he experiences. I spoke several times with the guy who wrote that article. It seems he wanted to get the facts straight.

I know you probably get this a lot, but would you mind sharing your thoughts on Ronnie Van Zant?

Ronnie was two people. When he was straight, he was one of the finest people I'd ever met; when drunk, he was a madman. Unfortunately, towards the end of my tenure with the band, he was drunk the whole time. That's mainly why I left. Working with him just wasn't fun anymore—and he was the only reason I wanted to join the band anyway.

One of my fondest memories of Ronnie, one that displays his genius, was in January 1975. I had written this entire musical piece in my hotel room. We were working on *Nuthin' Fancy*. He came by the hotel room to hear it and all I told him was, "It sounds to me like the song should be about a train." It took him only 15 minutes to write "Railroad Song" that night. Ronnie never wrote anything down—*ever*. But as long as the band could remember the "groove" of the music, the lyrics would always come back to him.

One other thing comes to mind—and this is so cool. Many times, in rehearsal while writing, the band would be playing, it'd get loud, and Ronnie, after completing a verse or two of lyrics in his head, would walk over to me. He'd cup his mouth to my ear and sing me the song! On at least three occasions I was the first person to hear what he'd come up with. I remember hearing "Saturday Night Special" this way and my jaw dropping. He was an inspiration. I wish we could've parted on easier terms.

Tell us about the original reunion of the band, why you left, and what you know about Artimus' leaving.

I guess I stuck with the reunion band because I was chasing some kind of dream. I was under the impression that just maybe we could write some music that mattered, and that maybe Johnny Van Zant would do a good vocal. I was misguided, I guess. I did it to myself.

The '91–'93 version of the band was fun. Custer was a great drummer, and we had some great live shows. Artimus left the band because...you'll have to ask him. It's way too complicated and I'm not sure I understand why. But that version of the band Ronnie would've been proud of. We were tight, energetic, and inspired. Every night was a musical surprise. I had a blast.

In September of '95 I went into congestive heart failure while on the road. I had been diagnosed with an enlarged heart back in late '92. I caught a really bad cold and the infection landed in my heart. The only remedy is a heart transplant. I held my own from '93 through '95. Though touring did get a bit rough at the end.

I had hoped to get a new heart and rejoin the band eventually. But the band kind of deserted me and maybe it's just as well. The doctors say my health is doing a lot better than they expected, and that I may not need a new heart for five years. By that time, they say, new technologies might be available so that I won't need the new heart at all. Who knows?

I had thought the guys in the band were closer friends. I was mistaken. Took me a while for that to sink in. I didn't expect them to support me financially, but I didn't expect them to forsake me either. The way they handled my "leave of absence" was a disgrace. I should be grateful to be away from their influence, and I am. I wish I was 20 again, but there's no going back. I am enjoying this time off. I do some writing, play with my dog and my toys, enjoy an "island" smoke once in a while, take a ride in my Jag convertible, it's pretty damn good. I'm doing just fine, thank you.

Would you contrast for us the equipment you used in the early '70s and what you prefer to play these days?

In the '70s I used several old Strats—rosewood-neck models—and a great amp given to me by Hartley Peavey, a prototype Road Master. During the reunion tour I used two custom-made Strats by John Suhr and a Peavey Mace, and later used PRS guitars. Now, I'm back to old Strats, maple-neck models this time. Almost any amp that can pump 70 watts is good enough for me, tubes only.

Did you hear the story about me getting my stolen 1959 Gibson Les Paul returned to me in August '97? The whole story is still posted on the *Nashville Scene* website. It tells how my stolen guitar was returned to me. I think my health did a major turnaround when that happened. I was in the midst of this lawsuit against my "friends" and was really down in the dumps big-time. Getting "Lester" back was a real lift, as you can imagine. I never, *ever* thought I'd see that guitar again.

What were your favorite Skynyrd songs to play?

"Sweet Home Alabama," "Simple Man," "Saturday Night Special," "Needle and the Spoon"...I had a lot of favorites. "Curtis Leow" was a good one to play. The original version of the band only played "Curtis Leow" one time onstage. We were playing in a basement in some hotel and thought we'd try it. We never played it again until the tribute tour with Johnny. But the songs, they were pretty much all good ones.

What would be your advice to a young, hotshot guitar player or other musician who thinks they have what it takes to make it in the music industry?

Of course, we live in a different world than we did when I was 15 years old. Back then, rock guitar was still in the pioneer stages...of which I'm proud to say I was a part. But one thing is probably still important. I always felt that, even though I wasn't the best player around, I had style. Most people could pick my parts out on a record and identify them. The intro to "Sweet Home Alabama" will always be a radio staple. And how many songs can you think of that can be identified within the first two seconds? I'm really proud of that one.

So, if you're really convinced you have style and that you have something to say musically, then you don't let anything hold you back. I didn't, although I could've quit many times. I had confidence in the little things that I know I can do well. It also helps to learn and hang out with as many musicians as possible.

If you could have one wish granted, what would it be?

I think my one wish would be to write the title track for a "Grade-A" movie. I'm working on it. •

Artimus Pyle

1999

He was the second drummer for Lynyrd Skynyrd, but most fans know him as "the" drummer for one of the South's most popular bands. Artimus became the band's drummer on their third release, Nuthin' Fancy. *Before and after Skynyrd, Artimus formed and rocked with several bands, including Studebaker Hawke, Those Guys, a few variations of the Artimus Pyle Band, and All Points Bulletin.*

Multiple vehicle wrecks, the loss of another friend and bandmate, Allen Collins, and hurt feelings regarding former bandmates had deeply saddened Pyle. In my 1999 interview, he opened up to share some of his innermost feelings.

MBS: Artimus, where were you born?

Artimus: Louisville, Kentucky, in 1948. I was born in St. Joseph Hospital. I was raised in Tennessee, on horseback, basically. I don't even use a saddle. I ride a horse with a blanket and a bridle. That's all I need. I like to feel the horse under me. As much as I love horses, I was lucky to be born in Kentucky and raised in Tennessee. When I was a little kid, I would go with my grandfather, Guy Williams, to cattle sales. One of his best friends was Al Gore, Sr. He brought his son, Al Jr., and he and I used to jump around in cow crap all the time. It was really hilarious. We're about the same age. I remember this little kid that used to be with this other man, and I'd be with my grandpa. I guess I never dreamed that he'd grow up to be Vice President.

I was raised in an area of Tennessee that Sergeant Alvin C. York, the World War I hero that captured all the German soldiers and saved American lives, was from. In fact, I am related to him. Remember the old black and white movie with Gary Cooper and Walter Brennan called *Sergeant York*? Walter played Pastor Pyle down by the store. That's my family. We were related to Sgt. Alvin York, and that's where I was raised in Tennessee. I ran bulldozers for my grandfather's road-building company when I was 9years old, every summer until I was about 18. So, my Tonka toys were real. And I helped build roads in Tennessee.

My father was an architect. He followed the architectural building boom north in the fifties. We got as far north as Columbus, Ohio. That's why I have no accent. I finished high school in Columbus. I went to Tennessee Technical University, and then joined the Marine Corps expressly to go to Vietnam. Four years later I was in the aviation program ready to go to Vietnam and the war ended. My dad was killed in a mid-air collision in Albuquerque, New Mexico, in the early '70s. I was a sergeant in the Marine Corps, training as an E-5 sergeant to go to Vietnam at the time. My dad was hit from above and behind by a B-57 bomber. Dad was in a Cessna 150, brand new, flying over some land that he was going to build on. He was flying with a man named Robert Stuttlefield, who had about 36,000 hours of flying time. He was an aviation pioneer. Both of them were killed instantly.

After that, my mom moved back to Knoxville. I had met a girl from Spartanburg, South Carolina, named Patricia Diane Williamson and married her. She is a wonderful person, and we are still best friends. After all these years. She lives in Bat Cave, North Carolina. She went to school with George McCorkle and Doug Gray and all those from the Marshall Tucker Band.

I was in the Marine Corps with Toy Caldwell. I had heard about this big guy they called "Toy." And they were messing with me because I was a "Pyle." So, they were calling us "Gomer Pyle" and "Toy." Boy, did they mess with us in boot camp! But we all hooked up, and they turned me on to Charlie Daniels, who in turn turned me on to Lynyrd Skynyrd—and the rest, as they say, is history.

That's something I wanted to ask you about. Charlie Daniels told me he was involved in all that somehow.

Absolutely true. It was exactly like this. I drove to New Orleans during the early '70s fuel crunch. I was at Mardi Gras. I went down there to audition for Charlie. He had two drummers at the time and he was pushing his new album. He had that song out called "Uneasy Rider." So, I went to New Orleans with a friend named Sonny Matheny, who eventually ended up working for Charlie for years running sound. Then he went back to Tennessee Tech and got his degree, and now he's the principal of a high school in Roanoke, Virginia. But Charlie loves Sonny. So, Sonny and I were at Mardi Gras. Charlie came up to me and said, "Artimus, the drummer that was going to quit decided not to quit, and if I took two weeks off right now to go back to Nashville and work you in, it would hurt my album sales something awful. And I need to keep these dates." So, Paul Riddle from the Marshall Tucker Band, another great person, called Charlie and said, "Boy do I have a drummer for you." So, Paul was pushing me to Charlie. But this drummer Hoss Allen that was gonna quit didn't, and Charlie was just honest with me.

Instead of giving me some big ring-around-the-rosy, some big story, he told me the truth. He told me he knew of a band that needed a drummer and he was going to hook me up. This was when Charlie couldn't even afford it, but later, after I left, I found a fifty-dollar bill in my pocket, and I didn't have a dime. Sonny and I probably had just enough money to get us back home to Spartanburg in my Volkswagen bus.

So, Charlie played his gig at The Warehouse, there in New Orleans, off the beaten track, away from the French Quarter. There were thousands of people, and I watched Charlie and his band play. Charlie's bus pulled out of town, and Sonny and I were gonna leave town, too, after Mardi Gras. Sonny got a gig, driving a bus and working on the road crew for Charlie. I didn't get a gig, but Charlie had invited me to come to Atlanta to a club called Richard's and jam with him that night. Dickey Betts also jammed with him. There were two sets of drums, and Charlie let me set up a third set of drums. So, when I left out of New Orleans, I found this fifty-dollar bill in my pocket. There's no way anybody else could have done it. It was Charlie. Then he turned me on to Skynyrd. There was this gig in Atlanta at the stadium, and it was Marshall Tucker, the Allman Brothers, Charlie Daniels, Wet Willie, Lynyrd Skynyrd, everybody. Paul Riddle invited me to go to that show after Mardi Gras. And I had jammed with Charlie at Richard's and everything was great. Then I left town and went home to Spartanburg and was working construction. Then I was working at an airport installing aviation electronics at the Spartanburg Airport. Then Paul called and said, "We're playing a big gig in Atlanta, do you want to come?" And I said, "Sure." And I went and that's where I met everybody that day. I met Ronnie Van Zant and everybody. Ronnie's face was all beaten up. They had just been in San Francisco and got into a big fight. Ronnie looked like the devil, all black eyes and cut up and everything. He had taken on a whole gang by himself because everybody else hid under the bus, I guess. And between Charlie Daniels and Paul Riddle pushing me and talking me up, saying, "This is the boy for you," which was unbeknownst to me, I went home and I got this call from Ronnie, and he said, "I want you to play drums for my band. I was gonna fly five drummers down to Jacksonville, but what I want to do is have you come down to Atlanta and play with Ed and Leon." I said, "Sure." So, he hired me over the phone. He said, "I need a fire set under this band, man. Can you do that? We are right on the fence. We're getting there, man." So, I went to Atlanta where I was supposed to meet up with Leon and Ed King at Alex Cooley's Electric Ballroom. I drove up there in my bus with my drums in it. Well, two or three blocks from the place, my engine overheated and vapor locked. I just pulled up my emergency brake, unloaded my drums, rolled them up the street to the Electric Ballroom, left my Volkswagen bus sitting on Peachtree Street with the emergency blinkers on, and went in, set up, and played with Ed King and Leon. Ed took me next door and made me a Caesar salad, and I ate. I figured enough time had gone by, so I went back to my bus. It had cooled down, so I started it up and drove up to the Ballroom and got the gig. So, it was Charlie Daniels and Paul Riddle believing in me and being good guys. And Ronnie said after he had met me, he realized that he was talking to somebody that talked to him on the same level. I wasn't talking up to him; I wasn't talking down to him. We became friends. I watched Ronnie whip everybody in the band's ass—Leon, Billy, Allen, and Gary. I used to go to their defense all the time, because Ronnie couldn't whip my ass. He was tough for a musician, but I had just gotten out of the Marine Corps. I was young and wiry. You'd have to kill me at that point. Ronnie was the same way. He respected me, and I respected him. I could have argued with him 24 hours a day about some things, Michael. About some of the policies. It was *his* band. But when he would start getting drunk and abusive, I was the only one who could talk to him.

What's the truth about you after the crash? There are so many rumors and urban legends about you running for help and getting shot by a farmer.

Those are all true.

Do you talk to the band now?

I have not spoken to the guys in the band for some years now. I left the band because I wanted Blue Cross insurance. I wanted dental plans for our families, of us survivors. I wanted us to lead the band with integrity.

I used to come to all your APB shows in Spartanburg during the early '80s, when you put out the two MCA albums. Remember, we used to talk all the time? I loved the band you had then. Karen Blackmon, Rusty Milner, and everyone.

Oh, yeah. At that point in my life, I was doing a lot of alcohol and drugs. Everybody thought I was doing a lot more than I really was. It was one of those things where I had survived that airplane crash and I was a living legend, people thought, I guess. I believe people thought that they would get some sort of knowledge from me by being around me, or offering me drugs. I mean, every good ol' boy that I met had a big baseball-sized hunk of cocaine. There were gorilla biscuits, Quaaludes, seconal, and just cases and cases of Heineken. The best pot a person could possibly smoke, that a friend of mine was bringing in from Hawaii. I was just trying to kill myself. Obviously, I didn't care about anybody or anything. I was stabbing my family in the back by spending so much time…you know, if I could trade, right now, for five minutes with my family, with my first wife Patricia in my little house on Wall Street in Campobello (S.C.) for months, and years of hanging out with [bad people] doing drugs and alcohol, I'd do it. But you can't do it.

You can't go back.

Exactly. What's done is done. You can't go back. You can't change things in the past. All you can do is kind of look at what's happening around you at this time. I now realize that the real heroes are like Thomas Edison, Henry Ford, Charles Lindbergh, research scientists that take children out of pain—these are the real heroes. It's definitely not rock-and-roll people. There are a few good ones. Like attorneys. There are very few good ones. The rest are blood-sucking weasel attorneys. They are the lowest form of human existence. But the few good ones are amazing. And there are a few good music people, but you could probably count them on your hands and toes, the people who have made worthwhile contributions and helped to change people's lives for the better. I have now been in the business for a long time, and I realize that all the people that I thought were my friends, that I thought loved me, have stabbed me in the back and stolen every penny they could ever get from me.

But you still have certain people you consider true friends, right?

I have a few. Real friends are few and far between. But I have my wife Kerri, and a new son, River. He is eight months old. My other two sons came over here the other day and held him. I'm standing right now on the intercoastal waterway. It's about four miles wide where I'm at, and I'm looking across it like a wilderness. There are sailboats going by. It's about 82 degrees. (Laughs) I bring my son out here on the deck all the time, and the other day, Chris and Marshall came over, and they were holding little River, and I'm looking at the three of them. It was amazing! His name is River Eugene Pyle. And then Christopher Chapel Pyle, and Marshall Daniel Pyle.

How old is Chris now?
He's 28.

I remember him sitting in on drums with the APB when he was ten years old. Does he still play?

Oh, man. He tours the world. He just did 40 cities, including Rome, Italy, and Barcelona, Spain up to Norway, and everywhere in between. London, Paris, all the normal places. I just did 27 cities in Europe, eight different countries, and ended up a hundred miles from Russia at the Arctic Circle in Finland during the war. Every day that we were there the U.S.A. was bombing Belgrade. It was pretty wild to experience being an American in a rock-and-roll band touring Europe, eight countries, Holland, Denmark, Belgium, France, England, Germany, Finland, while we were at war. While we were bombing people. That was a unique experience. But my son has a band called Royal Trucks. This is a man and wife that lived in New York and had a band called Pussy Galore. They moved to San Francisco and got into heavy heroin, wrote songs, and did all this stuff within a period of about five years. When they were kids. They got it all out of their system, got clean, and have been writing ever since. They are about 30 years old now. They've got a bunch of albums. Jennifer Hererga sings lead vocals. Neal Haggerty is on guitar and vocals. And they put together a band with my son on drums, a man named Dan Brown from Jacksonville Beach, Florida, on bass, and a Kenny Nasta who was also in one of my alternative groups that I put together called the Fenwicks, with my sons and my daughters. At one time, I had five of my children onstage with me performing in front of 10,000 people opening up for Foreigner in Jacksonville at the Metro Park down there. We called it A.P.B./The Fenwicks. I've had All Points Bulletin together for a long time, and we're still playing as APB. We played Europe under that name, All Points Bulletin or Artimus Pyle Band, whichever floats your boat. Marshall, my middle son, is 23 years old. He was named after Marshall Tucker and Charlie Daniels. Marshall Daniel Pyle, and he is a singer and songwriter and plays drums. Chris is a drummer, and plays flute, trumpet, and guitar and he's amazing. But Marshall concentrates on acoustic guitar. I picked him up a Texan from Gibson. They gave it to me in the factory in Nashville, and I said I don't play guitar, but they gave it to me anyway, so I gave it to Marshall. He's been writing a lot of songs. Kind of a reggae, hip-hop, rock thing that he does. He's real knowledgeable about his lyrics. They are about the environment and good things. His songs are real positive. He loves Bob Marley. He was definitely one of the good ones, Bob Marley. And I was in a band with what I think would be considered a rock-and-roll star, Ronnie Van Zant. I think that Ronnie, for me at least, it was like being onstage with Elvis. It was a phenomenal feeling. He had a real stage presence. That, of course, was the real Lynyrd Skynyrd, with Ronnie out there, and Allen Collins.

And then Ronnie hired Steve Gaines and brought him into the fold. He loved Steve. He wrote with Steve. He would actually leave the stage, in front of 200,000 people, and let Steve sing a song by himself. Now, most singers are not that confident. They're afraid to get their little wiggly ass off the stage, because somebody might forget them. Ronnie had total confidence in himself, his band, and Steve. It didn't bother him a bit to take a break and walk offstage. I'd sit on the drums and look over and watch Ronnie admiring Steve playing with his band. What kind of self-respect, and respect for others, is that? It was the best!

So, I continue to play music because of people like Ronnie and Steve and Allen and Mozart and Beethoven and all of these people who inspired me—Jimi Hendrix, John McLaughlin, Miles Davis, John Coltrane. These were great musicians. I continue to play. I'm 51, and my chops are basically as good as they've ever been. I enjoy playing now as much as I ever have.

I'm sure everyone asks this, because of the shirt you wore on the *Street Survivors* LP, but are you a vegetarian?

There was a period of time when all I ate were fruits and vegetables and lots of nuts. That's why I'm so nutty now. (Laughs) Then I had airplane crashes, car wrecks, and motorcycle wrecks and it became necessary to resume eating fish and cheese for the benefits of the oils and minerals. You know, bone-building stuff. Then, my children were wondering why they couldn't have turkey on Thanksgiving. So...Seeing that I like turkey and chicken—white meat only and well done—I began including them in our family diet. Red meat and pork are unhealthy for me to consume; however, I don't dictate anyone's diet. For instance, my wife Kerri, who is the best "eater" I know, is an ovo-lacto vegetarian. Our new baby, River, is a total vegetarian. But when I am ordering a meal in a restaurant, for the sake of simplicity I tell the waitress I'm vegetarian. It's easier than sending everything back to the kitchen because it has beef or pork stock in it.

What do you think about the new Skynyrd CD, *Solo Flytes*?

I love it, and there's a new one from Steve Gaines as well. On Lynyrd Skynyrd *Solo Flytes*, I wrote a song on that one. They digitally remastered two of my old APB songs, one from each album. There's one that Karen Blackmon sings that I think is great called "Red Hot Light." And there's one I wrote called "Makes More Rock," that talks about sitting in the Torch Club in Tryon. I put my name on very few songs, but I am very proud to have a song that I wrote words and music to on a nationally released Lynyrd Skynyrd album. They say on Amazon.com that it's doing very well. I'll tell you a secret about that song. There's a drum break in that song. That lick is a lick Ronnie Van Zant inspired me to do. He told me one time, "Artimus, I want you to come up with a drum lick." I didn't perfect that lick until later. I use it every night. It's a combination of half of a triplet that I picked up from Billy Cobham and Ronnie's inspiration. And the last verse says, "Sitting in the Torch Club/Thinking of a tune/The heavies are trying to bury me/But that won't happen soon/You can blow up our buildings/But that just makes more rock." That was from my experience living in Jerusalem, Israel. Seeing how the buildings over there are just rock. It seems like when they blow up a building it just gives everybody more strength. It just makes more rock. So, that song comes from my life in Jerusalem, my friend Jack Miller, life in the fast lane, and just give me my music. And with "the heavies are trying to bury me," I was kind of seeing into the future. Because eight years ago I was facing life in prison for a charge worse than murder that everyone knew I was innocent of, and everybody turned their backs on me. I faced it alone. You find out who your friends are.

I was going to court every day for two years and fighting. So, that line means even more to me now…"the heavies are trying to bury me." And it's on a nationally released Skynyrd album and I'm so proud of it, man. Things do come around. You know, after I left the band, they tried to pretend like I didn't exist. Then, here comes *Freebird—The Movie*, and *Behind the Music*, and because I articulated in that stuff my feelings, and they felt that it was heartfelt, they used much of my interview in both the movie and the TV show. So, I'm like, the main guy.

I spoke first on the thing. I said, "Ronnie Van Zant's the man," and the last thing I said was, "Ronnie Van Zant's the man."

I have been a loyal, hardworking member of the Lynyrd Skynyrd band ever since Ronnie Van Zant asked me to set a fire under his band. I continue to play music for the right reasons to this day. I miss Ronnie, Steve, Cassie, Allen, and Dean. I try to keep APB on the road against all odds; Mike Estes is a real trooper. Greg Baril is an unbelievable guitar player and they have to endure a lot of problems being in a band with me. They keep me going and I love playing with them. •

Rickey Medlocke

2001

These days Rickey Medlocke is touring the world as a member of the "three-guitar army" of Lynyrd Skynyrd, blowing the minds of Southern-rock audiences from Europe to Clemson, South Carolina, but before he joined the Skynyrd group he fronted one of the hardest-rocking bands in Southern rock, Blackfoot. In 2001, we spoke to Rickey about past glories and future goals, and the hot new Lyve *DVD and CD.*

MBS: Are you originally from Florida?

Rickey: Yeah, I was born and raised in Jacksonville and over on the west side. I went to Paxton High School, both junior and senior, and basically was raised there my whole life. My grandparents adopted me. They were my grandparents on my mother's side and they raised me like their own. I knew quite a bit about my dad and mom, where they came from and who they were and the whole bit. To be honest I was estranged from my real father. You know I learned to know my real mother as years went forward, because Shorty [Medlocke] was actually her dad. But honestly, I couldn't have had a better set of people around me. And I give my dad and mom credit. They did the best they could with what they had to do with. I couldn't have done any better because Shorty taught me how to play and taught me the values of music and that is why I really owe him everything. He really was the cat's ass to me when it came to being a real musician. He lived it, breathed it, and loved it. He had some successful times in his life, I guess. I think he would have liked to have gone further in his life. He did some sacrificing for me when he was a kid. I was very sick and had a respiratory problem called bronchiectasis and a lot of people get it confused with bronchitis, and now I come to find out it was a generic form of cystic fibrosis. That is what it is. I had a bout of it and was born with it and grew up with it. He tried to do the music thing and make a living at the same time and afford my doctors. I had a major operation at age 9, and really what it comes down to is that I have only one lung in my body right now. If it had not been for him and my mom I would have probably been in deep shit. They were great parents and they let me do what I wanted to do.

At what point did you first decide that you wanted to do music as a career?

Well, my dad Shorty was basically a Mississippi Delta blues country player. He was on a television show called *The Toby Dowdy Show* and it originated right in Jacksonville out of a radio station called WJXT and used to be called WMBR. It had a lot of different guests on there. What happened was that as a kid I learned how to pluck around on a banjo when I was, like, three and my dad got me a miniature and strung it up. I was actually a left hander. So, he strung the banjo up for me and taught me some stuff on it and we would go on the TV show and it was kind of a silly, novelty thing. From age 3 to 8 years old I stayed on that show with him. He also did some stints with Roy Acuff Band touring at one time. Then he played with Toby and his bands throughout the southeast. Me and my mom used to go on the road with him a little bit and I hung around musicians basically really all my life. At the age of five I got interested in playing guitar and started learning how to play the guitar and a couple of guys in his band who played guitar started teaching me. Actually, my dad taught me three chords, G, C, and D. Watching other players and plunking around on the guitar and stuff I started playing guitar at that time, and I played and kept playing. That has always been my main instrument of choice, although I did learn how to play drums, but only out of necessity. I played with my dad's bands when I was very young and he had a drummer named Charlie Saddlewhite. He helped teach me, and was a really cool guy. I used to think he was like Ringo or somebody. I actually took up playing drums in my dad's bands for quite some time, just as a teenager and going in and out of bands. I got into rock and roll early after seeing Elvis at a baseball park between the ages of 6 and 7 years old. My parents took me to see him, and if mom was alive today she would be the first to tell you that I kept telling her when we left I wanted to be a musician. It stuck with me for my whole life and I didn't care too much of anything about any other stuff. Playing probably kept me out of trouble, and kept me from doing lots of things that wouldn't have been good for me.

I am still unclear as to when you played for whom, between Blackfoot and Lynyrd Skynyrd, in those early days?

Well, Blackfoot had relocated up into New Jersey and what happened was some of those stupid little tiffs that bands get into and we were not really going anywhere. For me, I was just frustrated not going anywhere or doing anything and everything just going awry. I actually called Ronnie up after I had gotten ahold of Allen Collins first and told him that I needed a gig. I told him that I would be able to drive a truck, load equipment, or "whatever y'all need done." Then Ronnie asked me if I still played drums and I told him, sure, I could do that, but in reality, I had not sat on drums in a long time. We had a great drummer, Jakson Spires, at the time. So, I opted to go because Bob Burns was leaving and he says that you can come in and do the bill. So, I took off for Jacksonville and got with Lynyrd Skynyrd right there in 1971. You know from 1971 until 1973 I opted to leave and do that. I sold my gear and kept my guitars and a few things and hung around this band house we had in Princeton, New Jersey, and I kind of brushed up on playing and all that kind of stuff and they sent me a plane ticket down and flew me down to rehearse.

In Jacksonville that night I was sitting in rehearsal and working up the material that would later come out not only on the *Pronounced* album but also on Lynyrd Skynyrd's *First and Last*. That's what started it.

Tell me a little bit about what life was like during Lynyrd Skynyrd at that particular time, maybe contrasting with what it is like now.

(Laughs) When you are young and full of piss and vinegar and trying to do something, to be honest with you, I don't really think that anyone knew at that time what the band was really capable of. It was very raw back then. We had an incredible writer that we were playing with named Ronnie Van Zant. When I first started working with him, he had the most unusual way of writing songs. What we would do is go out to Hell House, and we would play those songs over and over again without him even singing. He would just kind of sit in the corner in a chair and keep thinking about writing the lyrics in his head. He never even wrote anything down on paper; it was all in his head. He would just step up to the microphone and start singing. It was incredible. When I look back on it, because we have some good writers now, but with Ronnie it was, like, genius. It was like an artist painting a picture. He could see it in his head, and I think it was a gift he was blessed with and just genius. Some of my favorite writers have been Bruce Springsteen, Ronnie Van Zant, Bob Seger, Sting, and Don Henley. People of that caliber. These are guys that paint the picture and allow you to see it in your head.

Let's talk for a minute about Blackfoot because I think that was one of the greatest rock-and-roll bands ever. Can you tell me a little bit about how

the band was formed and maybe a couple of high points that you recall from the days of the band?

I told some people this before and will always maintain this, because a journalist asked me recently, what did I consider one of my greatest accomplishments? I told him that the fans had a lot to do with it, and the record sales, and the traveling and playing shows but really to me probably the greatest accomplishment that I had in my life was being able to share the stage with some of the world's best and legendary rock musicians. Jakson, Greg, Charlie, Ronnie, Allen Collins, Gary Rossington, Leon Wilkeson—and these are some of the guys that I have had the pleasure of standing with and making music. The Blackfoot years were just incredible. We did something that I don't think anybody thought we were going to do. To think about those years of struggling and beating our heads against the wall and traveling like we did, and the hopes that we had in our heart that we would do something, those are some of the best years of our lives and nobody can ever take that away from us.

We impressed somebody from a record company. Then we moved up north to get out of the South because there was limited work around where we were. It's kind of ironic that we were a house band in Gainesville, Florida, and Tom Petty had a group called Mudcrutch, which was there in Gainesville and Skynyrd used to go play there. It's kind of funny because we went to the northeast and Tom went to the west coast, and Skynyrd stayed in the South and everyone went to seek their fame and fortune. We hit the big city of New York and stayed in a two-room apartment. It was big, with a small bathroom and one small bedroom. It was in the Village and this woman had brought us there. It was her apartment. It is still in the Village because I was there recently and saw it. We were right around the corner from Fillmore East and a block from the Electric Circus. We struggled and starved. We bit the bullet. Then we moved out to New Jersey and that was when I went with Skynyrd. Then I went back with them later. Jakson and Charlie had met a bass player named Lenny Staddler and they were in North Carolina. Jack asked me if I wanted to do it again and I told him absolutely, so I went and joined them. Lenny opted to leave the band because of health problems and he was a born-again Christian. So, Greg came back with the band and all of a sudden we were back doing it again. We were up there for years. The Island Records and Epic Record and Atlantic deals all came out of there. Blackfoot, for me, in all sincerity was a band that was way ahead of its time. We never considered ourselves the typical Southern-rock band, but were a very heavy band. Heavier than what is on record. We used to give people hell opening for them. There was basically no one that could stand up to us. We were fortunate to have some hits during that time in our lives. We had "Train, Train" and "Highway Song" and others that really made a mark and a dent. We were playing arenas and touring overseas and having the time of our lives. Then for whatever reason it all unraveled. I do know that there have been things in the press said about whose fault it was, but to be honest it was all of our faults. I don't think that it was any one person. When you are a band you should have control of it. I have the utmost respect for the guys that played in that band. Great musicians like I told you a few minutes ago. They are very talented. For whatever intents and purposes that it all came down, I do know that the business got in our way. The record business is the most ruthless business that I can even think of. It is funny how some record executives can talk out of both sides of their mouths. The business got in the way. We got caught up in the middle of record-company wars and it was a shame. It took people downhill. There were some hurtful things exchanged between some of us and to me I don't even want to go back and think of those things. With Blackfoot we shared some incredible years together and made some incredible music together. Skynyrd had a magic and Blackfoot had a great magic. We were hellbent for leather that we were bad-asses of the South.

I have an AC/DC book that has Blackfoot and AC/DC posing together. How did you feel about those fellows?

That was one of the cool things about Blackfoot, we were able to open for some of the heaviest rock bands that came out of Europe and around the world. We were the darlings of opening acts at one time. We took pride in that and started headlining our own stuff. The guys from AC/DC I am still friends with today. We struck up a good thing with lots of those guys—Nugent, Foreigner, AC/DC. Those are some years that I am very proud of.

Being a friend of Jakson's and I know Charlie pretty well, too, all three of them have said in the past that they would be open to do a reunion performance. Do you think that there is any way that you would do something like that?

I have lots of responsibilities now with Skynyrd and am counted as one of the main guys in this band. In order to do any project that you are going to do, you can't do 3 to 4 things at one time and make one certain thing great. I think that you can do two projects at once and make them good, but after it gets beyond that it takes away from both and takes away from the other two or all three. I know that the fans are interested in seeing a reunion between the four of us. I can say that right now I would have to take myself out of Lynyrd Skynyrd—and there are many people that count on me here—and immerse myself in Blackfoot. I don't know that at this time in my life I am able to make that kind of move. We would also have to sit down and lay a lot of stuff out on the table as far as the past goes. I am not saying that I am not willing to do that. I have taken a lot of negative rap from a lot of people. I have never commented about it. Jakson Spires is my brother-in-law and is married to my sister. I will not say anything negative about anyone. Things happen in life that you cannot understand or explain, but you know what? Life is too short to sit there and dwell on it. I am not going to dwell on the past. I have nothing but respect for those guys' playing and their musicianship. Right now is a very, very up and busy time in my life. I have a lot going on right now and just agreed to do another feature film with Maggie Gyllenhaal and it is one of the lead parts in this film, and it looks like I may be considered for a role in *Halloween 9*. The Skynyrd thing is going on into October. Is Skynyrd taking a break? I really don't know. They have committed to doing three more CDs for the record company. I am heavy-duty involved in the writing process and the recording and being there. I guess only time will tell. We have to wait and see how this whole thing unfolds. I appreciate all the fans. I am 54 years old and one of the main reasons that I love to play is to see the fans come out and have a great time. They can forget the blues for a while. I appreciate everyone's thoughts and sincere efforts to get to me and say that they really want it badly. I will say that if people can think about how they remember Blackfoot standing on that stage and playing, the one thing that I would never want to do is to tarnish it or make it less than what people remember it being. Four guys that had an incredible magic and incredible team on that stage. I would never want it to be less than what it was. The memories I have of it is kickass. We have a live record that proves that. It was voted the best live record of the decade. For me that says it all. This is not a thing where I am saying never, but there is a lot to be done and considered and then take it from there.

After having seen all these guys play, it seems like everyone could still do it. The thing about it is that if one note was missed somewhere, nobody would care. I know Jakson works a lot and keeps so much going and Charlie

as well and Greg—and then seeing you in Clemson... Lots of my friends feel as I do that you are doing great in Skynyrd, but you are a front man and we all would like to see you singing in the show. Even to do "Train, Train" as an encore—what about that?

I will be quite honest with you, when I got back with Skynyrd, I was very beat up. I had been slugging it around in a van and riding around with guys in a truck at 46 years old, and that is not an old guy but the thing about it is when you are sleeping overnights and sleeping in a seat straight up, you wonder what you are doing. When I got the chance to come back with this I took advantage of it. My dad says that "you can't drive a car until you learn to ride in the back seat." Those words are constantly repeated in my ear all the time. That is why when I took a break from lead singing it gave me a chance to play guitar. I have great confidence in myself but I am not going to come from an egotistical place. I play guitar and think I am good, but then I listen to Clapton, Hendrix, Eric Johnson, Van Halen, and then I realize I am not as good as some of the other guys. I am not one of those guys that brags about his playing. I learn constantly from other people still today. The greatest compliment that I have had in the last probably 25 years of my life came from Billy Gibbons. We did that tour with ZZ Top, and I used to eat dinner at the crew meal every night with Billy Gibbons and he looked straight across the table at me one night and said, "Hey, Rickey, I have got to tell you something. I was just listening to you play...man, you have the butter tone." I said, "Yeah, those old Marshalls are really something." He said, "Let me tell you why they are the butter tone. It's because you have the butter spreader in your hand." He said, "Your hand is smooth as buttermilk and don't ever forget it." He looked at me over those dark sunglasses and said that I was a really great guitar player. It blew me away.

How do you like working with the current lineup of Skynyrd?

Honestly, this is the best lineup of the band that I have seen. Not because I am in it. This is one of the best versions of this band since the original group. Its impact is unbelievable. It comes on with a forcefulness that doesn't let up. We questioned a lot when Leon died and questioned whether we should stay together. The decision lingered and we had to go out and finish what we were doing for that tour. Leon would have wanted that. He gave all his heart and could never say no. Do we miss him now? Absolutely. We have Ean [Evans] in the band and he is doing a great job for us. He and Leon sat together for a long time and became friends. When he got sick there were times when he just couldn't go. At least we had someone that had spent time with him and revered him as his hero. Everyone in this band rides down the road together all the time. And in a bus, there are always going to be times that we get on each other's' nerves. I know I do, with all my hyperactivity. The band does get along fine.

What would you say, since you have been in the band this time, has been the high point?

One of the biggest high points for me of this besides the ZZ Top tour with this band, would have been that I had long wanted to play the Royal Albert Hall. Everybody and anybody who was anything in music had played that place and stood on that stage. That is where Cream did their farewell gig. When you walk down the halls and see who has been there it gives you the chills. I stepped on that stage and couldn't believe that I was there. It was basically like when I was in Blackfoot and stepping out in Hammersmith Odeon or playing the Monsters of Rock or the very first tour date when we played "Train, Train" and "Highway Song." Everyone came alive—and we had no idea at that time we had a hit song.

Probably in Skynyrd the high point of my life was the first gig with them. Since I got back with them, the Royal Albert Hall and many other times with them were memorable. I love my role with this band and love getting on the bus and rolling down the highway and being able to get up and play those tunes every night. I love getting in it and taking off and doing it.

It seems like everything with Skynyrd is peaking again. *Vicious Cycle* was a great record and the DVD is exciting, and the live one that I just got in yesterday. Tell me your thoughts on the new live album.

I will tell you that the price of it is worth it just for "Tuesday's Gone." With the string section onstage, and we had Jim Horn who had originally done the horns on all the old stuff, and to me it was just an incredible and magical night for the band. I am happy and proud to say that first of all there was a DVD that came out last year that is now gold, and then the *Lynyrd Skynyrd Thyrty* record that came out is certified gold and just short of being platinum right now.

Sum up what's on the drawing board for you and the band.

The band has just confirmed dates through October 16th. We just confirmed 8 to 10 shows with us and the Allman Brothers. That will be the first time those two have shared the same stage. That's in October. Then we will take a break and start writing new material and start planning another CD. We have dates off and on through the first of the year. As far as me, I could be involved in 2 to 3 films this year and I have gotten into acting lately and really enjoy it. This first one is a dramatic character with Maggie Gyllenhaal called *Shall Not Want*, and another film called *Sweet Deadly Dreams* that could be coming out before the end of the year. So, there is a lot going on. •

Jo Jo Billingsley

2002

As one of Lynyrd Skynyrd's Honkettes, Deborah Jo Billingsley White enjoyed worldwide fame, playing stages from Japan to England, as well as all of the best venues in the good ol' U.S.A. In an exclusive interview back in 2002, "Jo Jo" spoke about her days with Lynyrd Skynyrd, her friends, and how she came to become a born-again Christian with a musical ministry.

MBS: Tell us about how you first came to join Lynyrd Skynyrd.

Jo Jo: Bob O'Neil was doing their lights, and he was a friend of mine from back in Memphis. He told me that they were going to be hiring some singers, you know. I had just seen them perform with Eric Clapton, and I thought they were really good. At first I thought he was saying they were going to hire the three black chicks that were on the album. Lo and behold, they called me! (Laughs) I was just so thrilled to get to go up there and everything. That's how it happened, Bob gave them my name and they called me and I went to Nashville where I met them.

Did you have to audition?

No, I just walked in and Ronnie saw me and said, "She'll do just fine." (Laughs) Hired me on the spot. And I knew Cassie [Gaines] because we worked at a restaurant called Ponchos in Memphis together. I knew she was a singer and she knew I was a singer but we never sang together. I thought she was real cool, and I had seen her sing in a play and I knew she had done some Broadway stuff. So, after they hired me, they asked me if I could help them find another girl singer. I had tried to be friends with those other girl singers in Memphis but they wouldn't give me the time of day, so the first one I thought of was Cassie. I called her, and she had already moved back to Oklahoma, where she was living in a Victorian house on this farm for $45 a month, and working at a country club. I told her about Skynyrd and everything and she literally had to go and buy the album because she had never heard of them. She listened to the album and she called me back and said, "Hey, they're pretty good." I said, "Yeah, they are." I asked her to go with us, and she said, "Should I?" and I said, "Yeah, let's go, let's do it!" We both had two weeks to pack up and move to Jacksonville. We had a few rehearsals there in their studio in Jacksonville, and then we were in London, England, on tour. We were rehearsing there in the theater owned by Emerson, Lake, and Palmer. It was a big theater with no seats in it. It had a huge stage, and upstairs were all of Keith Emerson keyboards and equipment. It was really a cool place.

You kicked things off in style, huh?

Yeah. Then we went to the British Isles and then over to Glasgow, Scotland, all those places in Europe. It was cool.

What was life like as a member of one of the hottest rock bands of the day?

It was fantastic. I thought I had died and gone to heaven. They were really my favorite band anyway. But getting to literally be with them onstage was amazing. They're such awesome musicians, and great guys. They treated us so good. Ronnie was such a gentleman. He wouldn't let anybody mess with us. And every show was sold out, and the energy was just awesome. The fans just loved it so much, so the energy was outstanding.

The *Freebird* movie was based around that Knebworth concert, which was huge. How was that for you?

There were 250,000 people there that had paid. And there were another 150,000 people around who had not paid, that had just gathered. They had a flea market set up there. People came in on every mode of transportation, from bicycles to Harley's, planes, cars parked all the way back to London on the side of the road. No kidding. And the stage was huge—we were playing with the Stones! [Excited] We were playing with *the Rolling Stones*! They had that stage built all up, and you had to have a special pass to get anywhere near the stage. It was really cool, 'cause me and Cassie were coming up the platform, and who other than Paul McCartney was coming up at the same time! We stuck out our paper for him to give us an autograph and he snubbed us. I thought, uh! We were both heartbroken. I thought, the nerve! I've loved him all my life. We were all backstage—there were so many entertainers there, because it was Hot Tuna, 10cc, Todd Rundgren's Utopia, us, and the Rolling Stones. They had hired entertainers to entertain the entertainers. There were jugglers and clowns!

Was that the show Jack Nicholson was at that Gary was telling me about?

Yeah! He had this cane that opened up and he could sit down on it. He was already a star, but that was before he really hit it big. Later on, backstage, there was a tent for just the artists, the people who were performing. There was a champagne fountain. We were in there, and then Paul McCartney wanted to come over and talk to us. So, we snubbed him! (Laughs) Cassie did, I promise she did. But we had a ball.

I bought the dress that I wore at the flea market that morning. I went out there and found that dress and grabbed some scissors and split it down the front, because I had that leotard. Allen and I were close, and I remember him trying to decide what to wear. He didn't even want to take a bath. I said, "Allen, there are 250,000 women out there who paid to see you." So, they all got cleaned up, and he had that red shirt and red pants, and I said, "Wear that!" It was perfect for the day because they had those big red Stones lips everywhere.

One time we were doing a show with Peter Frampton and Bill Graham was the promoter. It was when Frampton had the big live album with "Show Me the Way." I never did get it. But anyway, Bill Graham was the promoter. We were up on this high-rise stage, and we were looking down at about fifty black limousines and one white Rolls Royce. And I asked Mr. Graham, I said, "Mr. Graham, who's so special to get that white Rolls Royce?" And he just kind of smiled at me. When we got done and were ready to leave that white Rolls Royce pulled up to pick me up, alone. And inside he had a bottle of champagne and some roses just for me. That was so special to me. All the promoters just took such good care of me. Alex Cooley, and my friend Bob Kelly from Memphis. Tom Dowd was the producer the first time we recorded. I had never recorded before in my life, never been in a studio. He pulled me aside, and I didn't know who he was. He said, "Jo, you're a natural. Just go with it." He made me relax. Later on, when I found out who he was I just said, "Man!" And then later on when we saw him in Atlanta for the world premiere of the movie, we ran up to each other and got pictures and all, and I said, "What are you doin' here?" And he said, "I produced the movie." And I said, "Okay." (Laughs) I really put my foot in my mouth. He was just so precious.

Tell us a little about Ronnie Van Zant, from your perspective.

Ronnie was awesome. He was just such a gentleman. He was brilliant and very quiet, at least to us, the girls. Until he got high and then he got pretty rowdy. But he was a gentleman. He would never mess with anybody, unless they messed with him. And he'd always try to warn them. He'd warn them two times, and the third time he'd just hit 'em. He called it "cold-cocking." He was a Golden Gloves champion in Florida. He gave his dad, Lacy, a black eye when he was, like, three years old. Lacy would get down on his knees and box with him. Ronnie was in good shape, he really was. He was strong. And he was so creative. He was a great man. I really, truly believe that he was a prophet of God. And early on Satan got his focus off track. He was proud, too. I remember one time they told us that we could no longer continue to ride in limousines because it wasn't in the budget. Ronnie said, "We will always ride in limousines. I will ride in limousines 'til I ride in the back of one with flowers on top." It was a very prophetic moment. Everything he ever said came true and that's the sign of a true prophet. I knew then that there was greatness in Ronnie. He was just so charismatic, people were just drawn to him. I was praying one day, and the Lord told me, "Ronnie's with me." That blessed me. I thought, "Thank God."

Let's talk about the plane crash. You had a prophetic dream about that before it happened, right?

They had played those four shows without me. They let all of us girls go in Las Vegas. That was my last time to sing with them. That was August of '77. I had a stomach virus, so I went home to my mom's in Mississippi. I was under a doctor's care and just wanted to rest because we had 286 days that year that we were booked. We had about 55 days off, and about 30 of them were traveling. Leslie went first and asked for her job back so Ronnie hired her back. Then Cassie asked for hers back. Then they did those four shows without me, and then Ronnie called me. It was the night before Greenville. My brother and I had made plans to go over and meet them in Little Rock a couple of nights later to party with them. He called and told me he wanted me to join them in Greenville and come back into the band. I thought, well, that's music to my ears. I said, "Yes, of course." While I was talking to him I felt this strange feeling and I heard this word, "Wait." My spirit was talking to me. I said, "Well, we were planning to come to Little Rock anyway. Why don't I just meet you there?" And he said, "Good, bring all your stuff." I went back to sleep there at my mom's, and that night I had the most vivid dream. I saw the plane smack the ground. I saw them screaming and crying, and I saw fire. I woke up screaming, and my mom came running in going, "Honey, what is it?" I said, "Mama, I dreamed the plane crashed!" And she said, "No, honey, it's just a dream." And I said, "No, mom, it's too real!" They had already sent me the itinerary, so the next day I called Greenville, South Carolina. I called everybody on the list. Finally, late that afternoon Allen called me back. He said, "Jo, what in the world is it? I've got messages all over Greenville from you." I said, "Allen, it's that airplane." And I told him about my dream. He and I always sat in two seats up front, facing each other. It was a customized aircraft. We always sat there. I said, "Allen, please don't get on that plane." He said, "Jo, it's funny you'd mention that, because I was looking out the window yesterday and I saw fire come off of the wing." I asked him if Les Long had checked it out. Les had flown that plane for years, and knew it like the back of his hand. But he had been training these two new pilots. When he told me who the pilots were, I thought, "Oh no," because they had been on tour with us and I thought they were unprofessional. Instead of sleeping while we were getting ready and playing and all, I'd see them down at the bar and such. One of them asked me one night if he could come up to my room with me. I said, "No! Don't talk to me!" But when he told me it was those two guys, it really scared me. I said, "Please, please don't get on that plane!" Well, when they left Greenville they took a vote that it was going to be their last time to fly on that airplane. They were going to start flying commercial. They were gonna fly from Greenville to Baton Rouge and then to Little Rock. And of course, it crashed in Mississippi, my home state. Ronnie always called himself "the Mississippi Kid," we never knew why. And then he died in Mississippi. I was completely devastated. I was up celebrating with my band from Memphis because I was going back on the road with Skynyrd. We were all upstairs at my drummer's house, and she came upstairs and said I had a phone call. It was my mother, and she said, "Honey, I don't know to tell you this." She just started crying, and she put my brother on the phone. He said, "Honey, the plane has crashed and Ronnie is dead." My heart just sank. About that same time, a news bulletin flashed across the screen, and I thought, oh, my God. I drove home in the rain and nearly had a wreck, I was so upset. We made arrangements and flew down to Jackson, and we were some of the first to see Allen and them. The first thing I thought was, God saved my life. The Lord gave me that dream to warn me, and I did the only thing I could do and warned them. It was so weird because some of them thought that maybe I had something to do with it, but I had nothing to do with it. At the funeral, Ronnie's daughter Tammy was hanging around me, and I told her she needed to tell her daddy goodbye, so I took a rose off of his casket and gave it to her. I was standing there beside Robert Nix, and I'll never forget it, Lacy came up and reached down and scooped up a handful of the dirt and wiped it across my mouth and said, "Kiss this ground you're walking on." And walked off. I thought, my God. And Robert is a big guy, I guess 290 pounds and six-foot-five. He just picked me up and put me in the limousine and took me to his and Susie's house in Atlanta and I stayed there for about two weeks. It really disturbed me that I wasn't on the plane and was saved from it, but somehow got the blame for it, it's just weird. But Robert took me into his studio in Doraville and played me a new song. He told me if I felt moved to sing along, to go for it. He dimmed the lights and gave me a glass of wine and played "I'm Not Gonna Let It Bother Me Tonight." Pretty soon, I copped the attitude, and decided I wasn't gonna let it bother me neither. I started singing, and I looked up and Robert and Rodney were dancing in the control room, and he said, "Baby, it's a smash hit!" We finished it. But he made the mistake of calling someone to tell them, and the next morning when we went in, the musicians had changed everything. They turned me way, way down. Robert was one of the songwriters for Atlanta Rhythm Section and their drummer, and he had played for Roy Orbison. Later he found out a lot of things that had been going on he didn't know about and he quit the group. But they had it out for me after that; they thought I caused that, too. One of their roadies tried to kill me backstage in Savannah, Georgia, at a show my band Alias did with them. I was raped and nearly killed, and I quit singing for a long time after that. Seven years. I thought if this is what music is all about I don't want no part of it. My husband and I were married in 1981, and he knew I had sang but he had never heard me, until I started singing again in 1986.

What singing did you do between Skynyrd and the night you quit singing?

I did that Atlanta Rhythm Section stuff, and I sang some with Molly Hatchet at the beach. I did a Billy Joe Royal project, Leslie and I and this other girl. We were the "vicious voices." Robert produced it. Then Alias recorded *Contraband*, and we had some of the Skynyrd guys on it. They could never really acknowledge the Skynyrd guys for playing on it. Who knows, if they had done that, Mercury may have given us a better shot, more promo-tion. But at that time, it was us and John Cougar Mellencamp, and they put their money into him.

What happened to cause you to return to singing in 1986?

A friend of mine came to my house and saw all my gold and platinum albums, and she asked me, "What are you, a movie star or something?" (Laughs) I said, "No, I used to be a rock-and-roll singer and now I'm a born-again Christian." She said, "I am, too." We talked for a long time, and she called me the next day and asked if I would come and sing at her church and I said, "No!" And she said, "Why not?" and I said, "Because I don't have a way." My husband and I only had one car at the time and he was working at night. She said, "I'll come get you." I was making excuses like I couldn't read music and couldn't play an instrument. She said, "You go to the Christian bookstore and charge some taped soundtracks to me." She came to pick me up for a Valentine's banquet, and I had on a red dress and red shoes and she had on a red dress and red shoes and I got into her Cadillac and I thought, "This is too weird!" (Laughs) I went into a room and prayed and I came out and sang three songs and gave my testimony. God has blessed me so since then, I have sung at probably thousands of churches. It just blesses me so much. I had been searching for that my whole life. I have been writing songs, and I hope to get in the studio soon to do some of them. •

Jo Jo would later join old bandmates Ed King, Artimus Pyle, and Leslie Hawkins in a band called Saturday Night Special, a tribute to Lynyrd Skynyrd. She released a wonderful gospel album, I Will Obey. *She also recorded with the author on his 2006 release* Something Heavy. *Also in 2006, she performed with the surviving members of Lynyrd Skynyrd during their induction into the Rock and Roll Hall of Fame. Jo Jo died on June 24, 2010, after a battle with cancer. She was 58.*

Randall Hall

2001

Lynyrd Skynyrd has showcased some mighty fine musicians over the years, from the original band to the current lineup. One of the finest guitar slingers ever to perform as a member of this legendary band was Randall Hall. Hand-picked as his replacement on the famed "Tribute Tour" by the late Allen Collins, Randall brought his fire to the stages of the world, and appeared on three Skynyrd albums, including the smoking hot live set, Southern by the Grace of God. *When we spoke with Randall in 2001, he was heading up his own all-star band, with an ever-changing line up, the Randall Hall Band. He was also a member of the revolving Artimus Pyle Band lineup, and was set to release a new RHB album later in the year. Hall spoke with me about his friends Ronnie Van Zant and Allen Collins; his days with Lynyrd Skynyrd and why he left; touring with folk rocker Melanie; his fascination with Jimi Hendrix; soloing alongside Stevie Ray Vaughan; and growing up in the Sunshine State.*

MBS: I know you were born and raised in Jacksonville, Florida, where all the great guitar players came from. Did you come from a musical family?

Randall: I think both sets of grandparents had some musical ability, both sets on my mother's side and my father's side. My dad just dabbled on the guitar, but my mom used to sing in church quartets and stuff when she was a youngster. My grandfather on the Hall side, who I never knew, he was gone long before I was born, played fiddle, I believe. And my grandmother, who I knew up until I was ten, she played a zither. You know, you sit down and play it with a quill. And my mom's parents, my grandfather played a little guitar and grandmother played the organ. Like I said, I never heard 'em play, except for my grandmother that played the zither. I've still got that thing. I don't know how old it is, man. She died in 1964, and it was a fairly new one then. I don't know much about 'em except they've got those pre-tuned chords.

A zither, is that like an autoharp, like Mother Maybelle Carter played?

Yeah. Sure is. They have a few different styles of playing them.

When did you become interested in playing the guitar, and who were your earliest musical influences?

I can tell you that easily. You ever seen that tribute tour video we made? I dabbled a little on that question there. My brother was kind of interested in guitar. He really wanted to be a drummer, but they didn't want to foot the bill for a set of drums. And I don't know if they really wanted to hear them around the house. (Laughing)

Nobody wants their kid to take up drums. When I was a kid, I had a set of drums for a week, and they mysteriously disappeared one day.

(Laughs) He had one of those little Silvertone guitars with the amp built into the case. He was messing around with it, and I picked around with it a little bit. So instead of drums, they bought him a motorcycle. So, he got rid of the guitar, and I was just starting to get interested in it. We had one of these little Magnus chord organs around the house. I started dabbling on that, and it seems like everything I could get my hands on I could pick up and start learning something on it you know. That went on for about a year. Then when I was about fourteen years old I went to see the Monkees. Jimi Hendrix opened the show. I was excited about hearing the Monkees play "I'm a Believer," and Hendrix came out. I didn't know who in the hell he was. I went, "My God," and my jaw just dropped, seeing this wild man out there. This was two weeks after the Monterey Pop Festival.

That's like taking a kid to a strip show.

[Laughing] That's how a lot of parents were treating their kids, covering their eyes up. Me and one of my buddies went to that, our parents dropped us off. We had good seats. And Jimi, that was it! "Purple Haze" just nailed me. I loved that song, it was so wicked sounding. We had these little AM radios, and they had an underground radio show and they'd play "Purple Haze" every once in a while, and I'd flip. After that, my interest in guitar skyrocketed. Poof! There I went. So, within a year or two I was out doing gigs. In fact, my first paying gig I ever had was on the very day Jimi Hendrix died in 1970. I was, like, sixteen or something. It was over on the west side of Jacksonville. Most all of us came from the west side. It was Woodstock Youth Center.

So, actually, you played Woodstock. (Laughing at my own joke)

(Laughs) Yeah! Really!

And you played with Don Barnes' band, Alice Marr?

Yeah, I don't know what the deal was, but Don was out of there. And I went over to rehearse with 'em for, like, two weeks. They had their songs pretty much together. I don't know if I just didn't learn the songs quick enough or what, but they ended up getting Don back. They didn't last long after that, they just went their separate ways. Then I got hooked up with a couple of guys and got into one of my first good bands, Running Easy. It was Ken Lyons, who was 38's first bass player; a left-handed guitar player named Jim Harrison; and Joe Cramp. We formed Running Easy. We got a keyboard player who was in Alice Marr, Kevin Nelson—he produced Journey, and the band called Europe. He's a sound man today. Oh, my God. He mixed for Michael Jackson. He went out with us and Skynyrd. And he was a Skynyrd sound man and roadie back in the seventies. In Running Easy we were doing all instrumentals, and each song was as long as about three songs, they had so many changes in 'em. We ended up opening for Skynyrd. That was on the tribute tour video. That was on the first day that I met any of them guys. It was like 1972. Downtown there's a place they call Friendship Fountain on the river, and we opened up for 'em. That's the day I met Allen Collins. He came up to me and said, "Hey, you ol' hot dog, you, you're damn good." After that we started getting gigs opening up for Skynyrd before they were even known about. That was when they had two drummers—Rickey Medlocke was drumming and Bob Burns was drumming. And Ronnie helped us get on the "chittlin' circuit" with one of the agencies out of Atlanta—Paragon, I think. He just believed in us. He introduced me to Alan and Phil Walden there at Pinocchio's in Atlanta. We went up there to audition. We were gonna do our audition after their show. Before we could do it, Ronnie took me upstairs to one of these little balcony booths, and Phil and Alan were sitting there. Ronnie said, "I want y'all to meet Randall Hall. He's 17. Mark my words, you're gonna hear from him some day." We had to start doing cover songs. We had been doing original instrumentals, but we said, well, we'd better start singing something. (Laughs) One time we went over to Ronnie's apartment he had at the time. He said, "What do you feel like hearing?" I said, "What about some Allmans, live *At Fillmore East*?" And he said, "You don't want to listen to them guys. Why don't you listen to Merle Haggard?" I said, "Merle Haggard?" (Laughs) I wasn't into it then. I was just interested in guitar at the time. But he said, "You don't know what you're missing."

I wanted to talk about Ronnie Van Zant. He's become such a legend. What was he really like?

Mine and his was always a great relationship. I never saw the bad, because I never worked with him. He treated me, like, with a little-brother kind of attitude. He took me under his wing, like I said, hooking us up with agents and trying to get us going. He did anything he could on his end to help us. Sure enough, he got us on some gigs. I remember doing one with Bloodrock up in Atlanta. It was alternating sets all through the night. But as a person, he was always like, "Hey, good to see you again, man." The last time I saw him I was not working a whole lot playing, so I was working at an apartment complex as the in-house landscaping guy. I was digging a hole out in front of an apartment, and he just wheeled up. Him and some of the other guys, coming to get one of the roadies that lived there. And I was digging a hole with filth and dirt all over me, you know. And he said, "Randall, what the hell are you doin'?" I said, "I'm digging a hole." (Laughs) I had to knock the dirt off my hand to shake his hand. He said, "Man, you're too good to be doing this shit. Why are you doin' it?" I said, "I got to make a buck right now, you know?" A few months later his plane crashed. On that night, we were gigging out towards the beach, and at the time there were conflicting reports. Nothing was really accurate. They were saying Leon was dead, but he wasn't. We didn't get the full report on what really happened till the next day.

I was at his last show here in Greenville. We were all devastated. We still are. On your website, I read that you played guitar with the '60s folksinger Melanie?

Yeah, back in '79. You know who was responsible for that? Rickey Medlocke. At the time, I was living next door to Shorty [Medlocke]. We were playing at a pub in Gainesville, a college club. We got a call during one of our sets. He said, "Look. I'm staying in the same hotel with Melanie, and she's firing her band."" And he said, "I know some guys that can fill your bill right now. She took three of us out of the band. She already had her bass player that she wanted to keep. We hated not taking the one we had because he was a helluva singer. We ended up playing with her for just a few months. Like at the Copa Cabana, and we went over to Switzerland and played. It was a folk festival. Ry Cooder was on the bill. It lasted about, like, four days.

So, you got to play "Brand New Key."

Yeah, man. I didn't know much about Melanie at the time. We had to cram on all these songs, get every album she had and learn a pile of songs. We met up with her and she was real nice. She told me about flying with Jimi Hendrix. You know, when I got with Skynyrd, I ran into so many people who had worked with Jimi or something. And I had to ask every one of them about him. She flew from London to New York sitting right beside him. She said, "Randall, he was just a perfect gentleman." She said he was just like the song "If 6 Was 9." "Mr. Business Man, you can't dress like me." The suits would just look at him like, "Who is the weirdo?" He was just great.

Tell me about coming to join the Allen Collins Band.

That was just a few years later. They had the Rossington-Collins Band in about 1980. I was a candidate for that, too. Gary and Allen used to tell me, "We're putting this thing together, and we're gonna do some of Skynyrd's songs and some of ours." It was between me and Barry Harwood. It was me one week and Barry the next. Finally, they just decided on Barry. Then that ran its course. They did a couple of years of that and two albums. Then Gary and Allen parted ways. I guess Gary started hooking up with Dale or something, I don't know. So, Allen came out to see me playing locally, him and Barry Lee Harwood. And it happened that Jimmy Dougherty was playing drums with me in this band the Moody Brothers, an old-time lounge act that had been around for years. I learned so much from those guys. They said, "Man, you gotta come join this band." So that's where that came about. We rehearsed out at Allen's house. His six-car garage, one of them was made into a studio, you know. We did that album, and we were starting to work on a second one, but Allen was just losing it. He had been through so much tragedy in his life. The worst was losing his wife. After that it was just like he didn't care anymore. He began to party to the extreme.

What happened to his wife?

She died in '80 or '81 of complications due to pregnancy. It really devastated him. After that it was like he had a death wish. He didn't care. He'd drive like a maniac, drinking and everything. He just didn't care. That was just the demise of the band there. If he wasn't too drunk, he was too messed up. I hate to say that. We did a few gigs and just canned it. He just lost interest in keeping it going. We all loved him to the end. He was one of the most brutally honest people I have ever known.

I wanted to ask about Allen. He's one of my favorite guitar players.

He was a guy that had perfect pitch. He was real hyper as a kid. They used to give him Ritalin to combat the hypertension. He had such a tolerance level. He could do more of everything than anybody. I remember having a contest between him and one of the road guys to see who could string a guitar the quickest. He beat the roadie! And he had it in tune without even putting it on a tuner. I was going, "My God."

And it was Allen that got you on the Skynyrd tribute tour, right?

Yes. My wife and I were at the place where we used to live in Jacksonville. We'd heard some talk about it, the possibilities of something happening. Then out of the clear blue he calls me up one day, all hyped up. He said, "Hey buddy, are you gonna be there for me?" I said, "Yeah, sure. What is it?"

He said, "You gonna be there for me?" I said, "Sure, what is it, Allen?"

He said, "Oh, it's this Skynyrd tribute thing they're putting together. I just don't feel like going out there in a wheelchair. I don't feel like playing as much. I know you got it. I want to know if you'll be there for me." I said, "Well, of course." He said, "I told them guys if they don't use you I'd shut the whole m.f. down." He said, "I told 'em I want you and nobody else. I've got people calling me from all over that want to do it. I want you and you only to do it." I said, "Alright, man, I'll do it." So that's how that happened.

I remember seeing y'all on TV on Charlie's [Daniels] Volunteer Jam in 1987.

Oh, that was great. That was the day I met Charlie, the day I met Bill Graham. I played onstage with Stevie Ray Vaughan. When Charlie finished his set, he pulled all of the guitar players out onstage for a jam. There must have been seven or eight of us. We did something straightforward, like "Johnny B. Goode," I don't remember, or "Kansas City." He'd introduce the guitar players one by one and we'd take a solo. Stevie Ray was right next to me and he took a solo. Then I had to come out right behind him. I said, I'm not going to let this boy intimidate me, I'm gonna go for it—so I did. I gritted my teeth and took off. Turns out, me and Stevie Ray were the same age. I thought he was older than me.

I know Toy Caldwell played that show, too.

Oh, yeah! He did a lot of shows with us. He was on the live Skynyrd album. He did a lot more than just what was on the album. Like playing on "Call Me the Breeze" and "Sweet Home," stuff like that. He just traveled with us.

How many albums did you do with Lynyrd Skynyrd?

Three. *Southern by the Grace of God*, *1991*, and *The Last Rebel.*

Why did you leave Lynyrd Skynyrd? What happened?

Well, I can talk about it now. We had a lawsuit that ended a year ago. It took six and a half years to resolve. But it's public knowledge now. At the time, I couldn't say nothing. They were contriving other reasons, saying it was something it wasn't, but in essence, they wanted to cut my money in half. After being with them almost seven years at the time, they just wanted to take half of my percentage of the gross, and I said, "No way." None of them came to see me. They had their manager call my attorney about it. I said, "Call me and talk to me about this." My attorney said, "No. I don't see any reason for you guys to do that. Randall is there. He does his job. I don't see any legitimate reason for you to do that." And it wasn't everybody in the band's decision either. Months later Johnny called me and said, "I want you to know I fought for you tooth and nail." He said, "If my name wasn't Van Zant, I'd probably be gone, too." (Laughs) It was about them making more, and me making less. I was an equal shareholder at the time. They tried to say it was because I was late for rehearsal. Bull. I was the one that had to pick up Billy all the time, because there was no driving for Billy. And Billy would want to stop on the way and pick up something. And we'd be late. And they tried to use that as an excuse. It was more than that. I think it was greed, man. It all happened conveniently after Allen was gone. Because if Allen had been around he would have fought that tooth and nail. I think it was more Ed and Gary, I'm not sure.

Tell us a little about the Randall Hall Band.

For the past two years, we have been calling it the Randall Hall Band. It consists of Barry Rapp on keys; Sammy Buonocore on drums; Tim Lindsey on bass. We had the old singer from Allen Collins Band, and we recorded three songs with him. But Jimmy is not with us anymore. We have some more songs we want to record. And we have been going out a lot with Artimus Pyle, calling it the Artimus Pyle Band, or Randall Hall Band with Artimus Pyle. Who cares what it's called? We're out there making people happy. We do everything from blues to Skynyrd, you name it. We hope to finish the album this year, and we've got a lot of dates coming up here. In the meantime, we're keeping our meat-and-potatoes gig when we're in town. We're doing well. We'll be at Planet Hollywood in Nashville for a couple of nights at the end of July, and they want us back in September. When we were there in May, we did two nights and packed the place out both nights. It's in the works, man. Dead in the middle of the works. But on the band, the lineup varies like it does with the Southern Rock Allstars. Mike Estes does some, and Rapp will be on some and not on others. But the basic core is always there, and it seems like we can't go wrong. We play some Skynyrd songs, and they're cheering us on before we play the first song. And we have the waiting list for our CD on the website, and people all over the world are on the list. The reason I named the band the Randall Hall Band never was anything to do with me being a tight-fisted leader. It was just my name, and if some people recognize it, then that helps pull people in. Artimus said it was the same way when he did APB. •

Mike Estes

1999

Born in Kentucky, raised in Ohio, and currently living in Nashville, Mike Estes has enjoyed quite a varied career so far, taking guitar lessons from the late Allen Collins; playing in Lynyrd Skynyrd; heading up the Southern-rock-meets-NASCAR band, Drivin' Sideways; playing with the Artimus Pyle Band and the Southern Rock Allstars; recording with his band Brave New South; acting as lead singer for the Blackfoot reunion; and now heading up Skinny Molly. The red-hot guitarist spoke with me back in 1999 about his past, present, and future.

MBS: A lot of great musicians live up and around your area there on the outskirts of Music City. Charlie Daniels, Marshall Chapman, Ed King, and Allen Woody...

Mike: I haven't seen Allen in a while. At one time, me and him and Ed King, Owen Hale, Johnny Neel, and Billy Ray Cyrus played together. We were gonna put a band together. You wouldn't have believed it. Billy Ray Cyrus is a better Southern-rock singer than he ever was a country singer. It was going to be great. It was the best band I was ever in, and it lasted two days.

That Ed King can play, too, can't he?

Yeah. He's one of my absolute favorites.

I saw him down in Macon about a year ago in an all-star jam, wearing a Hawaiian print shirt, a pair of Bermuda shorts, and a big ol' stogie hanging out of his mouth. (Estes cracks up laughing.) **He led the band, which also featured Jeff Carlissi, through a series of Lynyrd Skynyrd songs. He was awesome. He didn't even pause between songs.**

Yeah. Ed's one of my best friends. And me and Carlissi are good friends, too.

How did you first become interested in music? Did you always know that was what you wanted to do?

I guess I did, actually. The first music I remember ever hearing, my dad had bought me a tiny little phonograph to play 45s. He had a great collection of Hank Williams records he bought when they first came out when he was in the Navy. He's from Harlan County, Kentucky. It's hillbilly heaven, to say the least. He kept that collection, which I still have. Then when I was about twelve years old, I heard Lynyrd Skynyrd and ZZ Top. To me it just sounded like Hank playing through Marshalls. The same kind of feel, just more of a rock-and-roll deal. But, yeah, I always felt like I wanted to do that. Then I learned a couple of chords on the guitar, which my dad showed me. He played and sang a little bit. He's a really good singer. He had the talent to do it if he'd wanted to, he just didn't want to take it as a profession. I kind of got it from him, I guess.

When and how did you form the band Helen Highwater, and talk a little about the Allen Collins connection.

Allen was always fabulous, I thought. I was so intrigued, I had to find out where he lived and everything. I wasn't a stalker, but I guess I was just short of being a stalker. When I was in high school I went to a library and found a Jacksonville phone book and looked in it. The Rossington-Collins Band was listed in it. I couldn't believe it. So, I called it up, and this guy named Craig Reed answers the phone. I was living in Ohio at the time, and it turned out Craig's from Ohio, so we just got to talking. He was their production manager. I was a junior in high school at the time, so I'm sure I aggravated him to death. I told him I had a band, and needed a name for my band. So, he got Allen Collins on a conference call, because Allen was coming up with all these cool names, but Craig couldn't remember 'em. Imagine this. My favorite guitar player. I'm a junior in high school, on the phone with Allen Collins. I said about two words. But he says you can have that name Helen Highwater, but you gotta swear to God you'll do something with it. So, I did. I played under that name, and opened for Allen, and he showed me all kinds of stuff. He'd come and sit in when we were playing clubs down in Jacksonville. This was just at the start of the Allen Collins Band. He showed me everything on the guitar, and moved me up to the next level. I was lucky, I got to learn from him right there at his house. He had so much patience with me. To this day, I still don't know why he let me hang around, but he did.

He probably saw the potential in you.

Maybe he did, I don't know. I was also writing a lot of songs and he liked those. He just wanted me to get the guitar part together. (Laughs) But

I'd stop by and we'd play for hours. I took an eight-hour guitar lesson from him on Easter Sunday in '83 that I'll never forget. That's when he showed me how to play "Free Bird." It was absolutely unbelievable. That probably had something to do with me getting the Skynyrd gig when I did, because I could play all those songs.

Do you remember what you were doing when you heard Allen had died?

I was at work and I heard it on the radio. I knew he was in bad shape, but I didn't know it was that bad. I had tried getting ahold of him a month earlier, but couldn't because he was in the hospital. Nobody would tell me where. So, when I found out about it at work, I took the next week off. It just about killed me. It was terrible. It wiped me out. I actually had a gig that night that I had to go play. It was very hard. I went and saw his grave after that and had the closure thing. But I had told him while he was alive how much he meant to me. I still miss the crazy guy. He was so much fun to hang out with. Always on fire. I always said when I had that Skynyrd gig I'd give it up in a minute if Allen could come back. And I would have.

How did you actually end up playing with Lynyrd Skynyrd?

I'd been knowing Gary and them for a long time, and Ed King had me come out on the road with them for about a year between '92 and '93. I was writing a lot of songs. Randall Hall was still in the band then. Right after that they fell out with Randall. I don't know what happened. He told me they fired him. They told me he quit. Only they know the truth, I guess. But I was out there and I got comfortable writing with Johnny and Gary and Ed, mostly Ed. When Randall left, we were down in Florida doing pre-production work on the *Endangered Species* acoustic record. They were gonna just do it with two guitars. I was running their board for 'em as a paid engineer. I'd never engineered in my life. One night Ed had to go out of town for something. I was staying at Ed's house. Gary called me over to see if I wanted to write. We started playing at about eight o'clock that night and didn't finish until five in the morning. I knew all of the Skynyrd songs, and we jammed on some of those and some Free songs, all kinds of different stuff. He had actually asked Greg Martin of the Kentucky Headhunters to take Randall's place, but Greg was undecided or told him he couldn't do it. Well, we'd had a little too much to drink that night and Gary turned to me and said, "Hey, man, you want the job?" So, I told him I'd give him until tomorrow and let him ask me again. I didn't want him to make a decision like that drunk. So, he called me the next day and said, "Hey, I meant everything I said and I want you in the band." The next few years were the wildest ones of my life. I went from running their board to playing in the band.

What caused you to leave the band?

When Ed got sick with that congestive heart failure, we were finishing a tour up. I had to learn all of his parts in one night. Which, I need a year to learn all of Ed's parts. I got by, but it just wasn't the same without Ed. They hired Hughie Thomasson to come in and play for Ed as a temporary replacement, supposedly. I was a lot happier playing with Ed than with Hughie, and I made it known. Then I was told that Ed wasn't going to be in the band anymore. I went off the deep end. I didn't quit, they fired me. No doubt about it. But it may have been because I was fighting hard to keep Ed in the band. I thought that he was a big part of the sound and the history. Not that Hughie isn't a great guitar player. In his element with the Outlaws, he is wonderful. But it just wasn't the same. It didn't have the same feel. I was just dissatisfied with the whole deal, and maybe the feeling was mutual. But now I have Ed on two songs on my new record. He's great. When I played with him, I just stood beside him and sometimes it was just unbelievable.

I wish I'd been able to see the band when you two were playing together.

Oh, it was good, man. There were nights when we'd go out and we could do no wrong. You live for those nights, man. You *play*, you know what I mean?

You've been sitting in a lot with the Southern Rock Allstars. How's that been?

I've been playing with Jakson and the Allstars for the past four or five months. I haven't joined the band yet, but I probably will at some time.

Filling in for Dave Hlubek, or playing with him?

Playing with him! I started out filling in for him when he was having surgery, but then they didn't want me to go home.

They are great guys. Jakson Spires is the salt of the earth.

Jakson is great. Just great. We have gotten to be good buddies.

I opened for them in Spartanburg, and they brought me up onstage to sing "Can't You See?" It was awesome standing there watching Hlubek lay down those Hatchet licks of his. But they are great.

They are good boys. It's been a riot playing with them.

You played some with the APB, too.

I played with Arti for two years, since '98. We played a lot of great shows together. I don't know what the future of that band is, but I'm open to playing with him forever. He's treated me like gold. He's done me a lot of favors. I hope to play with him in the future. I love him like a brother.

Tell us about the band Brave New South.

I have a couple of guys from my old band Drivin' Sideways, which shall rise again before it's over. That was a really good band. And I have a couple of new guys from around town. And we just started doing stuff, not pure country—some of it is. Lots of Southern influence. Like Dickey Betts said, and he was right, there are so many influences that make up Southern rock. To me it sounds like Waylon singing for Little Feat or Skynyrd. I'd always heard that Ronnie Van Zant was going to do a record with Waylon Jennings and Merle Haggard. Since that never happened, I thought I'd try it myself. That's kinda where I'm coming from anyway. It probably ain't as good as what that would have been, but it's just a raw, Southern-rock/country thing, and I wrote or co-wrote all of the songs on it. There are some great guests on it, like Greg Martin from the [Kentucky] Headhunters; Ed King on two tracks; a guy that used to play with Merle Haggard, Eugene Moles, on a track or two; Jeff Carlissi may be on a track if I can pull it together. He and I want to cut a new version of "Four Walls of Raiford" that he co-wrote with Ronnie. Hopefully we can get it on there; if not it'll be on the next one. I'm going to do a Europe tour by myself on July 30 and I'll be back on August 21. I'm doing Finland, England, and Sweden, it looks like. And when I get back, we'll release the album within a couple of weeks. I should have had it done before I went to Europe, but there was stuff that went on that I couldn't control. So, our official release date will probably be September 1. But I have a great backup band over there from Finland, good friends of mine. It's gonna be fun! Finland, here we come. •

Dale Krantz Rossington

2003

She may be in the background as a backup singer for Skynyrd now, but there was a time when Dale Krantz was the full-throttle lead vocalist leading the Skynyrd survivors' first major outing following the plane crash of '77, the Rossington Collins Band. In 2003, I spoke with Dale while she was on tour with her husband and the rest of Skynyrd in Glasgow, about her band, her memories, her family, and the man she loves.

Dale: It sounds good to hear your voice, I'm telling you. A familiar accent.

MBS: Thanks, I've really been looking forward to it. The first thing I wanted to ask is, when did you first become interested in making music?

My goodness. My daddy was the church choir director, and all my sisters and brother were very musical. So, it started in the church. As early as we could talk we were in the church singing the hymns. I grew up a couple of hours outside of Detroit, so when I was old enough to flip on the radio I began listening to old Motown and rhythm and blues out of Detroit. I think the very first time I looked into the mirror and pretended to sing it was probably to a Johnny Mathis record. I realize I'm dating myself here. But my mother always loved those Perry Como and Bing Crosby records. Both my Mom and Dad had beautiful voices.

What was your first professional gig?

I was a senior in college. I got a bachelor of music education, actually. My parents felt that I needed something to fall back on. I actually hadn't thought of professional music until I was a college senior. I started playing in a duet with a fine musician who was a music major. He played piano, and we called ourselves Sweet Seasons, after the Carole King song. We did a lot of clubs in the neighborhood, and I never looked back. I think I took a final on Friday, and left before they even handed out diplomas, with a traveling club band. I was hooked, but then again that was my last year. I had never really intended to teach music, but I thought it was a good education, you know.

Tell me how you first met Gary. Was it during the Rossington Collins Band or before that?

Actually, I had sung with 38 Special for a while. I had sung with Leon Russell in the fall and winter of '76, and the 38 boys had heard about that and decided they wanted some background vocalists at the time. We opened for Lynyrd Skynyrd in the spring of '77, which was an eye-opener for me. I had worked with 38 Special for several months before opening for Skynyrd, and I remember standing in the shadows watching Skynyrd and I was just overwhelmed by the sights and sounds—I was blown away. Then several months later after the plane crash, I was still affiliated with the 38 bunch, until they were ready to look for a new singer. And of course, that caused some feathers to be ruffled, I must say. When I quit 38 to go and sing with Gary and Allen, I mean. Of course that was just the beginning of a lot of feathers being ruffled.

When the Rossington Collins Band was first hitting big, were you as confident as you appeared onstage?

I was totally confident in my belief that Gary and Allen especially, but all of them, deserved their rightful place on the stage. I was only there. I totally understood all the grief they were going through, that they were consumed with over the loss of Ronnie and Steve and the rest of them. I couldn't understand why everyone was so tough on Gary and Allen and the survivors. So, a little bit of the cheerleader in me came out, and the Baptist preacher. The press had a lot of funny adjectives for the way I came off, but I was not educated enough in the Skynyrd history to know what I was up against. So, part of it was ignorance (laughs)—and part of it was an idealistic, almost worship of Gary and Allen and all they had gone through. I was gonna go out there and kick anybody's ass, if you'll pardon the expression, that didn't feel they deserved to be up there. You can hear that in the lyrics. "They're alive and well and ready—are you ready for the big boys?" That's a pretty simple statement. And "Opportunity," another of my favorite songs, was for those who doubted the reasons they had for going back to work. Everyone wasn't ready for them to do music again, except of course for them. They needed it. So, it was easy to be tough. You had to be tough standing between Gary and Allen, can you imagine? (Laughs) Have mercy!

You'd have to be sure your feet were firmly planted in place to keep from getting blown away.

And your buns blown away, too, buddy. (Laughing) They would take nothing less than 110 percent, and I would have never thought that I would have gotten by any other way. But fear can take you a long way, too. (Laughs)

I was telling Gary earlier, you were one of the first voted into the *GRITZ* Magazine Hall of Fame for Female Vocalists.

Great. Thank you. Awesome. You know, they used to call Gary "The Prez," and I'll never forget the most lovely compliment someone gave me was when they called me "The First Lady of Southern Rock." I felt a little guilty with my Yankee Indiana roots, but my affiliation with Gary and Allen really did put me in a special spot. I am so honored to be a part of this. I have seen your magazine and I love it. I saw it when we were trying to do this the first time, and you know the whole story there—bless his stubborn little heart. [Gary's hospitalization with heart problems] Clogged and unclogged, he's still the toughest guy I know.

I told Gary everyone had been praying for him, and I'm just so glad he's better.

Oh, thank you. I can't tell you how much that has meant to all of us. It was just one of the most frightening things I have ever been through, having to see my man there, going through all that. And the support of everyone is what brought us through—his daughters and myself. So, please, please tell your readers I thank them from the bottom of my heart for that.

Definitely. Dale, who would you say have been your major musical influences and favorite female singers?

Well, you're gonna hear the classics from me. I love Ray Charles, like no other. I love Aretha Franklin, like no other. I used to do the most wonderful Gladys Knight tunes, and I'm very, very much soul influenced. Oh, and Bonnie Bramlett. She rocks. She was at one of the Farm Aid shows one year and came out to sing on "Sweet Home Alabama." It was a dream come true. Bonnie Bramlett and Kris Kristofferson singing with us. And I love James Taylor. The more recent female vocalists, I adore Alanis Morissette. Oh, golly, I don't brave too many concerts unless I'm working them, but I'd go to see her. She's a tough little broad. And I love that big, big sound she puts out.

What's it like to be a mother out touring in a band?

I have experienced it since they were tiny babies, and now my eldest daughter at the big ripe age of 20 is going to give us a granddaughter this year. It is just as hard to leave them now as it was when they were babies. I remember thinking it would get easier as they got older, but it didn't because they're so magical and so wonderful, and you don't want to miss any of your time with them. That was one of the hardest things I had to do, but we had support from family, and all of the different gals we left them with over the years—the nannies, so to speak—were all just wonderful people. And each time that we left, we felt that we left them with the very best that we could at the time. And the kids have grown up to be little rock-and-roll girls. They totally understand their father, and our love for each other and what we are doing. Now that they are almost adults themselves—well, they are adults. (Laughs) Gee, even that was hard for me to say. I still miss them like they are my little ones, but I know we have their full support. I miss them, though. It hurts. We're trying to figure out who is gonna fill in for me so I can go home and be a grandmother for a few days this summer. And my daughter already understands that I'll probably fly in, be the cheerleader, and then fly back out to meet Gary on the road. This has always been our dream and they know it.

Tell us a little about your Skynyrd co-vocalist, Carol Chase.

She is tried and true and she loves the Southern thing. That's cool for a girl from North Dakota! She's another one that has embraced her "Southern-ness," if you will. She's a darling girl, very light-hearted and fun to be around. She's out of Nashville now, and has been there many years. She does songwriting. She has been a wonderful influence on us as far as health issues. She loves to read about nutrition and vitamins. She's one of those "up" girls. She's so happy to be with the Skynyrd bunch. We've seen a lot of people come and go over the years, and some of them of their own choosing decided to go ahead and go. But this child is so happy, and she knows how important Skynyrd is to the world. We just have a ball together. We just finished beating the streets of Glasgow, Scotland. She's got enough energy for six women. She's a good, good friend.

One of the guys I have become good friends with is Jay Johnson of the Southern Rock Allstars.

Ooooh, my baby.

Do you have any fond memories of the Rossington Band?

You'd better know it! Those were sweet times for us. There wasn't so much of the pressure. I mean, Rossington Collins was tough to have to leave. It was a difficult situation at the time. Allen had lost Cathy. We had been mourning her for over a year, and the music was getting further away, and unfortunately, drugs were the predominant factor in that after we lost her. It was tough to leave that band, but once we did that we still missed the music. This was a wonderful way to get our chops up and wail, and, God, Jay was a great rhythm guitar player, as well as a lead. He had a solid rhythm that could always take it right on up a few steps. We had a wonderful time back then. We believed in the songs we were writing and we enjoyed working with the younger guys. It's a judgmental business we're in, but some of the old stuff finally got to take a back seat for a little while. We needed that. I have to tell you honestly that in '87 when they started talking about a tribute to Skynyrd, I was very afraid of it, because I didn't want to see Gary going back to so much weight on his shoulders. But, oh, well...Thank God they didn't listen to me, huh? (Laughs) I have learned over the years that Skynyrd is bigger than all of us. It is way bigger than any one of us. It has a life of its own. It started out as six shows. It was going to be one show as a tribute, then it was six. Then everyone was saying, "Hey, there's fans in Texas. There's fans in Nebraska." Then a hundred shows later we decided we couldn't let each other go. It was too good. The rest is new Skynyrd history.

We have a really nice picture of you and Gary for the [GRITZ] cover. He's smiling.

That's an unusual picture. (Laughs)

I wanted to ask you your heartfelt thoughts on Gary.

He swept me off my feet, it'll be 21 years in July we've been married, and 22 years together. But after what we've been through these last few months, I can't tell you how much the love has grown. Deeper and stronger than ever. For a few days, I felt what it was really gonna be like if I lost him, and it was a very empty, lonely place. (Tearfully) I knew I'd always loved him, and I've always respected him, and I feel that is a big part of any working marriage. You maintain a respect for the other person. And then to have almost lost him like that. There isn't a well deep enough, or a sky high enough to fill it up. He's my soulmate and always will be. And it's *real,* too;

it takes my breath away. We're both healing from this. And every night, if he drops one note, or he looks a little bit different, I get this sick feeling of "what is wrong?" I forget that he's fixed, and he really is getting better each and every day. I am really in awe of what these doctors can do and what they did for him. He's my miracle man.

One thing we feature in our magazine is about home cooking. I was wondering, do you ever do any cooking?

(Laughing hysterically) Lord, have mercy. This is the best question of all. Let me explain by saying that my daughter has gone into culinary school as her chosen profession. And it was certainly not because her mother was a fine cook and she wanted to follow in my footsteps. Oh, dear God, in that aspect, I am ashamed, dear, to say that I am very much a rock-and-roll cook. Stouffer's does it so well for me. All those companies work so hard to put out those fine meals, why should I go through the strain? (Laughing) But Mary Elizabeth can cook. She's amazing. Pecan-crusted chicken. She used to grab different colors of peppers like other kids would go for candy. She's an awesome chef. I cook if I have too. I defer to my daughter the chef. I mean, I can cook—nobody has starved in our house, but I don't have much love for it.

Any messages for the Lynyrd Skynyrd fans?

Again, this has been the year for gratitude, and humility. The fans are our salvation and our strength, and I thank them so much for that and for their love for Gary. To the women fans, I would say, "It's all grits, girls." It's all about grits and guts and singing from the floor up. I used to say I am from the Ethyl Merman school of music, that the show must go on. And I firmly believe that if you are called to the music and it's your life, you've got to work it and not be ashamed of it. To my fellow musicians, I say work it and you go, girl!

Thank you, Dale, and my thanks to Gary as well.

Thank you, Buffalo, and you take care, and we'll see you soon in "God Bless" America! •

Derek Hess

2009

Derek Hess is one of the true "unsung heroes" of Southern rock. He was smack-dab in the middle of the whole Jacksonville scene during the glory days of the seventies, and after the Lynyrd Skynyrd airplane crash, when Gary Rossington and Allen Collins decided to form a new group called the Rossington Collins Band and Artimus Pyle was unable to play because of injuries sustained in a motorcycle accident, the job went to RCB guitarist Barry Lee Harwood's old friend, Derek Hess. The rest is history.

In 2009, I spoke with Derek about the short but brilliant career of Rossington Collins, his subsequent work with the Allen Collins Band, and his recent instrumental CD called Mainstream South, *recorded with Barry Lee and Steve Perez.*

MBS: Tell me a little about growing up. Where were you born and raised, and when did you first take an interest in music? What music influenced you the most? What was your first band?

Derek: I was born and raised here in Jacksonville. In my very early years my family lived in a small beach community called Atlantic Beach, where I attended elementary school until sixth grade. My father was somewhat of a musician. He played a little sax when he was in the service, and later bought a little guitar/amp rig—I believe it was a Gibson melody maker. My mother got myself and my sister going on piano lessons when I was six. I really moved along very well, playing in competitions and performing one on one with judges in an attempt, I suppose, to just ramp up my level of skill. And just a couple of years into that, I would say '57 or '58, my oldest brother, Paul, snapped up my dad's guitar rig, and the next thing I knew, his little rock-n'-roll band, complete with Baldwin organ and sax, were rehearsing in my tiny bedroom where our piano was, so they didn't need to lug that organ around, except for their few gigs around the beaches. Now bear in mind, this was the early goings of rock n' roll. Oh, my God, I was hooked and on my way, much to my mother's exasperation. However, when I started whackin' on the drums that would be left set up in my room, I was in heaven. I would throw on some 45 rpm's and rip. When my mother and my brother's band guys heard me, they wanted to run their drummer off, and Mother was quite proud. On a significant note, my brother and some of his buddies got to see Buddy Holly in a downtown armory just shortly before his death. Outrageous!

I probably didn't realize it at the time, but I'm sure a lot of the music I was learning to read and absorbing, lots of classical, really surfaced in several ways throughout my journey in music. Of course, we were all inspired by R&B and soul music and some of the pop tunes—I mean the really good ones, believe it or not—Connie Francis, Sam Cooke, Marty Robbins, on and on. And not just the vocal brilliance, but the whole production, instrumental parts as well as some of the marvelous background vocal arrangements. I mean, I liked Dion, Billy Joe Royal, Roy Orbison...then came the Beatles, the Yardbirds, the Byrds, the Rolling Stones. I'm not a huge fan, but "Honky Tonk Women" is without a doubt one of the most romping and soulful tracks ever recorded. Charlie Watts just lays way back and plays solid on that one—whew. I still play that one real loud. Then Jimi Hendrix and Mitch Mitchell came along, some of the most incredible guitar and drum work ever captured.

I would say that my style of playing kind of settled into a hybrid of Mitch's playing and some of the '60s soul music I cut my teeth on. I know that's out there, but people would hear me play and scratch their heads on all the funk that erupted when I'd play. I'm also a *huge* Stevie Wonder fan—of the early seventies masterpieces, *Music of My Mind*, *Talking Book*, *Innervisions,* and several others that followed. That guy is the bomb! I was a very devoted fan of The Band as well, you know, Levon Helm. Once, while in Cape Cod at Martha's Vineyard, I was fortunate enough to charm my way up onstage and sit in with what was left of the group. It was a religious experience for sure.

For a time, I bounced around in the early fusion/rock frontier, especially the Chick Corea and Herbie Hancock worlds. Man, I still eat up that early "Headhunters" stuff—it's killer. Lots of earthy and rhythmic grooves and mind-blowing percussion. I also have a very nice bluegrass collection. My influences just seem to come from everywhere.

The first band I was in was the seventh grade. My folks divorced, and I moved with my mother further into town, an area called Ft. Caroline, in Arlington. My sister and I stayed very much in touch with our dad. I attended a junior high school, and our little combo called "The Rockers" entered a talent contest where we performed two original tunes that were really quite decent. We had this guy who was from England who sure looked the Beatles part, faked playing the bass, but could sing okay, and the chicks went wild! And as the story goes, Barry Lee Harwood was in the crowd and later proclaimed, "That's the band I wanna be in!" I didn't know him at the time, but we later had an interesting first meeting.

So how did you meet Barry Lee?

Barry and I had a rather peculiar meeting sometime in seventh grade. As I recall, my school bus passed a really cool-looking red Corvair convertible that had been pulled over by the police, and upon further glaring at the situation, I saw it was Barry and his very attractive mom being ticketed. So, by the time he got to school just before homeroom, I was blabbing all about it to all who would listen, and the next thing I know, little ol' Barry Harwood—and I was pretty short then myself—was all over me, not physically, but he was all bowed up and he let me and everybody know I needed to shut my big mouth or else. Man, he was hot! Well, some time went by and I guess I heard he played bass pretty well; his dad and mom were in a country band that was a regular on a locally broadcast family entertainment/talent TV show. His dad, Clarence, played bass. So, we were seriously in need of a real player in the Rockers, so we ask him to come over and rehearse with us, and, oh, my God, that was the first time I realized what a band should sound like. I mean, it was like some new invention. I was gassed, so we begged him to join, and he did.

Sometime later, he wanted to switch to guitar, and I was really bummed because I knew there was no one else who knew the proper way to play bass. Believe it or not, as young as we were, there were no bass players to be found—*anywhere*. Well, eventually he made the switch, and we did find a good bass man, and then another… We changed band members a few times, and off we went. Through most of high school and beyond, we played dances, senior breakfasts, naval bases, really seedy and horrid old bars downtown, tried our hand at going in the studio, and some close-to-home road gigs, which were a blast. And looking back I feel so very fortunate and lucky for all of it. It was approximately at this time we meet the One Percent, which soon changed their name to Lynyrd Skynyrd, and I just loved the name. It instantly sounded "big-time."

Did you play with any of the Skynyrd "family" prior to the Rossington Collins Band?

I believe if my memory serves me well, just before Leon joined Skynyrd, there were some players hangin' around at the old Comic Book Club downtown, and that place was rough. Myself and probably Barry Lee, Leon, and some others were jammin' around one late Sunday afternoon just having some fun. I seem to remember that Ronnie walked in and sat around and listened. The jukebox had one of their very early recordings on a 45 on it. I remember it kept getting played a lot. The song was "Need All My Friends," and I liked it and was surprised it didn't end up on their first album. I thought it was as strong as or even better than the other tracks.

Can you offer any insight into what Ronnie Van Zant was really like?

I knew Ronnie just enough to know that he was a man of quiet dignity and honor. Unpretentious and unassuming and just knew his place. A self-confident man, he seemed to walk out of another time almost. A time of chivalry, and just a plain old gentleman. I truly liked being around him. Now of course I never had to endure any of his disciplinary actions as we all knew he was known for. Glad I never had to quit his band. It was usually your ass if you did. Fortunately, I think he respected me, and the level of playing our band was at. It's hard to believe he's been gone longer than he was alive. A true classic and stylist.

One day around Christmas in the early '70s, *Pronounced* had been out maybe a year or so, Ronnie and Gary Rossington walked into a music store I was working at—we were casual friends at the time—[and Ronnie] told me he was looking to buy a starter drum set for his younger brother Johnny for Christmas. And all through the conversation and transaction, the both of them would drop these little remarks, maybe hints along the way as to when was I going to start doing what I really loved and was good at. I didn't catch on right away, but as soon as we got outside to load the drums, he just matter-of-factly blurted out, "Would you like to play drums for Skynyrd?" Well, of course I was a little stunned to say the least. Then he stated they were thinking about letting Bob Burns go, and looking to replace him. What was my reply? There wasn't much of one, I think because Ronnie could see I was a little perplexed at the ambush, and he knew Barry and I were going at it pretty hard to get where they were. And I will tell you, that band busted their brains out to make it happen, such a shame to see it go down in such a way and at a time when they were heading for superstardom—America's Rolling Stones, you know?

Soon afterward, I heard "Sweet Home Alabama" and was blown away. I was like, where did that come from? So well put-together and well played, and, yes, I was listening to Bob Burns. I thought he must still have the gig. Later, it was suggested to me by several friends that maybe my missing that opportunity kept me on this earth for a while longer. It makes me shudder. That had to be fright beyond words.

I know you and Randall Hall spent some time touring with Melanie. What was she like to work with? Did you get tired of hearing "Brand New Key"?

Let me back up a little to a time around 1976 or so, and Barry Lee was picked up by Melanie, probably an offshoot of his time doing session work in Atlanta, and possibly New York. He called me one day when I was at work at the music store, and knowing what a huge fan of Stevie Wonder I was, just wanted to share with me that Stevie had just walked by him in the hallway at the Record Plant, I believe. Of course, I just got stupid. I'm sure I was foaming at the mouth, just without words. I was terribly envious. So later that year, I almost got a percussion-only gig with her and with Barry, just the three of us. I was going to get to play piano on a cool cover of "Tennessee Waltz" during the show, too. They were going to Australia and New Zealand. I was so stoked. However, at the last minute, again the plug was pulled on me. They cited financial reasons.

A couple of years later—sometime in 1979, I think—our band Running Easy was playing at a Gainesville hotspot and on one of our breaks we got a message that Rickey Medlocke of Blackfoot had called and left a message for Randall to call him, somewhere up north, I believe. The message was that Melanie Safka was looking for a new band; she wanted to go electric. We didn't know what to think. The kicker was that she had a bass player she really liked and wanted to keep. So somehow it got worked out with Gary, our bass player, and about a month later we were rehearsing with her at her summer cottage on Ft. Meyers Beach in Southwest Florida. We played a few theaters in New York and New Jersey, then played a killer electric folk festival in Switzerland. Man, that was one of the most incredible things I've ever gotten to do. It was like Woodstock on Lake Geneva. Wow! We also took a train to the Montreux Jazz Festival. That was a gas. As far as "Brand New Key," we didn't stay together all that long, so I played it just a couple of times. I think she just did it solo, short version. She was probably sick of it for sure. She only did a few of her older classics like "Candles in the

Rain" and "Laydown Laydown," which were great live tunes. That relationship was over pretty quick. She loved the band but her manager husband said they could no longer afford us. Oh, well.

Can you tell me where you were when you heard about the Skynyrd plane crash, and what your thoughts were at the time?

Our band Running Easy was playing at a bar, and I got a message to call home; my wife had called. So, when I got the news from her, we really didn't have much information, didn't know if it was a commercial flight or whatever, and I felt some worry, but honestly thought that maybe there were no major casualties and certainly not what was to come. So, we all went home, not knowing anything else, and on my ride home I tuned in to our local FM rock station, where they were pretty hard on the coverage. By then it was revealed that in fact it was a charter, that the whole band and crew were on board, and there were fatalities. Of course, I was sick at my stomach at the sound of that. They had no names as of yet—this was about 2 A.M. in the morning. So, when I got home, I sat up and just listened and took it all in. As I recall, there was huge anticipation and word they would report the list of fatalities soon, and when the time came, I just shuddered. It was so unbelievable. It was terribly sad to hear the names, but I really couldn't believe Ronnie's was one of them. You just thought he was invincible. We attended the funeral and I remember seeing Billy Powell with the damage to his nose, but he seemed quite receptive and friendly. I was able to approach him and tell him how sorry we all were. Maybe a year or so later, I was in a backstage area at a Blackfoot concert, I think, and who would walk up to me, and I really didn't see him until he was right up on me, but it was Billy. He seemed genuinely happy to see me, and equally candid. Just very warm and friendly, just wanted to say hello. I asked him how were things, and he said just doing it day by day, and looking forward to getting back to playing on the big stage. I knew then what a great man he was, and he was so very engaging and wanted you to know you were his friend.

It seems Artimus would be the first choice as drummer for RCB. How did you land the gig?

I had heard of the formation of a new band and knew that Barry Lee was going to be a part of it. Again, I was very envious, but also happy for him. I think they had been getting it together up in North Carolina, at a place called Bat Cave N.C., where Arti was recovering from a motorcycle accident. I'm not sure if I knew it was his kickdrum leg then or not. It would've been irrelevant to me at the time anyway. I think I knew they were trying a chick singer, the 38 Special backup singer, Dale Krantz. I didn't know anything about her. Seems that Arti wanted the band to listen to and consider a friend of his who was lead singer in his band, Studebaker Hawke. I don't know if that ever transpired, but I believe they were pretty impressed with Dale and her lyric-writing ideas and ability. I think when she opened it up, they were sold. And it was very intuitive on their part; no one could stand in Ronnie's place. Good move. It's a bit gray here, but from all of the hearsay and opinions flying all about, it was said that Arti wasn't too happy with his bud being out, and wasn't sure about the chick-singer thing. Nothing personal, I'm sure. I don't think there was any question about it as things came along. And the leg was certainly an impairment. Very frustrating for him. Out of the blue, very early in the morning, middle of the week, I was jolted awake by the phone that was ringing. No answering machine or voicemail back then. So, I finally answered it, and was floored to hear Billy Powell's voice on the other end. You can't imagine the surprise. I had to stop and reassure myself I wasn't dreaming, really. He proceeded to tell me that it was looking like Arti was not doing it with them this time, or at least not now, and everybody was back in Jacksonville and they would sure like me to come out that next afternoon to Allen's rehearsal studio, bring my drums, and see if things could work. I couldn't believe my ears. I was up the rest of the night. At the time, I was working for a ship chandler, which is the business of supplying commercial ocean-going vessels with food supplies and just about everything you or I would need to survive. That job surely sucked. I would do deliveries in the freezing rain and cold in these derelict trucks. It was so depressing. So, with an aura of "this can't be happening," I made my way out there.

What was that first get-together or rehearsal like?

I was warmly welcomed and we proceeded to drop the hammer. It was awesome and powerful. Those guys rehearsed at almost stage-level volume. I'm thinking, we plowed through what was later to become "Prime Time," and the fellas were just grinning ear to ear. I was trying to remain conscious, don't you know? Allen blurted out, "Now that's what I'm fucking talking about!" They were signing me up in less than an hour.

What was your initial reaction to Dale's singing?

I could hear the woman had chops, but didn't realize how incredible her delivery was until we were cutting the first album. She would sing along for scratch vocals as we laid basic tracks, and when we played it back we were all just juiced to hear how much energy was there. I think she only re-sang parts of two or three tracks. Amazing. Allen always called her "you wailing bitch!" With affection, of course.

What were some of the high points of the RCB days?

There were many, but for me one of first things I recall was when we were nearly finished with cutting tracks on the first album, and some over-dubbing had begun, some of the brass from MCA Records came out to hear their new artists, and how the album was coming along. The president of the company along with some of the A&R folks came along. We all gathered in the control room, and Allen says to the engineer, "Don't be shy" —meaning the volume he played it back at. So about 30 seconds into the track, Allen charges up to the console, switches on the big playback speakers, and jacks the throttle up. Meanwhile the co-owner is standing there with us, and very much concerned. Then Allen reassures him that MCA will cover the damages, with an intimidating chuckle. Well, we just howled, and those tracks just rocked the house. It was awesome. They all looked at each other when it was over, just flabbergasted. You could tell they were just stunned and blown away at how great it was.

Another memorable highlight would've been some of the large shows we did. The New Year's Eve, 1980–'81 transition. All of our families came up to Atlanta at the Omni, which was probably the largest indoor facility of the time. My dad was there with my oldest brother, my family, and my two kids who were 11 and 5 at the time. At the stroke of 12 o'clock, the kids all came out onstage with us, my daughter was up on my shoulders, fireworks were going off, the front of the stage had this great firework effect that sizzled like a curtain of sparklers. When the thing heated up, it sort of raised up from the heat, like a curtain would do. Some of us were standing at the very front cheering with our fans, and I almost lost my balance while leaning back to get me and my daughter away from the monster. It was all good, though, and we cleared the stage and went into the renowned instrumental "Free Bird." And you know how that goes over. The entire spectacle—the pre-show and everything the simulcast DJs could think up—was broadcast nationwide. It was fabulous. I actually have a board mix from that show.

And it is strong. Don't tell anyone, though. (Laughs) Three days later, we came home to a front-page write-up with a huge color live photo, and a sold-out coliseum. I can't say enough about that feeling. There are many wonderful highlights of our very short existence, but one more I must share is when I received my first gold album. I was thrilled, and almost as thrilled when I gave the adult family members their very own gold records. I think a few of them cried. I had arrived!

How did the band break up, and what happened next? Didn't you join the Allen Collins Band? Tell us about that group.

That is a rather delicate subject. After an incredible first year, an album that was holding its own in the charts—I believe it got to #9 in some very worthy company—we were having so much fun. It kind of had a euphoric sensation swirling around the whole miraculous happening. After tragedy struck again with the passing of Allen's wife, and just getting caught up in all of the trappings of the big-time rock-and-roll lifestyle, something just went out of the bubble. We were convinced by the record company to get into the studio in a rather hurried fashion; we would pick up a nice bonus if we got our second record out by a certain deadline. So, we bit on it, were really unprepared. Allen had a pretty serious car accident a week before we were to go, and he was really struggling with the loss of his wife. He absolutely adored her, and had two young daughters. He just seemed lost. It was very hard to see this happening to him. About this time, it became evident that Gary and Dale were in a pretty serious relationship, and that seemed to drive a wedge between Allen and Gary, and the normally free-flowing productive juices just bogged down. There was a lot of bad behavior to get into out in El Paso, and that just further worsened the entire situation. It was a catastrophic crash-and-burn outcome, and it just got worse when we got down to Criteria studios in Miami for mixing and mastering. Every imaginable poison that could be thrown our way was, and we barely got the album finished. After lots of anguish and discontentment everywhere, multiple canceled shows two and three times, RCB performed a benefit concert here at home. Little did we know, it would be our last. Man, that was hard to swallow.

A few weeks passed, and Gary announced that he and Dale needed to get away to clear their heads and think about the future. We got a call from them from somewhere in Wyoming, and they said they were done. I was stunned. Such an awesome new beginning for the survivors, and just a tease for the rest of us. And it was all over. It was very hard to deal with it, I assure you. A few months went by, and I guess Allen, Leon, Billy, myself, and Barry wanted to carry on, so we tracked down my old bandmate Randall Hall, and somebody thought about Jimmy Dougherty. We became the Allen Collins Band. We recorded one really good record, and at the time of its release our record company, MCA, was now in the arms of Motown Records. I think they went, "Allen Collins Band—who?" Very little album support from them. They just cleaned house, so we were pretty much on our own. We toured a little, a couple of uneventful shows. It just seemed that Allen wasn't into it. I know he was just beaten down. It was over.

Would you share your thoughts on Leon Wilkeson?

God, where do I start? Leon and I, once we were laying the lumber, musically, were like old long-lost pals that found each other again. When we played together it was like a freight train. It was with little effort for our parts to just lock in like a rock. It was like a mental telepathic communication. We rarely discussed or hashed out how to make our parts come together. We could lay down our basic tracks in record time. When we were done, it was depressing. We really rolled. At soundchecks most of the time it would be me, Leon, and Barry, with Billy some of the time. We would have some very productive moments. A gas.

On a more personal one-on-one relationship note, I would have to say that Leon was really my favorite. We hung out a lot; I would drag him out in the boat sometimes, and actually got him to go camping with Billy, Timmy Lindsey, and myself once. He loved it. We rode around in the river most of the night and had a ball. He had quite the moral conviction tucked away in his being, and it would be hard to realize that sometimes, and I know a lot of people didn't perhaps see that side of him, though there was no doubt with whoever was fortunate enough to spend some time with him. He was all ears, and loved to talk at length about just about anything. And he would make you feel very comfortable. We really hit it off great, lots of shenanigans from the two of us. All through the Skynyrd reunion years, he was always very mindful about calling me on my birthday and at Christmas. He would end the call with, "Love your guts." I loved that man. How I do miss him.

Is it true you were initially asked to be on the reunion tour in '87?

Yes, that's true. We, the remnants of the ACB thing, were sitting around at the band office listening to Gene Odom talking up this grand idea of putting together a quasi-Skynyrd show, with the ten-year anniversary of the plane crash approaching. After we all thought about it for a bit, and we weren't doing anything at the time, we thought, hey, yeah, that might appropriate. God knows who else was thinking about it, but the next thing I know I'm on the outside looking in, and the rest is history.

Are you friends with the surviving Skynyrd/RC Band members? Are you close with Artimus or Bob Burns?

Sadly, with the passing of Billy Powell, he was my last remaining good, good friend of the whole crew. I've known Rickey Medlocke for a long time but really don't have the opportunity to associate with him at all. I have no contact with Gary or Dale, no choice of my own. We'll leave it at that. Artimus and I are friends, though he's not around much for me to see him. However, I had a nice visit with him at Billy's funeral, got to hand him off a copy of the CD I just did. I did see Bob Burns—we know each other from way back, but unfortunately, he got away before we could chat.

What did you do next? Tell us about playing with Derek Trucks.

Derek and I are both from Jacksonville, and when he was just starting out he'd come out to these weekend deck parties at various waterfront locations in Jax. I knew his dad a little, and when he was showing some real progress, I guess at the age of about 12 or 13, they put a band together for him, and a couple of years later I jumped in and did some ramblings around Canada. He was outrageous, at any age you could say. But at the tender age of 16, he played like a well-traveled and cultured musician. The coolest thing that happened when we were together, and we had a damn good band, we did a couple of Bob Dylan dates, and ol' Dylan invited the young guitar whiz up onstage to play with him. Got to see that up close, and it was really great for Derek. We eventually got into the studio and did some tracks for Capitol Records. Jimmy Hall on vocals and harp, and Chuck Leavell on some keys and producing. That stuff kicked ass. Don't know why it got shelved. It's pretty cool to see him having such great success. I guess he's followed every tip I've given him, eh? (Laughs) No, just funnin'. I talk to him from time to time. We always kick around our alter-ego musical association of the past as "The Derek Brothers Band."

Give me your thoughts on *Mainstream South* and your bandmates Steve Perez and Barry Lee Harwood.

From the outset of this studio project, I don't believe Steve or myself saw it as a viable piece of work that would travel beyond our own gratification and sharing it with some friends and family. Initially, it was partly envisioned as a way to get our old musical ideas, with our old bandmates, involving everyone that we crossed paths with back in the early days, and have some fun. We knew we wanted to get Randall Hall doing his original parts on the new retooled material, along with some new ideas of Steve's and Barry Lee with his off-the-chain guitar mastery, and whoever we could persuade to come and do it with us. Well, most of what we wanted to happen did transpire, and so with tireless effort on Steve's part, we were pretty happy with the result. We understand it does get a little busy, and sometimes a bit crowded, but there is no denying the energy and good intentions the music does convey. Steve Perez has a rather crafty knack for coming up with ideas that are fun to play on. They do develop through the arrangement very nice. They do inspire. He's a very good player, one who Billy Powell had loads of respect for. I'm very happy he came up with this whole idea, and that I got to be a part of it. I would have never seen this a couple of years ago.

What are your thoughts on the state of music today, especially this thing we call Southern rock?

I've always maintained an open mind to any and all music that has something to offer. It is remarkable how music's creative forces, styles, and message simply evolved and altered its path over the years. You find yourself at some crossroads several years and many new bands later wondering, just how did we get to this point? It amazingly slips by, doesn't it? Wish I could write a song or poem to capture it. I am perplexed at some of the simple and angry culture that is depicted in some of the new bands today. Now there are a few that are really good at it. Hip hop and the anti-social venom that's everywhere doesn't make me think about having a good time doing much of anything. I don't want to come off sounding ignorant, but there's no doubt some new artists do say it in a good and inspiring way. Funny that I never considered myself a "Southern-rocker" type, but I am very honored to have been right in the middle of one of the most renowned and legendary bands of our time. And I had the privilege of being a part of a nearly impossible resurrection of sorts to come out of a terrible tragedy, and one that clearly stood on its own merit, and on its own very big stage.

Who was the greatest drummer that ever lived?

Now you know that's one impossible spot to be put in. I'd have to say Mitch Mitchell, Ringo of course, and those early big-band drummers that just kicked the band along. Huge energy, that stuff. Talk about the wall of sound. I'd have to say I have always keyed in on any track that overall just cooks along. It's hard to name a favorite, there's just too many. Oh, yeah, Stevie Wonder had one of the great groove drummers of all time, really.

Any words of wisdom for aspiring musicians out there?

Keep your nose clean. Have fun and don't fall into the traps that are laid for you, which are many. Be considerate of your bandmates and have fun. It can be a great ride, even with all of the disappointments. •

Donnie and Johnny Van Zant

2001

Perhaps no other name in Southern rock conjures up as many images as that of Van Zant. Like the Petty's in NASCAR, their family name is forever etched into the rock-and-roll family tree. From the legendary Ronnie Van Zant of Lynyrd Skynyrd, to his baby brother Johnny who would one day take his position at the front of the Skynyrd band following his untimely death, to their middle brother Donnie, a veteran rock-and-roller with his band 38 Special. The Van Zants are icons of the American South, and musical heroes to millions around the globe.

When we spoke in 2001, two surviving Van Zant brothers had once again come together to record a follow-up to their highly successful Brother to Brother *release of 1998. We caught up with the brothers for a telephone interview the day after Valentine's Day.*

Donnie: Johnny will join us in one second. He's having a house built out here, and somebody came up unexpectedly.

MBS: That's great. How have you been?

Donnie: Just great, man! It's good to hear from you again!

You, too! What inspired you guys to return to the studio to do this second record together?

Donnie: You know what, man, I think it was just the success we had from the first one. It went out there and did well for us. Like the song "Rage," it was, like, a Top-10 song for us, and it did well selling-wise. We were very happy with it, and CMC offered us a deal to go back in and do another one. We didn't really know if we were going to do another one or not. But when they came back with an option to do a second CD, we jumped on it, you know.

The first song on the album is very compelling. Can you tell us the story behind "Oklahoma"?

Donnie: It came from watching the news. It's about the devastating tornados that those people have been through out there. Robert Johnson, Chris Peleer, and myself wrote a song about it. We were inspired by the people. They didn't seem to be complaining, you know? They just showed an incredible amount of faith and strength. They just pulled together to help each other. There wasn't anybody out here trying to be heroes, you know? They were just trying to help their neighbor. It was a pretty heavy song.

There's a lot of great songwriting on the album.

Donnie: Thanks, man.

I noticed Kenny Wayne Shepherd plays on the album. How did that come to be?

Donnie: Well, Michael, Kenny Wayne was opening for Skynyrd. They were playing some big sheds a couple of years ago. So, Johnny met him on the tour there. After that, Kenny Wayne started dating my niece Melody, which is Ronnie's youngest daughter. About two and a half years ago, and he came over to my mother and father's house for Thanksgiving, and had dinner with us over there. That's when we hit him with it. (Laughs) "Hey, we're thinking about doing another record. Would you be interested in playing on it?" We kept him to his word, man! (Laughs)

Do you have any favorite songs on the new album?

Donnie: You know, I'm really proud of all of 'em. If we weren't proud of them, they wouldn't be on the record to begin with. I mean, I like "Oklahoma" a whole lot. "Alive," I like that one a whole lot because Johnny and I wrote that with Jim Peterik. Jim was actually flying to Nashville to write with us, and he had a real difficult time. The plane that he was in had to make an emergency landing. So, when he got to Nashville, he was real upset. Real nervous and the whole nine yards, you know. I just mentioned the line "Ain't it good to be alive?" and that just triggered something. The song just came from that one little statement.

Who would you say influenced you the most in your songwriting and music?

Donnie: I think our brother. He was definitely a big influence. He was very underrated as a songwriter, and as a performer and a singer. He was a big influence. Michael, we've got Johnny here now. (Laughs)

Johnny: Hi, Michael!

How are you, Johnny?

Johnny: I'm just fine, thank you.

Johnny, let me ask you the same question I just asked Donnie. Who would you say influenced you the most as a songwriter and singer?

Johnny: Oh, God. Tiny Tim? (Laughs) No...Ronnie and Donnie were my biggest influences, me being the youngest of the three. And I loved Paul Rodgers from Free. And I loved the country people, like Merle Haggard. Of course, I loved Marvin Gaye and Ray Charles, as far as singing goes.

Donnie: I just gave him a dollar, Michael. (Laughs)

Make a buck any way you can, brother! Johnny, could you address the Internet rumors that Lynyrd Skynyrd is planning on breaking up in 2002? Is there any truth to that?

Johnny: Not that I know of. But that's how the rumors get started—the Internet—ain't it? No, as a matter of fact we are writing for a new album. Actually, I leave on Saturday to go and write some. We'll be cutting demos for the record in April. And we've got 72 shows planned for the outdoor amphitheaters this summer. After that we'll take a little break, and between our break, me and Donnie will go back out, I'm sure. (Laughs) And then we'll start on the record after the first of the year.

I just wanted to throw in that I thought your Christmas album was just great. I hope you'll do more duets with Dale Krantz Rossington. Your duet on the album was awesome.

Johnny: Thank you. Yeah, that was my idea. I've done opened up a can of worms with that. (Laughs) I always thought she was a great singer, and I had that song for a long time, so when we decided to do a Christmas album, I just hit 'em with it on the bus one night and it all just fell together. But that was a fun record for us, because we got to produce it. We didn't have any jerk in there going, "You can't do that."

Donnie, what's the status of the new 38 Special album?

Donnie: We're working on it right now, Michael. It's got some good, rocking songs on it.

If it's as good as this Van Zant album, it'll be great.

Donnie: I hope it's better! (Laughs)

We were all deeply saddened by the recent death of your mother, Sister Van Zant. I just wondered if you'd each tell me the most important thing your mom ever taught you?

Johnny: Everything.

Donnie: She was the glue. She held this family together. I think Johnny and I realize it more today than we did when she was living. We always felt that way, you know. We just lost our best friend, that's it. She was someone you could just go to and talk in confidence, you know? She would just listen to you, and not judge you.

Johnny: Like Donnie said, man, she was just everything to us. We miss her a lot, and we know that she's with us every day of our lives.

How's your dad, Lacy, doing these days?

Johnny: He's doing good. He keeps me and Donnie hopping. (Laughs) He just turned 86 years old. He had a birthday and we had a cake over there for him the other night and he was in good spirits.

Lacy's almost as popular as you guys.

(Johnny and Donnie laughing)

Donnie: You know what I always said… If he could sing and play guitar, we'd be out of a job! (Laughs)

I wonder if each of you would give us a special memory of your brother Ronnie.

Johnny: The last day I spent with him, Donnie was there, too, just being out there at his house. He really had his stuff together right before he passed away. We'd gone out there to do a *People* magazine interview. That was a special day for me. There were a lot of them, to be honest, but that one, maybe because it was the last one, sticks out in my memory.

Donnie: He was physically in good shape, too. So many years before that, he wasn't. But he had been lifting weights and swimming.

And you could hear it in his voice. It was so strong at the last concert here in Greenville. We all miss Ronnie for sure, but we're so glad we have you guys to carry on the tradition.

Both: Thank you.

Do you think 38 Special and Lynyrd Skynyrd will ever tour together again?

Donnie: Johnny, what do you think about it? (Laughs)

Johnny: We have done shows in the past together, but never a complete tour. I would love to see that happen, of course. That would be a great thing.

Donnie: We actually both have the same management now, so we're going to be working on that, especially on 38's end. (Laughs)

I think it's a great package. And 38 is going out on the Volunteer Jam Tour this summer, too.

Donnie: We're gonna do, I think, 15 to 18 shows with that. From what I understand it's doing great already.

Has the Van Zant tour started, or getting set to start?

Johnny: We just started rehearsing—for my birthday, February 27. And I expect to get a birthday present. (Laughs) No, it starts, Michael, March 6 in Orlando.

How do you feel about doing this together?

Donnie: It's exciting but scary. I know, for myself, I've been playing with the same guys for 27 years, you know. I've never been outside of 38 Special as a band. But it's a dream come true for me and Johnny.

Johnny: Hey, man, I figure I'm just gonna have a lot of bruises on me. (Donnie laughs.) Donnie running around. I'll be that pole that he always runs into. (Laughs) But I'm looking forward to it. I told him we should have started off somewhere like South Dakota where nobody would come see us. But we're starting in Orlando where all the family will come see us. We'd better be on it that night, either that or be loved really well. But fans are great. The way I look at it, when I first went out with Skynyrd I was scared to death. But now doing something new is real adventurous to me.

Will you be doing any of your 38 Special or Lynyrd Skynyrd tunes on the tour?

Johnny: Well, man, they need to come and see. (Laughs) We wouldn't do a show without giving 'em a taste of both.

What's next on your agendas for each of you?

Donnie: Right now, we're concentrating on getting *Van Zant II* out there and going as far as we can with that. Also, there's 38—that's my band there—you know what I mean? I really want to put the effort and time into that, too, and come out with a great CD there, too. We're pretty busy, man.

Johnny: Myself, just writing for another record. That's the end of the cycle; we put one out and then do another one. We have 72 shows we are doing this summer. We start out in May in Canada, where we're going out with Ted Nugent. But Donnie and I do this because we like working together and hanging out with each other. And I think we're putting out some pretty good music, too.

It's great.

Johnny: I'll tell you what it is, it's Rock 105 here, and they suck because they don't play us! Radio is so confusing these days. They have active rock, mainstream rock, and classic rock. It's all a bunch of bullshit. They should just have "rock."

Donnie: Thanks. I want to encourage your readers to call up the radio stations and ask for the new songs. It just means so much. I'll just tell you a "for-instance": We have a radio station in my own home town. They just play classic rock music, and it's hard to get our new stuff played on these classic rock stations. I just wish they'd play all good music.

...Play good music, old and new.

Johnny: Right. Just play good music. It just makes it hard to get new music played here, whether you are 38 Special, Lynyrd Skynyrd or Van Zant, or Van Halen. If you come out with a new record, you're not gonna get it played in Jacksonville, Florida. But you would think—between the two of us, we have how many years?

Donnie: About 40 years?

Johnny: Forty years, I figure we're as classic as they come. Play our damn music! (Laughs)

Donnie: But we would appreciate the fans calling up the radio to request our music.

Johnny: Yeah. We do love the fans. Without them, we'd be mowing grass. •

In 2005, the duo Van Zant went country, got a major deal with Sony, and put out an album that spawned a Top-10 country hit. Their father, Lacy, passed away in 2004. Johnny continues to front Lynyrd Skynyrd and Donnie continues as a member of 38 Special, although medical issues prohibit touring. •

Don Barnes

2000

One of the hardest-working bands of the '80s and '90s, still going strong today, is 38 Special. With a string of Top-40 hits a mile long, the band just keeps getting better and better. Along with co-bandleader Donnie Van Zant, Don Barnes rode the wave of success from the very beginning, playing guitar and singing with one of the finest voices in classic (or Southern) rock.

Back in 2000, I spoke with Barnes by phone from his Atlanta home about the band, his past, his future, and Donnie's brother, Ronnie Van Zant.

MBS: When is the new studio album coming out?

Don: Well, we are probably doing it in sections. Six songs this spring. Danny just got off the road with Gregg Allman and Friends. He needs some time off the road. We will go out and do six weeks of shows and then come back and finish it. But we have some great stuff, really powerful songs. We just put everything on hold and did this live album. That was pretty much the strategy to reacquaint the public with the history of the band and all the singles through the years.

Let's jump back to the very beginning. Where did you originally come from, and where do you live now?

I was from Jacksonville, Florida, and live in Atlanta now. I moved up here about 1984 after spending 32 years in Jacksonville. It was hot and humid and flat. We did a lot of records up here at Doraville, Georgia. It is a pretty historic place. I would come up here and drive a rental car around Atlanta and get lost. I liked the change of seasons and the terrain of the area, and over the years we have all migrated up here from Jacksonville. There is a whole different attitude here. This is more of a hub. When the plane lands in Atlanta you can just go on home.

When and how did you get involved in music?

My family was musical. My dad was the musical director in the Baptist church growing up. My brother and sister and I were all steeped in the church music. My dad played the piano and we learned some of that from him. My brother was four years older than I am and he went on to be a big musical guy in high school with the hootenannies. I watched him, and of course the Beatles were a big influence on the *Ed Sullivan Show*. Over the years my sister sang acapella in the choir and there were some simple piano chords that we knew, and then I picked up some guitar chords. Donnie Van Zant and I have known each other all these years. There were about 15 to 20 bands before 38 Special. We've known each other since we were 12 years old.

Speaking of earlier bands, was he in Alice Marr with you? What's the story on that, and where did you get that name?

Donnie had come across an old encyclopedia that told about an old ghost ship. Legend had it that all of the people on the boat were dead of the plague and it was an old, odd name, so we used that. Billy Powell was actually on the keyboards in that band. We offered him to join us and we played a few gigs and then it was not long before he started being a roadie for Skynyrd.

What is the story about the van you got from Ocean Way Auto Parts?

There was an old truck called Big Blue that kept falling apart. It kept eating up all of our profits. I remember coming home with $30 after fixing this truck. Donnie and I would ride around and try to find an obscure place to rehearse. We would find these places for fifty bucks a month to rehearse; of course, we had day jobs then. The guy could not figure out why we wanted to rent this place. There was manure, and we had to shovel it out of there and then get some pallets to stand on for a floor. We had the place fortified and had it vaulted up with 2x4's and a big motorcycle chain that went through the hole in the door to lock it with this old rusty lock. Then we had to climb in a window to get in and out. One night we were rehearsing and heard someone banging on the door and when we looked, there were 12 constables banging on the door to get in. We were yelling and telling them we couldn't open the door and one of them yelled that he had a .38 special to use on the door if we wouldn't let him in. So, when we had our first show, we had not thought of a name so we decided to use that name.

Wow, with just a little shift of fate you could have named the band "Rusty Lock"!

(Laughs) That's right.

But you would have had to be a heavy metal band.

(More laughter) We became friends of some of those officers after that. Over the years, we had moved into town and these officers looked after us.

You guys have had some songs on movie soundtracks. How did this affect the band?

For a while we had a lofty position with A&M Records and they had A&M Films and they wanted us to do a song for their movie *Revenge of the Nerds*. So we did "Back to Paradise." It was a good song, not a great movie. Before that we did "Caught Up in You" in the movie *Spring Break*. And we did a song in *Teacher, Teacher*, with Nick Nolte and JoBeth Williams.

We would just stop in the studio and do a couple of days recording and whip out a tune for a song track. They wanted you to do a three-track recording so they can remove the vocals if necessary. That was a good vehicle to propel a song forward.

During the time period you were not in 38 Special, did you do solo albums?

There was a period of time when I was not involved with the band. You tend to put your personal life on hold and we had achieved lots of our dreams, money, and success, and I felt like I needed to leave for a while and take another path. I did a solo album with A&M and then they were bought out by Polygram. The solo record was not released at the time and it is still there. It could be released in the future. I was able to write with lots of other writers and it was a good growth period. John Bettis and Jim Valance and Randy Goodrum are just a few of the guys I got to work with. I was able to absorb those different influences and come back to the band with much more creativity. They were able to explore many more avenues with Max Carl and Danny Chauncey. This was a good break, and I had met my wife during this period. I have been married for five years now and bought a boat, learned to ski, and gotten some balance and reflection on my life and creativity.

I let some of the readers know that we were talking with you, and some of them wanted to know if you had hung out with Lacy Van Zant, and what do you think of him?

Lacy has been a big mentor of the band. Ronnie (Van Zant) was a tremendous mentor. Coming from the wrong side of the tracks, he made the whole world listen to him. He had such strength and fortitude and perseverance. This was an influence we took and there was no other band that experienced that.

Lacy was so supportive when we were just sleeping on a mattress in a van. He would talk about perseverance and keeping your chin up. Lacy is a great guy and we go back to when we were kids. We all grew up on the same street; Donnie and Steve Brookins were all friends. Lacy was the patriarch of the whole group. He is a great man, and when the tragedy happened [the Lynyrd Skynyrd plane crash of 1977] and I was the one who flew out with Lacy to identify the bodies, the strength that this man displayed was monumental. Lacy was in denial on the plane and hoped that there was a mistake and that his son was not dead. I had to find out who was where and we had to get to the funeral home to identify the body. After seeing Ronnie at the funeral home and paying last respects with Lacy, I felt changed because this man had helped me at an early age. He had co-signed for me to get an amp when I was young. He felt I wanted it bad enough to make something of myself as a musician. Up until then I was giving about 80 percent of my talent, but after seeing Ronnie dead and remembering his kindness, I try to give 100 percent.

We then went to the hospital and see all the other people who were hurt. They all looked at Lacy through stitches and swelling and he told me not to say anything about Ronnie. He just stood there and said that Ronnie was fine and you just get better and rest. This man had just been to the funeral home and seen his son dead and decided to keep that to himself for these guys to heal. I told him that it was the strongest thing I had seen a man do. They were ripped from their life and career and there is justice that they can get back out there. Johnny does a great job and they perform very well. Everything was taken from them so quickly. Ronnie would have wanted them to go on. I have nothing but great respect for him and the Van Zant family.

What else do you remember about the early days of Skynyrd?

I used to ride my bike over to Allen's house and listen to records. His mom was great and very sweet. I remember walking into his house and he had this Vox amp there and she would just smile and be really proud of him. At the time, you are part of history in the making and we were just kids together. They were one of the first bands from Jacksonville to make it on their own material. There is a lot of musical history in Jacksonville.

Moving into the present time and have been enjoying this *Live from Sturgis* CD (CMC International, 1999). I heard that the weather was not very good when you recorded this show.

We did not have the luxury of taking music from several shows. The logistics of getting a camera crew and audio trucks in the midst of this biker rally was not easy. There are 5 to 6 stages going and the day we pulled up there, there were 40-mile-an-hour winds blowing sideways and rain. You would think that it would have been mild but it was cold and nasty weather. We had this giant 32-foot backdrop made and it was like a sail in this 40-mile wind. It almost pulled light trusses down. There is some mist coming out where we are singing. The guy with the camera was a distraction, but people did come out and we had a great time doing the show. Then everyone got drunk on the bus on the way out of town—stress relief. This was something that came out good considering all the problems.

Personally, how did you feel about this album?

I felt like there is a meaty sound there we captured on tape. The last show of this tour was at Myrtle Beach and we blew the roof off the place. I wish we had recorded that one, too. It came out great considering all of the obstacles we had to overcome. There is a lot of truth in all of our songs. Ronnie taught us that. He was a true down-home poet that put his poems to music. "Hold on Loosely" was written about a woman that I was married to and she was not letting me be myself. Jim was talking about the couplet line "but don't let go." I can't get anything done because I'm caught up in you all the time. We tend to find the destination first and write it into that. Other songwriters say they come up with a melody line and then write the lyrics and add the music. For some other people, it works the other way.

So, you really were heavily influenced by Ronnie Van Zant?

Basically, you can listen to Ronnie and get a biography of Ronnie through his music. Like I said, he was a true real-life poet. The "Ballad of Curtis Leow" song was written about a house that was literally up on concrete blocks, just a wooden shack. It was a little store and there was an old black guy that sat around there and sang.

What can you tell us about the new album?

The last studio album was a different departure for the band. We wanted to show some growth and evolution from the band and were trying to reinvent ourselves. This was a much more diverse record. We used some other instruments on there, some 12-strings—we did this with Joe Hardy out in Nashville. We used 12-string mandolins and all these odd things from around the studio. We were layering and overdubbing unusual instruments. We did address some issues about redemption and family spousal abuse. At this point we felt like our fans were surprised without the usual in-your-face guitars. We are going back to "in-your-face guitars" with muscle and melody. Our trademark is the congenial snarl of the guitar and that great melody that is sing-able and memorable. The muscle and melody is something that works for us.

How do you feel about the fans?

We have a strong fan base throughout the country. We like to let our fans come backstage and get an autograph and pictures. We know that without our fans we would not be working for 25 years. We are flattered to have longevity. We were the flavor of the week at one time and now it is nice to hear our songs that are 20 years old on radio. That was our goal in the first place. We have been very proud and happy to have achieved that. We have had some fans that have grown up with us. We have had some really good experiences. One of the songs off of the last studio album was debuted in space. A few astronauts came up onto the bus in Houston. You know how they wake them up with music, and they had picked one of our songs and we were invited to the Houston Space Center to sight-see. Then the astronauts came to the bus and were real quiet and nice and said, "Do you mind if we come on your bus?" We said, "Are you kidding? Anytime. Mind if we come on the space shuttle?" (Laughs) •

Greg T. Walker

2014

Greg T. Walker co-founded Blackfoot back in 1969, playing bass and singing backup during the band's entire run. But during an early break in the action, he became a member of Lynyrd Skynyrd, before reuniting Blackfoot a bit later. In our exclusive interview, Greg fills in all the gaps on the history of one of Southern rock's heaviest bands, Blackfoot, and tells us all about his days with Ronnie Van Zant's band, as well as his brand-new project, Two Wolf.

MBS: Greg, there was so much happening in Jacksonville at the time of the formation of Lynyrd Skynyrd and also of Blackfoot. Would you give us an accurate timeline as to when you formed Blackfoot and when you joined Skynyrd? And if you don't mind, detail it with who was in the band at the time, and what Skynyrd recordings you played on?

Greg: I formed Blackfoot the last week of August 1969 and we played our first show a week later in a Battle of the Bands. A few months earlier, Rickey Medlocke (RM), Charlie Hargrett, and me had a band with a keyboardist playing seven nights a week at the Comic Book Club in Jacksonville. RM was on drums at the time. The One Percent played there sometimes if we had a night off. Our keyboard player was having some issues and sometimes we played as a three-piece. I had an idea to let our keyboardist go and recruit two other guys I had known since kindergarten and had been in various bands with growing up. I called them where they were playing in Gainesville and, as luck would have it, they were having issues with their guitar player. I suggested we each eliminate a group member and merge the two bands. RM moves out front as the singer, Jakson took over drums, DeWitt Gibbs became the new keyboard player, and the rest is history. But there were a few hiccups in the early years. Six months after forming we moved to New York City for three months, then out to the country area of New Jersey where, after three months there, DeWitt left the band and returned to Florida. By then Rickey was already playing more and more guitar and often doing dual, harmony leads with Charlie so we had a good thing going. It was now summer of '70. We moved a couple of times and by the summer of '71 we were sharing a big band house with another band near Princeton, New Jersey. RM left to join Skynyrd and we all parted ways. Six months later I joined Skynyrd and was in the band from October 1971through May 1972. We recorded a lot of music during that time in Muscle Shoals, and I think we were the most well-rehearsed band in the country. That's all we did, like a job, six days a week. Eventually we lost the first "Hell House," a condemned house on the St. Johns River across the "bridge to nowhere," and began rehearsing at my parents' house in what was formerly my bedroom. RM and I had grown up together since around four years old and he was already like family, and Ronnie, Gary, and Allen were always polite and my parents liked them very much. It was a great time. We played gigs here and there, but I was really missing Blackfoot and told RM I wanted to get Jakson and Charlie back together and resume where we left off. I told him I wanted him to go with me, but if he chose to stay it was perfectly okay with me because we would always be friends. He chose to leave with me so I (we) reformed the band again. It didn't last very long as RM wound up going back to Skynyrd. Charlie was not with us anymore, we got another guitar player (Bobby), DeWitt came back in, changed the name and kept going for a while. We spent the late spring and summer of 1972 in Atlanta recording all original songs with the hopes of getting a record deal. DeWitt and Bobby went back to Jacksonville but Jakson and I remained, sleeping on packing quilts in the studio for two more months. Jakson and I were writing most of the songs and finished the record, with he and I running the board and playing different instruments. I even played a sax lead in a song. Imagine that! We regrouped in Gainesville, played some shows in Florida and Georgia for a couple of months, and things fell apart again. Late fall '72 I bought a one-way ticket to New York, walked into the Brill Building at 49th & Broadway, and landed a gig with The Tokens of "The Lion Sleeps Tonight" fame. We had met them a couple of years earlier when living in New York; they remembered me, had just inked a deal with Atco Records, and brought me into the fold. We did a brand-new record, had a huge hit of a remake of Wilson Pickett's "In the Midnight Hour" and it reached #14 in Billboard. It was a ballad, acoustic version, which was very cool, believe it or not. During this time, Charlie had joined a band in North Carolina called Blackberry Hill who had lost a guitar player. A few months later the drummer left so Jakson was brought in. A few months later the other guitar player quit and RM was brought in. Now three guys from Blackfoot were in a band with another bass player. The bass player got sick and the guys wanted to get me back so it would be the original band again. I was making $50 a week and $75 when we played a gig and I had to think about it. But, the guys came up to see me and I knew I wanted to come back to the band, so I agreed to make a trip down to North Carolina to spend a week and really talk about things. While I was there I called The Tokens, and gave my two-week notice. Everyone in the band was pissed except Jay Seigel, the lead singer. He knew where my heart was and was very happy for me, giving me his full support and blessings. We are still great friends to this day. Thank you, Jay; you are a great human being. This was the summer of '73. Blackfoot stayed intact with me, RM, and Jakson to the very end. A keyboard player (Ken Hensley) was added in 1982, Charlie left the following year, Hensley quit soon afterward, and Bobby Barth was brought in to assume both guitar and keyboard duties and vocals. Bobby was, and still is, a great talent who brought a lot to the table. This lineup played its last show in December 1985, and everything came crashing down the last day of January 1986. Took me ten years to get past that, but I never have gotten over it. Like I said, I got past it.

Did you guys consider Blackfoot Southern rock, hard rock, or metal? Seems you were always on shows with AC/DC, Scorpions, etc.

We always considered ourselves hard rock. When we began in 1969 the only terms around were simply "rock band" or "rock-n'-roll band." It was several years later when "Southern rock" began to apply to the bands coming out of the South, especially northern Florida. Somewhere around 1980 or 1981 the term "Southern Metal" was coined and used to describe us, as we were a harder-edged band to have come from the South.

What was the biggest show Blackfoot ever played?

In August of 1981 we played the Monsters of Rock festival in England with AC/DC, Whitesnake, and others to a crowd of 80,000. That was the official paid attendance and estimates of 90 to 100 thousand were the unofficial estimates. It was insane, a day I will never forget. There were a few others with different lineups in Europe with the same numbers.

Who were your favorite bands to tour with? You were pretty tight with AC/DC, right?

We got along great with everyone and the list is long, so forgive me if any bands feel left out. In no particular order: Foghat, Nugent, Peter Frampton, ZZ Top, Iron Maiden, Scorpions, Deep Purple, The Who, Cheap Trick. This barely scratches the surface. Touring with AC/DC was unique because we did a lot of shows when Bon [Scott] was alive. Bon, Jakson, and I raised many an elbow together. When Brian came into the band it was instant friendship as well. Those guys were very kind and gracious to us every single night, as well as their crew. We had a blast. As far as pure fun, it was Nazareth that made our tours a riot. From day one we hit it off, hung out on- and offstage, rode on each other's busses at times. laughed, drank, swapped stories, and had the time of our lives.

We'd love to hear a funny road story or two.

Once in a while I think of something funny but never seem to be anywhere with a pen and paper to write it down. So, each time I am asked this question I have failed to come up with a particular story. At least something printable. I apologize for this. Life was a party for many years and all the memories are happy ones.

You guys played a lot with Molly Hatchet, too. Did you all get along?

Dave Hlubek and I go back to around the age of 12, so we had been friends many years during our youth before the touring began in the late '70s through early '80s. We butted heads now and again on some shows, depending on which one of us was headlining that particular night, but all was forgiven the next day. It was a great package. Danny Joe [Brown], Jakson [Spires], and I shared a close bond because of our native connection. Riff [West], who we just lost, hung out with Jakson and I on a daily basis and were genuine friends on- and offstage. Bruce [Crump] shared a love of sports and was a good athlete and we loved playing ball with radio stations' teams. Duane [Roland] and Steve [Holland] were just great guys as well. Dave and Bruce are still very close, dear friends of mine.

Why did the band break up?

MTV changed the complexion of music and the way it was presented in the early '80s. Many of us ignored it at first, but the new breed of bands was using it to their advantage. Videos began to be scripted and musicians were asked to play roles; about one in a thousand has that natural ability. Hair bands came in droves, most being one-hit wonders, though a few were actually very good and had a longer and more lucrative shelf life. Record companies began to panic to a degree and began looking at bands like us as old-school. They wanted a pop hit because that was where the quick money could be generated. Our label began pressuring us to modernize, change our wardrobe and persona, and make a leap into the new sounds coming out. I am certain each era faced the same set of problems. We were getting pulled in many directions by the record company and management. Truthfully, lack of management. A keyboard player was added against the wishes and full agreement of most of us. Our sound changed. It was a double-edged sword. We pissed a lot of fans off and gained new fans at the same time. There was still a lot of good music coming from us but it wasn't the guitar-based, power-driven material that had gotten us well known. We became disjointed the more things unraveled.

What did you do after Blackfoot broke up? I recall you were in Southern Rock Allstars at one point. Tell us all about the various projects. Something called NDN...right?

In February of '86 I suffered a major back injury that left me having to decide between surgery or therapy. I opted for therapy and went six days a week, then five, etc., for three months. In 1991, I moved to northwest Montana for a year, four miles from the Canadian border. One of my best friends there had a band but it was not what I was interested in. However, we began to write songs together. I returned to Florida, did a few commercials, then recorded demos for some of my songs. I got an offer to do a video for one of my songs so I invited Jakson to do it with me. We flew to Wisconsin in January and filmed the entire video outdoors in a blizzard. Kind of rough on Florida boys. He and I then went to Michigan and recorded a lot of songs, most of them his, and some we had written together. He had been in the Dixie Allstars since '88 with Charlie, and was working on a fairly regular basis. I moved out west again in '96. The next few years I began doing shows with him and now the band was called Southern Rock Allstars. Jakson, Dave Hlubek, Jay Johnson, and me. It wasn't full time but I did a number of shows with them when schedules permitted. It was a revolving door of players but Jakson, Dave, and Jay remained the core. I played four songs on their first CD, then started working on my solo CD.

In 1999 I released my CD titled *Warrior's Pride* and the band was NDN. Jakson co-wrote four songs and my Montana friend, Richard Luciano, co-wrote the others. It did great right out of the box in the native community but never got distribution in the mainstream market. We were nominated in four categories by the NAMA association. A few years later one of the songs, "Times We've Had," was nominated for Video of the Year by the NAMA people and it was the video Jakson and I had done. I recorded a new, different version for the CD but they knew that.

In the fall of 2000 I moved to Texas, did a few shows here and there with all-star lineups with friends like Mike Estes, Randall Hall, Tommy Curiale, Dave Hlubek. I had horses and began doing rescue work and wound up with eight at one point. It was my therapy for not playing full time. In 2002 and 2003 I joined Pat Travers for a few mini-tours and had a blast. The last two we did I brought in my friend Simon Wright and we had a hell of a power trio. October 2003 I moved back to Florida and the first half of 2004 did a few more all-star gigs with some of the guys I mentioned earlier and with others like Steve Grisham, Barry Rapp, Kurt Petro, Bob Burns, Jakson.

There was a lot of excitement when you, Charlie, and Jak first came back out with Bobby Barth. What were you feeling at the time?

We had always stayed in touch on a regular basis through the years and often talked about a reunion. We were not sure if the public would support it so a friend of mine in Texas took it upon himself to start a petition to see what interest may be generated, or not. Over 1,000 signed the first week, quickly went to 10,000, and then through the roof. Not all of us had computers yet or knew anything about electronic networking other than a website, which we did not have and they were very expensive at the time. RM was contacted but was with Skynyrd and wanted nothing to do with it and said for us to do what we want.

Jakson, Charlie, Bobby, and I had multiple phone conversations and agreed to have a rehearsal and made a promise to each other. Despite how much we wanted to do it, no matter how much our hearts were into it, we agreed to accept the possibility it may or may not have the magic of former days. We met in New Orleans at Bobby's studio and within 60 seconds of the first song were grinning ear to ear. It had that "Wow!" factor we needed to validate it all. A few trips later we had a ninety-minute set ready to go and poised and ready to hit the road. We were on cloud nine!

We played the first six shows and were booked months in advance. Show number six was at House of Blues, Myrtle Beach, South Carolina. Jakson and I had driven up from Florida, spent the night with our friend Billy Kitchens in Savannah the night before. The day after the show we returned to Billy's and stayed the night. The following day Jak and I headed back to Florida, stopped in Jacksonville to say hello to one of my sisters, continued on where I dropped Jakson off at his home in Ft. Pierce that afternoon. It would be the last time I saw him alive.

How did the death of Jakson Spires affect you?

Well, two days later Jak went to North Carolina for a few days to finish tracks on his solo record. He called twice to tell me how it was going and that he had been using a bass player friend of ours in the studio. He wanted me to go next time and add acoustic, a little piano and vocals, because he wanted me to be part of it. I was excited. On Sunday morning, he called from the airport in Nashville to say he would be home that afternoon and would call. I told him to get some rest and call me the next day. The next day never came.

He landed in Orlando and told his girlfriend on the way home he had the worse headache he'd ever had. A few hours later he was unresponsive, rescue was called and he was rushed to the emergency room. I got the call and drove straight to the hospital where he was already on life support. He had suffered a massive brain hemorrhage. Four days and nights I remained by his bed, slept in the room beside him, and on the fourth day he was gone. It was March 16, 2005.

My world was shattered, it was devastating, my brother was gone. A piece of me died that day, and I can only equate the feeling to the day my dad died in 1973. We all have, or in the future will suffer, monumental losses like this. We never completely get over it, just spend the rest of our lives trying to get past it.

Amen. That is so very true. I myself think of Jakson almost daily, and I only knew him for a few short years. I'm sure it is hard on a lifelong friend. You guys tried to keep it going. I saw a couple of great shows with Jay Johnson joining in. And there were the Mike Estes shows. Tell us why and how you quit being Blackfoot. Also, please tell us your thoughts on Rickey's "new" Blackfoot. Inquiring minds want to know.

Losing Jakson really knocked the wind out of our sails. But during our rehearsals preparing to start performing again, we had many discussions about the future, including what to do if someone broke a finger, arm, or leg and was out for a couple of weeks, months, or permanently. Do we keep going? Do we keep going if one of us dies? The immediate answer was always "yes" and in unison. We recruited a drummer who was a friend of Bobby's that we all got to know, who became good friends with Jakson. One year after losing Jak, Bobby got sidelined from losing feeling in his arm at any given time, so we asked Jay Johnson to come in. Jay did an outstanding job taking over lead vocal and lead guitar. After six months Bobby improved enough to come back in but at about 50 percent. Now we were a five-piece with three guitars and two lead vocalists. As Bobby got stronger month by month he was eventually able to function at 100 percent and we had to ask Jay to step aside. It was painful but necessary. Three other drummers would play with us the next four years. In 2010 Bobby had another setback and this time had major, almost emergency surgery and would be out for a long time. Mike Estes came in and soon afterward the drummer left so we brought Kurt Pietro in. We remained with this lineup until July 2011, then Charlie quit and we brought in a replacement but it all came crashing down December 31, 2011, when we lost the rights to perform under the name "Blackfoot" forever. For the second time in my life I saw the band I formed end, resurrect, and end again. Two of the worse heartbreaks I have suffered in my life.

I don't have much to say about the so-called "new" Blackfoot. It's acceptable for a band to continue if, one by one, original members die and are replaced. It's another thing when three of four original, founding members are alive and well and a new band is assembled with four young, non-original members.

What have you been doing since Blackfoot ended the last time?

During 2012 and half of 2013 I was in a project called Monsters of Southern Rock, which was me, Mike Estes, Charlie, Jay, Kurt, and Jimmy Farrar. We had Bruce Crump join us on a show, which was great. I did a few "one-offs" with all-star lineups also. January of this year I recorded a CD with a band in Paris called Lloyd Project. Great bunch of guys, great writers, and there is talk of doing another CD sometime next year, which is not far away. And, I have been rehearsing with a new band recently.

I saw you in French magazine *Bands of Dixie*, playing with a band called Natchez. Who are they and how did that come about?

Natchez is a Southern-rock band from France. These guys are killer! I was introduced to them in a venue in Paris last year and asked to come up and play a few songs. They told me they knew a Blackfoot song. We played "Railroad Man" from the *No Reservations* album note for note and a couple of other songs and it was a hoot! A few months ago, I was part of a studio jam and one of the Natchez guitarists was there. Of course, it was great.

I want to offer you a soapbox, Greg. I feel you have been kind of shafted in relation to royalties from original Skynyrd recordings you played on. Am I right?

This has always been a bit of a sore spot with me. To answer your question…yes, I do feel like I got shafted for never receiving any kind of royalties from the songs I recorded that came out on many albums and CDs through the years. My problem was never with the band members; it's with the record company. They are responsible for tracking, collecting, and distributing monies to the band or their representative. Either the record company has money being held in an escrow account or it was given to someone else who never gave it to me. But, the fact remains I have never been paid for my part, nor received an explanation why not. It's never been about the amount as to how much or little; it's the principle. I have publicly stated countless times I always wished the best for the band, and told one member not many years ago I hoped they continued another twenty years and recorded twenty more albums. My wish continues for this, for them.

Do you have a list anywhere of all the songs and albums you played on with Skynyrd?

There are several that I am credited with playing bass on, and some I also did background vocals. It's difficult to list every release I am on as there are a lot of compilations: "One More Time," "Preacher's Daughter," "White Dove," "Comin' Home," "The Seasons," "Lend a Helpin' Hand," "I Ain't the One," "You Run Around," "Ain't Too Proud to Pray," and "Wino." "Wino" was a song I originally wrote in Blackfoot that RM helped on with lyrics. Ronnie and Allen added more parts to the song which were great, so now there were four writers on the song and that was fine with me; their parts made it better. In 1975, I received a call from one of the producers in Muscle Shoals to let me know these and other songs recorded a few years earlier were going to be on a new album. The most important reason he called was to verify who wrote, played, and sang on each song. He had the original track sheets and we went down the list song by song and everything he had was correct for my parts. There were two other songs I had originally recorded but Ed King came in after me and played a new bass track—and he did a mighty fine job. Between the time of this conversation and when the album was finally released, my name had mysteriously disappeared from the writer's credits. My name had also been removed for background vocals.

Hmmmm...... Two of these tracks were only RM and me singing the entire song, with everyone's blessing, of course. Twenty years later my name finally appeared with vocal credits on a re-release but never the writing credit. You think *I* got screwed? Jakson Spires co-wrote four songs and never got credit.

Albums/CDs: This is a partial list and in no particular order: *Street Survivors, Skynyrd's First and Last, Gold and Platinum, Lynyrd Skynyrd Boxed Set, All Time Greats.* There are another six to eight, but they are compilations, best of, etc., and released by independent labels under a license, some with new packaging or cover art. These contain songs from all the catalog up to when that particular release came out, and I may be on one track, nine tracks on another, and anything between on the remainder.

What's next for Greg T.?

Call it luck or timing, it's interesting you asked this question and it could not have come at a better time. Just three days ago (as of right now) I announced my brand-new project called "Two Wolf." We have been rehearsing, selecting material from our catalogs, and working on new material. The response has been overwhelming and quite humbling from friends and fans around the world. Offers started coming in from promoters here and in Europe within the first twelve hours, which surprised all of us. Two Wolf is: Brad Sayer/Lead Guitar and Lead Vocal; Tommy Curiale/Drums; Jimmy Sexton/Lead Guitar and Vocals; and me, just the bass player and vocals. I have a lot of work to do in order to keep up with these guys! We could not be happier with the results already and are excited beyond words about touring in 2015.

Thank you so much for the interview, Michael Buffalo Smith, my friend and brother.

Thank you very much, Greg, for sharing your time and your thoughts.

Jakson Spires #1

2001

Most people remember Jakson Spires as the hardworking drummer for the heavy Southern-rock band Blackfoot, but for years he was playing as hard as ever in a band called the Southern Rock Allstars, featuring Dave Hlubek (Molly Hatchet), Jay Johnson (Rossington Band), and Charles Hart. In our 2001 interview, "Thunderfoot" Spires opened up about the SRA, Blackfoot, Southern-rock controversy, and the importance of fans.

MBS: Jak, how did the Southern Rock Allstars come to be?

Jakson: This band has been playing for a little over two years. Of course, Charles (Hart) just came with us in October. We had several different incarnations of the Dixie Allstars before that. Charlie Hargrett was out with us for a while, and Billy Jones from the Outlaws. The Dixie Allstars was a band that just kept going out and playing the old stuff. We'd work up some of my old songs and get them to the point where they sounded good, but we wouldn't play them out live. We had cut "Ghost of You" and a song called "Cry of the Heart" back in 1992. We never got around to doing anything with it, though. We were off the road for about a year because of things that were happening with the person who was handling our booking and finances and stuff. I started coming to Muscle Shoals, and me and Jay (Johnson) were cutting some tracks that were originally going to be for his solo album. The stuff started sounding good, and people liked it, so me and him started thinking we need to throw something together and go out and play. We called Dave (Hlubek) and Greg (T. Walker), our old bass player in Blackfoot, and Mark Ray—and of course Charles once in a while. It really wasn't a set band until a little over a year ago when Pete Geddes called me and he needed a job. He was a guitar player and we needed a bass, so I told him I didn't really think he'd be happy, but he said he wanted to do it. He basically went to bass and did a good job. I guess it finally got to him, and he wanted to do other things, so in October, he left. Charles was our first choice anyway, but he'd just gotten this job at Muscle Shoals Sound Studio engineering that he'd been waiting on for years, and he couldn't just blow that off. We understood that. He would come out on occasion to play with us when he could. He's worked out a thing with them now where he can come back and work with them when we're not on the road. We finally reached a happy medium with that.

How's the new CD been doing for you?

It's been doing a lot better than we thought. We're already into the second pressing. We just got the new one week before last. It's all revamped, with Charles in it and all. We're getting big orders from Switzerland and Germany. It's selling really well, and there are a few places that are playing it, but you know how this programmed rock is now. It's like pulling teeth to get anybody to do anything.

What have been some of the more memorable shows you've done recently? It seems like it has to be an adventure out there.

Oh, yeah, it is. Both of the Danny Joe Brown benefits were good for us. Getting to see old friends and stuff, and play with people you more or less grew up with. We've had some killer shows lately. It'd be hard to pick just one. A couple of weeks ago we drove up to Indiana. We left here in a snowstorm and drove there in a snowstorm to play at a place called Doc Holidaze, believe it or not. D-A-Z-E. I mean we were in a blizzard. We got there and set our stuff up, and they were going, "We didn't even think you guys were gonna come, man." I said, "Man, we've never missed a show!" It was like a whiteout. We went to the hotel and unpacked, came back, and the place was packed! It was just killer. We walked in and the owner, Jim, said, "I'd never have believed that this many people would come out on a night like this." I said, "Me neither, man. I wouldn't go out on a night like this [for anything]." You've got to appreciate your fans for that. And some places we play, we hear about bands, some of them are friends of ours, where they're twenty minutes down the road, while the fans are standing out in the freezing rain or something, waiting to have their CDs and stuff signed. People just don't do it no more. They don't feel the need to be bothered with it. These are people that have kept me alive and supported my children. I've got four kids to feed and put through school, and if it weren't for these people, I couldn't do it.

What's it like playing with Dave, Jay, and Charlie?

Obviously, it doesn't make any sense to play with people you don't get along with. Not after what we've been through. That's one of the main reasons we do what we do. It certainly isn't for the money. (Laughs) Although we make a decent living, some of the bands we play with have full-blown crews and stuff, and buses. We pretty much do everything on our own, which, to me, is a feather in our cap. I don't know of anybody that could do what we do of any of the bands that are out there doing this right now. Me and Jay started this thing as a perfect deal for me and him. When I write stuff, I put it into my memory bank, and he runs the machines and stuff. I just come in and cut the drum track and teach him the part or whatever, or he knows the part and puts the guitars down, and we'll do dummy vocals. Then we'll bring Charles and Dave in to fill it out. The good thing about this band is we all get along. We don't have to close the door at night after a show and beat each other up to get to the next gig. And everybody plays the same; it's a hard-playing band. Jay and Dave and Charles attack their instruments the same way I beat my drums.

Let's talk for a minute about Blackfoot. How was that band formed?

We all kind of grew up together in Florida, and we were in different bands. Us and Skynyrd, the Classics IV, Johnny Van Zant, 38 Special, the Allman Brothers, Grinderswitch—all of us grew up together within a three-mile radius in Jacksonville. But we were in two bands that were playing a lot of the same places, and we just formed it like that in September of 1969. We were together until 1986.

Tell us about the personnel changes the band went through.

Rickey and Al Nalli kind of phased Charlie Hargrett out unbeknownst to everybody else while we were off the road, during the *Vertical Smiles* album. But we had Ken Hensley from Uriah Heep after that, and we burned him out in about two years. Bobby Barth from Axe, another band that Al Nalli was managing. His guitar player and him had been in a wreck in Texas and Michael was killed. Bobby was the bass player, and he was recuperating. When Ken quit the band, we rehearsed one night and played Chicago at the Vic Theatre the next night, and just kept going for the last two years. It was a great band and we had a great time and stuff. But to tell you the truth, Rickey was so in debt to Nalli and listening to stuff he wanted to do, he kept wanting to change direction and do this and that to sound like everybody else.

People wonder why the band isn't together, and why Rickey this and why Rickey that. I just tell them, "Look, the last time they had a song or album that charted, I was in the band." But that was the direction Rickey and Al wanted to go. They tried to change back to it, but it was too late. People could no longer relate to it. It wasn't Blackfoot, that was the thing. When we split the band up, it was put to me that I could hire another singer and guitar player, and me and Charlie and Greg could go out and call the band "Blackfoot," since I named the band. You know? They said you can do

this because we'll never use the name again. So, I go out and I'm doing sessions in L.A. for six weeks and when I come back Rickey Medlocke and Blackfoot was out. It was a mess. He even took an album that me and Greg and Charlie had done, and when we split the corporation up, he took the album we had done and put out Rickey Medlocke and Blackfoot.

I have a real hard time with bands who go out and play under the old name when they don't have any original members.

I just got told two nights ago by a promoter, "I know you're from Blackfoot. I saw you guys in Wisconsin a lot. But y'all don't have anybody important from Molly Hatchet; you don't even have the second lead singer. And you don't have the guy, Bobby Ingram, that replaced him." I said, "Wait a minute. Bobby Ingram don't sing a note. Dave started the band and wrote the songs." I said, "How unimportant is that?" I said, "Why don't you look at the back of their current album and look at the back of *Flirtin' with Disaster*, and tell me which one of the original band played on that new record? None! I told him to hire them for three times as much as he could hire us for, let them play sixty minutes, treat him like [dirt], and be happy. I told him, "We're going to go out here and play. If you don't want the band, don't hire us. But don't sit there and tell me what we ain't!"

What do you think of the current touring lineup of Molly Hatchet?

You wouldn't believe how many shows they've ruined for us. We'll get shows booked, and their people will come along behind us and try to undercut our prices and stuff, and say, "You're getting Molly Hatchet, man!" Yeah, right. It's like, when we would go out and do shows with Toy Caldwell and the Shadow Riders. He'd get up there and play his songs, and he'd say, "People wonder how I can get up there and play these songs when there's a Marshall Tucker out there playing them, too. Well, I wrote the damned things and I'll play them whether you like it or not!" That's the way I feel about this Blackfoot stuff. If you wrote it, get back and play it. I've about had it with all this crap. People come up to me and say, "How can you play this stuff when Rickey wrote it and Rickey sang it?" I say, "Look at the records Rickey did after Blackfoot split up, and you tell me who wrote the songs." As for these guys who are just in it for the money, all I can say is anybody who will screw their friends can stay away from me. Life's hard enough, Michael.

So, you wrote a lot of the Blackfoot music, too?

All of it. I've been going through that for years, but more and more people are finding out. It was put to me by Al Nalli that I had to put Rickey's name on songs. What I do is, I write on acoustic guitar. Everything's a ballad at first. Then I speed it up or slow it down. I'll bring it to the band, and I'll hum leads and stuff. I have the finished song in my head; I just don't have the ability to play it. I used to be a guitar player, but I got a really bad burn on my left hand, my cording hand, when I was 15. That's why I play drums. It took me eight years to get two of my fingers working for half-chords and bass chords, and that's how I've written every song I've written. With two fingers. But Al came to me and said, "These songs are great and they're going to be hits. But you know Rickey and his ego. If his name doesn't start getting on some of these songs he's going to freak out, and the band's going to break up." I said, "Al, like I give a shit. I mean, I put Charlie and Greg's name on songs that they didn't even hear until they were recorded, just to give them extra money. Like that new Skynyrd record. There are five songs that are my riffs from old Blackfoot songs. That riff from "Preacher Man" is right out of "Fire of the Dragon." And the whole melody line from "Preacher Man" is "Double Back Again" from ZZ Top. The current Skynyrd is just a mess. It's another band. If they called themselves "the Johnny Van Zant Band," they'd be playing the same places we are.

Who are some of the other Southern-rock bands you guys are friends with?

Doc Holliday, the Kentucky Headhunters, 38 Special, the *real* Molly Hatchet, Randall Hall Band, Artimus Pyle & APB, Mike Estes—that's all I can think of right now.

Who were/are some of your favorite drummers?

John Bonham, of course. Ian Paice, Michael Giles, Ace Allen, and Artimus Pyle.

What's next for the SRA?

We're workin' on the new CD, and basically touring all over.

What would you say has been the most rewarding aspect of your career so far?

I'd say, just being able to play with the people I play with. Jay is a godsend. And having a few good friends and my family, basically. My children are everything to me. I've got a 16-year-old at home; soon-to-be 19-year-old freshman, Ameek, at the University of Minnesota; a son that's in Worton College in Pennsylvania; and my other daughter, Salara, is a ballet teacher in Pennsylvania. They have just turned out incredible. I'm just lucky to know them.

Jakson Spires #2

The Blackfoot Reunion

2005

MBS: How was Blackfoot formed and when?

Jakson: I was in a band called Tangerine, and Charlie, Rickey, and Gregg, were in a band called Fresh Garbage. We did a lot of stuff together as a combo. When the Allmans first got together, they only had one drum set so they used mine for the double-drummer thing. We had a good thing going there and we had all grown up together since we were 5 or 6 years old; me, Gregg, and Rickey and I had met Charlie at age 15. We all had played around together and we felt that because we got along so well that it could transform into music that way. It did, and we just kind of took it from there. The two bands merged and the actual keyboard player for my band Tangerine stayed with us for about one year and then he went on to do other stuff and all and we just kept it that way. We called the band "Hammer" and then we heard about another band doing an album out on the west coast; this was September 1969, so we changed our name to "Free" and about one week later we sat around and decided that some of us had some Indian heritage and we came up with the name Blackfoot. We wanted a strong-sounding name. Blackfoot is actually the Blackfeet Indians and "Blackfoot" is the plural of that—it's reverse English. They were a nomadic tribe that moved seasonally and hunted and we were very nomadic moving every night. We played in the South and at the time the Southern thing was real big. Laidback, country blues or the real jazz influenced blues of the Allman Brothers, and then there was Marshall Tucker, Charlie Daniels, and Wet Willie and all Skynyrd. Even though we liked all that stuff we didn't play it. We were more influenced by the heavier stuff, like Deep Purple, loved Free and The Who, and The Move and stuff like that. So, we headed that way. There were not that many places for us to play in the South because we were too heavy for what was going on. So, we moved up to New York and did it up there for a while and then moved to New Jersey for a bit. After a few years, Rickey had gone with Skynyrd to play drums and then Gregg joined a little later on bass and the whole thing was maybe a year apart. We reformed and started the band up again, actually, with a different bass player for around not quite a year, in the early '70s, out of North Carolina, got Lenny Sandler. Gregg was working with another band in upstate New York and I called and asked him if he was doing anything. I went up and got him back and we stayed together like that for a while. Right up until Charlie left then we got Ken Hensley, then we got Bobby Barth from Axe right up until 1985. The Corporation broke up in 1986. Rickey did 10 years of Blackfoot with 11 different bands kind of thing. It was like a Nugent thing, band of the week. It was a great time and great band and we did stuff that people would not even believe or comprehend and we still can't talk about a lot of it.

When you think back to those days, what are some of the highlights that you can think of—of course, in the realm of those things that you can talk about?

Well, I mean touring with Ted Nugent, played with Kiss, the Scorpions are really good friends of ours, AC/DC, toured with Deep Purple, The Who, went to Europe for many tours and had a great time over there. Hopefully, we will be going over there this year, too. Touring with The Who was great because we had just come off of 18 months of touring at the time of the *Strike's* Tour. We were doing it worldwide and I thought we were going to have some time off. I do remember being offered the thing by their manager, Bill, at the time and falling and rolling around on the office floor laughing hysterically that we were getting ready to go to Seattle and start after we had just gotten home. We always seemed to get along with musicians from other countries better than we did with the ones from America. The exception would be Ted Nugent, because he took us out when no one else would get near us. That was then and this is now.

After all the Blackfoot years, you came to form the Southern Rock Allstars, which was called the Dixie Allstars then. Tell me how that came to be.

Actually, I had a farm in Ann Arbor, and had a country band called Driving Sideways. It was a great country band and we played everything from George Strait to George Jones, and then about half of the stuff we did was my original music. There were a couple of other guys in the band that wrote and we did some of their music, too. I also had a blues band called the Conquerors and a couple of other side projects. I had been asked to do this Dixie Allstar thing and they were doing a benefit in Lakeland, Florida, for the Florida Handicapped Foundation. I had been asked to do some shows before and I wasn't interested in doing history again. It was actually too close to the end of my version like 1989, 1990. About the last part of 1990, I decided that I would do the benefit with them. It was Billy Jones from the Outlaws, and Charlie Hargrett from Blackfoot, and a bass player, Ed Gaines, and Pete Frizzell the keyboard player that had played with a bunch of different people, and then Dave Hlubek from Molly Hatchet. So, I went down and we rehearsed and played the thing and we got a couple of offers, thinking we would never make a living out of this stuff. We ended up doing about 5 years of it. Then after four years Charlie left because he got married and wanted to stay off the road. Then we got Jay Johnson from the Rossington Band in it. Did a couple of years of that and then that kind of fizzled out. At the end of 1996, we didn't work for about one year and Jay and I were doing some demos for other artists at a studio in Muscle Shoals, and Jimmy Johnson, who is a producer from the Swampers, heard some of them and said that this was too good to give away for other people to do and that we should do it ourselves as a project. We cut the stuff ourselves and got a bass player, Pete Geddes, who passed away last year. He was with us for about a year and a half, but he was a guitarist, and Charles Hart had played some of the first album, *Crazy Again*, and so had Gregg Walker from Blackfoot. He was doing the solo stuff and then we asked Charles to come into the band and it just kind of formed from there, the Southern Rock Allstars thing. Dave Hlubek was in it until a couple of years ago and he left, and then we got Duane Roland and he had a hip problem. Then after about 8 months everything was going pretty well and he had to leave and then we replaced him with Scott Mabrey on guitar, and then got another front-of-the house guy and kind of kept that going. Over a period of time there was just about everybody coming out and playing with us at one time or another.

Well, what is the status of the SRA now that you are doing Blackfoot and Farrar is doing things with his old guys?

It's still up there. I have some offers, and if I am not available then I will have to get someone to sit in. I have had Mike Estes come in and Charlie and Tommy Crain—of course, it is still a revolving-door thing.

How did the Blackfoot reunion thing happen?

Well, we had been talking about it for some time and Rickey and Al had mentioned it to people and stuff. Nothing had ever happened and Rickey was with Skynyrd and doing his acting thing and we wanted to do it, and as far as we are concerned, he had an opportunity to do it and decided not to. That is fine with us and we wish him the best. We went out and got Bobby Barth, a friend of ours that is a front man, leader of Axe, and singer, guitarist for years, and had actually played with us for the last couple of years when we were on the road.

I was going to ask you how you came up with Bobby Barth, but you already knew him from playing before?

Oh, well, we had known him since the middle '70s and we had written a bunch of stuff together for Axe and Blackfoot. We still got stuff that we are talking about doing with this band, too. We went back and got the standard stuff we always did but we also put a lot of stuff in the set that we didn't do very much or hardly ever did. The mix of it has worked really well, according to the audiences.

How many reunion shows have you played so far?

We have played four so far and are getting a great response and having a great time. We sold out in North Minneapolis, Minnesota, and we sold out in 35 degrees below zero. Then we did Las Vegas, at the Fiesta Rancho Casino, and it sold out and they put tables up and we were out there about two hours signing stuff for people. They seemed to like us, and if we are having fun, you know they are.

What's it like, because I'm sure that you are having deja vu, but what is it like looking around and seeing the greatest part of your band up there, including Charlie and Gregg? How do you feel?

I feel lucky to be alive. It is horrifying enough that we are in our 50s and no one ever thought we would live up to 30—that was the cutoff, for sure. The way we lived wasn't always pretty. But to hear us still playing like this is incredible. There is no one touring right now that plays like this.

Jakson Spires passed away following an aneurism March 16, 2005. The world lost a great musician and songwriter; many of us lost a true friend.

Gov't Mule

1999

Following in the footsteps of bands like the Grateful Dead and the Allman Brothers Band, but with heavy influences ranging from Cream to Hendrix to Pink Floyd and Traffic, Warren Haynes, Allen Woody, and Matt Abts forged a power-trio that was moving straight ahead with a bullet—a band with elements of all the best classic rock and blues groups, but totally original. The power trio known for giving their heart and soul to the audience in extended jams and long shows that featured countless guest stars from Little Milton to Jimmy Herring, from Gregg Allman to Col. Bruce Hampton. That was all before the untimely death of Allen Woody in 2001.

After years of grieving for the loss of their fallen brother, Warren and Matt regrouped with a new Mule. Of course, it could never be the same without Woody. He was one of a kind. Still, the Mule of today kicks ass in a whole new way. What was to be the original band's final album together, Life Before Insanity *was about to be released, and all three band members were in high spirits when I spoke with them. I spoke with Warren in March of 1999, Woody in November of 1999, and Matt in October 1999.*

Warren Haynes, Guitar/Vocals

1999

As one-third of the hottest power trio playing today, Asheville, North Carolina-born Warren Haynes stays busy all year long, and up until a couple of years ago, he was juggling that career with his career as lead guitarist for the Allman Brothers Band. Then Warren, along with bassist Allen Woody, decided they had to put more time into their own band, pulling away from the legendary Allman group. It wasn't an easy decision, but as Warren tells us in an exclusive interview, it was something they had to do, in order to show the world just how important Gov't Mule is to them and their drummer, Matt Abts.

Speaking with Warren is as easy as talking to a cousin or a brother. His relaxed demeanor and kindness tend to put everyone at ease right off the bat. With tapes rolling, we spoke with the man that many are calling the best blues-rock guitarist and singer living today.

MBS: What would you consider to be your first big break in music?

Warren: I would say being hired by David Allan Coe as guitarist. I never thought about playing a country gig before, but they called and offered me this gig and it was my first chance to record on a major label and to tour on a national level and stuff. I talked to Coe on the phone, and I told him I wasn't a country guitar player, and I might not be right for this job. He was like, "Well, I'm looking for a blues-rock guitar player to add a nice edge to my sound." I thought, if I can play like me then I'll be into it. It was really through playing with him that I met Gregg Allman and Dickey Betts and all those guys. That was my first opportunity on a national level, plus I met a lot of the people I'd become involved with later.

I know you played with the Dickey Betts Band for a while, before joining the Allman Brothers Band reunion. Can you give us a bit of retrospective observation on those experiences?

I met Dickey and Gregg on the same night. It was late '80 or '81. I was always a big Allman Brothers fan, so it was a big thrill for me to meet those guys, and hang out with them and jam and stuff. Then a few years later, when I joined Dickey's band, I had just signed a deal to do my first solo record. In the same time, I got a call from Dickey, and he said he was going to do his first solo record in nine years, and wanted me to sing and play guitar and write some songs. It was two really great opportunities hitting at one time, and I was going, "Man, when it rains it pours." I had gone from having nothing to having both of these things. So, I had to choose between them. I made a decision at that point to join Dickey's band (who released an excellent album featuring Warren, *Pattern Disruptive*). I did that for about two and a half years. Again, that was stepping up to a nicer situation, and also, because of the musicians in the band—Dickey and myself, and Johnny Neel was playing keyboards and Marty Privette was playing bass, and Matt Abts, who is now in Gov't Mule, was playing drums. We had a really excellent band, and toured for about two and a half years. Then that thing was kind of coming to a halt, and I decided I was going to take that opportunity to do my solo record. That's when I got a call from the Allman Brothers saying, "We'd like you to join." It was really strange timing. Here I was preparing to do my own record again, and I got a call from the Allman Brothers. Once again, it was an opportunity that I couldn't turn down. I mean, getting a chance to work with an institution like the Allman Brothers, that's a once-in-a-lifetime situation. I never really knew that they were thinking about getting back together. And they never kept it a secret, they didn't want to get back together. They just said, "We're never going to play together again." But somewhere along the line, with Stevie Ray achieving success, and being so good at bringing blues back to the people, and Robert Cray coming into the picture, and the Grateful Dead was doing great, they started seeing opportunities for the Allman Brothers to be a valid entity again, and knowing that if the right combination of players could be brought in, it could be a great thing. So, they had a little meeting, and they brought me and Johnny Neel into the band. Then they auditioned bass players, and they auditioned Woody, and he got the gig. It was just a great feeling, that first year, knowing that the Allman Brothers Band was coming back full force. I had always been a big fan. I'd grown up listening to that music, and it was just a great opportunity for somebody like me to come in, and be allowed to interject my personality into it. That's about all you can ask for, as far as being in a band that's been around that many years. I can't imagine another band from my past like that who would give me that much musical freedom, and be so enjoyable to play with.

A lot of people felt that you and Woody made the band sound the best they'd sounded since the days of Duane and Berry.

We tried to bring that spirit back. I think Woody deserves a lot more credit than he got, because the bass player's role is more understated in most bands. But Berry Oakley was such an aggressive bass player, so unique, that when they lost Oakley, having just gotten over the loss of Duane, that was such a huge loss for those guys that a lot of people thought they'd never get it back. But they were gaining momentum from a fan-base standpoint, and they had some great bass players through the years. I mean, Lamar Williams, who passed away as well, was a really great bass player, too, but he didn't play in that style that Oakley did. Until they hired Woody, nobody ever did. He brought a lot of that fire back in, and deserves a lot of the credit.

I remember seeing Woody when he played with the Artimus Pyle Band in Tryon, North Carolina.

You bet! In fact, that's when I met Arty. I was eighteen years old, and playing in a band called Ricochet, not to be confused with the band that's playing now called Ricochet. We were playing at the other club in Tryon called The Second Level, and Artimus came to see us.

What was the real story behind you and Woody leaving the Allman Brothers Band?

Well, it wasn't nearly as complex as some would have you believe. When I joined the Allman Brothers—Woody and I joined in '89—it was just going to be a reunion tour. But it went so well, we decided to do it the next year. Well, that went even better, so we decided to do it another year. But they had this past history of never staying together over three years at a time. I don't think it was ever my intention to be in the Allman Brothers for eight and a half years. But it was a great experience and a great opportunity, and I wouldn't trade it for anything. I write a lot of songs that don't necessarily fit into the Allman Brothers bag, and I always wanted to first and foremost do my own music, and I was able to in the Allman Brothers. I was able to write songs in the band, and I was able to be one of the singers in the band, and given a lot of musical freedom, as we had talked about earlier. But I still wanted an opportunity to record and perform a lot of the songs that I was writing that didn't fit into that genre, so to speak. For three years, Woody and I juggled the two bands. We'd get off the Allman Brothers bus and get on the Gov't Mule bus, and we'd get off the Gov't Mule bus and get on the Allman Brothers bus. We went from one tour to another and another, which proved to be a very hectic schedule. It was rewarding, but it was tough, you know? Eventually we just figured out that Gov't Mule was really starting to gain some momentum, and that's where our heads were as far as a musical future. That's what we wanted to do, and we didn't want to pass up the opportunity to do it the right way. So, we thought about it, and the only way we could convince the world that we were serious about it, and that it wasn't just something we did when we weren't playing with the Allman Brothers, was to do it full time and allow it to gain the steam that it needs. Last year we left the band, and this was the first year that we've had the entire year to do what was best for Gov't Mule, and it's been a great year. We're really excited about it. It was great to make decisions based on what was good for the band, as opposed to saying, "Well, the Allman Brothers are working here, here, here, and here, and what's left we can figure out, if and when we want to work." See, to leave an institution like that is never going to be an easy decision. We had to do it to kind of show ourselves and the rest of the world that we were very serious about this. A lot of people read more into it than there really was, you know.

The rumor mill at work.

(Laughs) Yeah, probably a lot of them I haven't even heard!

Like the one where Dickey Betts drove you out of the band.

You know, Dickey and I played together for eleven years. He's the one that brought me into the Allman Brothers, and gave me some wonderful opportunities, so I have no regrets about any of it at all.

Let's talk about songwriting. I heard that you wrote a song for Garth Brooks.

I co-wrote "We're Two of a Kind, Workin' on a Full House" with Bobby Boyd and Dennis Robbins in Nashville.

Have you had other songs like that picked up by country artists?

Well, I've only written a handful of country songs, compared to the amount of songs that I've written. But they've been recorded by George Jones and Earl Thomas Conley, and David Allan Coe.

I didn't realize you were such a prolific writer. I mean, I knew about your great songs with the Allmans and the Mule, but I didn't realize you crossed over the genres.

When I was living in Nashville, I had a lot of friends who were country performers and writers, and we would get together and write songs and stuff. And there were even a few that I wrote by myself that turned out to be country songs. But the majority of what I write are rock songs or blues-based rock songs, things that fit into the Allman Brothers or Gov't Mule genre. But a lot of my stuff tends to go across the board. A lot of things that could be interpreted in a singer-songwriter sort of way. And I've had things recorded by a lot of blues artists. People that grew up listening to, like, John Mayall. He recorded a song that myself and Johnny Neel wrote. Gregg and Dickey both did some of my songs on their solo records before I even joined the Allman Brothers. And blues artists like Son Seals, Kenny Neal...it's very flattering to have people like that record your stuff, and they always do it justice.

Who would you say were your greatest influences growing up?

Well, I started out as a singer, so all my influences were soul singers—James Brown, Wilson Pickett, Otis Redding, the Four Tops, and the Temptations, that kind of stuff, you know. Eventually hearing Ray Charles and B.B. King, and getting the idea that, wow, you can sing and play a musical instrument at the same time. Then I heard Cream and Hendrix, which made me want to play guitar. So, I'd have to say Clapton, during the Cream days, and Hendrix were my two major influences. Johnny Winter, Dickey, and Duane were big influences a couple of years later. I really listened to everybody. All the blues guys, all the jazz guys. I tried to learn as much from as many different people as possible. The three "Kings" —Freddie King, B.B. King, and Albert King—were big influences. And of course, Otis Rush. I loved Howlin' Wolf, Muddy Waters, and Elmore James. I listened to a lot of great jazz players like Wes Montgomery and Joe Pass and Grant Green and Jim Hall. A lot of guitar players from all over the map, whether it be Southern guys like Billy Gibbons, or West coast players like Santana. Some of the British guys—Jeff Beck I always loved. David Gilmour, Steve Howe from Yes I always liked. I think any musician is really doing themselves a favor to not put any boundaries up, or to cut themselves off from any type of music. There's good and bad in all types of music. You can be influenced by something in a whole different direction from what you do, and sometimes it's those influences that add extra character to your playing or singing.

I heard a tape the other day of a 1988 show. It was the Dickey Betts Band at the Lone Star Café in New York. You were there, and Jack Bruce, Rick Derringer, and Mick Taylor all jammed with the band.

Right. You know, that was awesome. Just playing with those guys was a great experience, and they sounded great. You know, sometimes you get a chance to play with great musicians, but the environment's not conducive to good music. That was definitely not one of those times. The music was great. I've had the opportunity to play with so many people I grew up listening to. I played with Willie Dixon before he died. I played with John Lee Hooker. I played with Albert Collins before he died. A lot of people that I loved in blues and rock and roll. Hopefully there are tapes somewhere of those performances. Sometimes there aren't tapes, but a lot of times, there are tapes rolling to remind you of what a beautiful time that was.

Your album *Dose* really has some dynamic rhythm changes and oddball time signatures. Was that initially a part of the band's plan, and is that the direction you are heading with the music?

We are going to continue showing a little more jazz, acoustic folk, and other influences. We just want to show all of the different sides of Gov't Mule that we haven't yet revealed, while still maintaining the blues-rock influences. Take our first record, for instance. While we are extremely proud of it, we tended to stay close to that blues-rock, power-trio genre. Now the band has been together for over five years, and it's just kind of growing exponentially. We are able to show a lot more diverse sides of what Gov't Mule does. I believe *Dose* is the most diverse thing we've had released.

I'd like to get your thoughts on Derek Trucks and his band.

Derek is amazing. I've known him since he was eleven years old, and he was amazing even then. He's got the depth and maturity of someone three times his age. It's really a special gift he has, and to deal with it the way he's dealt with it, he's such a great person. He's so down to earth and genuine. I could tell in all the times we've been around each other and played together, he's going to always remain a student of music. That's what it's all about, learning. You're always going to be learning. When you're eighty years old, you're still going to be learning. He has such a great attitude about it, and he'll get up and play with anybody, anywhere, anytime, which is really what it's all about as well. I have a deep respect for Derek as a musician and as a person. For all the guys, they're all great musicians. He's fortunate to have a touring band of that caliber, because they're turning heads. People come out to see them live, and they say, "Wow, these guys are really great." We're really glad to have them on the road with us; we have such a great time. We always end up jamming together in their set or in our set, or in both. It's a great excuse to play together, and some really good things come out of those jams.

That's one of the great things about your band and Derek's, and of course the Allman Brothers... You're bringing back a lot of the magic that was so prevalent in the late '60s and into the '70s with Charlie Daniels' Volunteer Jams and stuff. Just everybody out there onstage having fun together, which of course, transcends over into the audience.

When I go to a show, and I see something special happen, that maybe only happened that one time, then I feel like I was a part of it. That's the way we want our audiences to feel. You know, in the late '70s and early '80s, bands got really mechanized into playing the same songs the same way night after night. Even down to a little rehearsed speech in between songs. You know, if you go see two or three shows like that, you get really turned off, and say, "Hey, I've seen it, I don't need to see it again." But a lot of bands these days are taking their cue from the late '60s, early '70s groups that played a different performance all the time. There are a lot of people who follow those groups around. There are people who have seen 75 to 80 Gov't Mule shows. It totally blows my mind.

It's a really cool thing, what's going on with the tapers and everything.

Our goal from the very beginning was to expand our repertoire to the point where we didn't have to play the same songs every night. Even though we were kind of baptized by fire, we jumped right onto the stage as soon as we knew eight songs, and we'd stretch those eight songs as far as we could. (Laughs) Then a couple of weeks later we knew ten songs, and a month later we knew fifteen. Now, we could probably do two or three nights in a row without repeating a song if that was what we wanted to do. It makes it more fun for us, and for the audience, and for the repeat offenders, as we call them, that keep coming back. They want to see a different show than they saw the week or the month before. It works out great for everybody, because, we get bored playing the same songs, the same way all the time. We break the set list up as much as possible, and we look for new ways to interpret the same song. Sometimes a song will start feeling stale and we'll quit playing it for a while. And then, after we don't play it for some time, you'll find a fresh approach to it, and put it back in the show. We want every night to be different, and we want the audience to feel like they were a part of something that only happened that one time. It's not a mass-appeal sort of approach to rock music, you know? We're making music for the people that like music for the same reasons we do. I never wanted to make a record that I wouldn't go to the store and buy. I never want to do a show that I wouldn't pay to go see. I think you try to maintain that attitude. If the band's bored, how do you expect the audience to be excited about it?

Around here where I grew up (Spartanburg-Greenville, S.C.), the most popular band to come out of the area is the Marshall Tucker Band. Can you give me your thoughts on the Tucker band?

Well, I was always a Tucker fan. I grew up listening to that stuff since the first album. The first concert I ever saw in my life was in 1972. It was the Edgar Winter Group, and Marshall Tucker opened up for them. Even though they were from right down the road, we didn't know about them. I was a twelve-year-old kid. We really enjoyed them. Then we started hearing about them; they were really getting a lot of regional talk. We became fans, and bought the first record, and listened to them through the years. And even though I mostly became friends with Paul Riddle and with Toy, I did know some of the other guys as well. And Doug was always such a really unique rock singer. He had such a smooth kind of folksy voice that fit perfectly into that band. I thought those guys had such a great chemistry, and that's really what rock music is all about. And they had it. Their sound was always so unique, you could hear the first ten seconds of a Marshall Tucker song and you knew who it was.

Allen Woody, Bass

1999

Allen Woody was playing bass with the Artimus Pyle band in Tryon, N.C., the first time he met Warren Haynes. It was a chance meeting that would change the course of both men's lives forever.

MBS: When did you first become interested in playing music?

Woody: Well, as a child, you know, hearing Elvis Presley play. And my dad was a big music fan. He didn't play or anything, but he was a big music fan. It was kind of weird, he was a truck driver, but he was into the blues. There's a great radio station here (Nashville), and Gregg (Allman) and I talk about it a lot, it's WLAC. It's still on the air now, but it's not the same as it was. It was a clear-channel blues station, and, man, they played Lightnin' Hopkins, Blind Willie Johnson, Howlin' Wolf, John Lee Hooker, Muddy, B.B., Freddie, Albert, they played all the blues stuff. And my dad got interested in it when he was in the service and he was out in Wisconsin. It was a clear channel, so it would reach all over the country. He was into that, and Hank Williams, Sr., country music, real roots music, and Elvis Presley and stuff. I was steeped in that when I was a kid, and then the Beatles came along, and that overloaded my circuit, you know. I was already primed for it, so when I saw them, I said, "This is what I want to do." It seemed pretty glamorous at the time.

Matt Abts told me that the Beatles were his turning point, too.

Yeah, I think anybody in our generation, from their mid-thirties to about fifty, that fifteen-year span there, the Beatles and that whole British Invasion would have to have some impact on you.

Was the bass guitar your first choice of instrument?

No, I played guitar. I still play guitar. But I'm not a frustrated guitar player. I'm okay with my guitar playing; it's my bass playing that frustrates me. It doesn't surprise me that Matt would say that, because I was used to seeing the instruments that you would see on TV. Like when I was a kid, there was a wealth of country music on TV, like Buck Owens with those glittery Telecasters and Jazz basses and stuff. And Flatt & Scruggs with their

Martin guitars and Gibson mandolins and banjos. As a kid, you're not really sure about the names, so you scramble to read what's on the head stock. You're familiar with names like Gibson and Martin and Fender, and Gretch, and to a lesser degree Guild, and things like that. But the Beatles came over, and Lennon had that little short-scale Rickenbaker, and of course George was playing a Gretch, and McCartney had that little weird-shaped Hofner—nobody knew what in the hell that was. To me, in a strange kind of way, McCartney and that little violin-shaped bass somehow really grabbed my attention. The tone that he had, and the way he went about playing it with a pick, more like a guitar player. It really got my attention. Then I found out what the bass was. I had a little Japanese bass, which I unfortunately no longer have. My first good bass I got in 1970 or '71 was a Hofner Beatle bass, which I still own; it's in mint condition. It's, like, a '64 or '65. And the first rock concert I ever saw was the Dave Clark Five. My dad took me. That whole stigma got me.

You said your dad didn't play. Were there any musicians in your family?

My mother played violin in the Junior Symphony or something before I was born, but that was many years ago and she didn't really keep up with it. I was an only child, so I was kind of like a pioneer.

Who were some of your major musical influences through the years?

I don't want to be tongue in cheek about this, but when FM radio came along, they began playing album cuts and stuff, and I was influenced, obviously largely by the Beatles and by the Stones, I loved them, The Who, I loved John Enstwhistle's bass playing. I was a huge Cream fanatic. I was really influenced by Jack Bruce. Of course, Mountain, and Felix Pappilardi, and Jack Casady certainly caught my ear. And not to sound tongue in cheek again, but when the Allman Brothers came out, me and a friend were driving around out by a lake near Nashville, and there was an FM station at the time that would just put an album on and let the whole damned thing play. So, me and this friend were out driving around the lake—we were underage but we had us some beer—and they played that first Allman Brothers record. It just knocked me in the floor. That was a major influence. I'd never heard anything like it. I found myself playing in some horn bands when I was young, too, so I was influenced by Jim Felder, who was the bass player for Blood, Sweat & Tears. Peter Cetera, before he went to Vegas. (Laughs)

The bass player in Chicago. The next big milestone for me was Mahavishnu Orchestra. I was a music major at MTSU, which is a little college in Murfreesboro, which is thirty miles from Nashville. This friend of mine, who was a classical guitar major, came in one day and said, "I got a record I want you to hear." It was *Birds of Fire*, which was the second Mahavishnu record. Behind the Beatles, hearing the Mahavishnu Orchestra really got my attention. It was the Beatles, and then hearing the Allman Brothers thing, and then Mahavishnu. Of course, I felt a connection to the Allman Brothers because Gregg and Duane were from Nashville. I was really proud that they were actually from this area, especially those two. They seemed like the real pioneering thing behind the Brothers. And Berry Oakley as well, he wasn't from around here, but the way he played bass really got my attention. But when I heard this Mahavishnu record, it was like, wow, this is a whole new level, something I haven't checked out. It's very much like the English bands. I mean, thank God for people like Clapton, and Keith Richards, and George Harrison, folks like that who were dropping names about all of these blues guys who were in my own backyard. I had some exposure to it as a child because my dad was into it, but when you start hearing things like that London Howling Wolf session that Clapton was on, and being a fan of the Beatles and Cream, you start saying, "Well, if these guys are into it, then I need to listen to them and see what's going on." It's a similar thing with John McLaughlin. You say, "Who has he played with? Who has his drummer played with?" Well, they both played with Miles, and Jerry Goodman had played with The Flock, and you start looking into who Miles was influenced by, this guy or that guy, and suddenly you find yourself listening to John Coltrane, and Charlie Bird and Charles Mingus. It's like going to music school.

It's the same with the old blues players.

That's a whole other level. You start hearing Robert Johnson—he and Willie Dixon and Muddy all influenced Led Zeppelin. You hear Page and people talk about all of these artists, and you get hit by Robert Johnson and it just blindsides you, because it's so raw. It's such emotional, from-the-gut music. You know, they weren't making any money back then playing that music; they never made a dime. What a terrible irony it is that when they became famous, they'd been dead for thirty years. We're especially bad about that in America. You go to other counties, like Japan and Switzerland, and you see what reverence they have for musicians. Let's face it, man, if you grew up in the South, that's where all of the classic American music forms were started. I mean country, blues, jazz, rock and roll. It all came from, like, three states, a tristate area, Louisiana, Mississippi, Tennessee, right there in that area. That was pretty much the hotbed for what would become all of these classic music forms. So, you have a plethora of this stuff, and some of these guys couldn't get arrested here, but in other countries they were highly respected and revered. What we choose to embrace musically never ceases to amaze and sicken me.

Some of the things the kids are buying is unbelievably bad.

Like MTV. Warren and I were looking at a *Rolling Stone* magazine on the bus the other week, and they had an interview with Tom Petty, who I think is just a marvelous artist. He was calling it like he saw it. MTV did do some good things, and helped to call attention to some people it needed to, but he said something in there about not being into game shows. Now if you turn on MTV, they have all these trite game shows.

It's all game shows, teenagers on the road, and gangsta rap.

Once again, they've shanghaied us. They slipped one by us. Now, VH1, which I guess is a part of MTV, has some great stuff, like the *Legends* series, and *Behind the Music*. In Canada, they have a TV show called *Much Music*. Man, they are worlds ahead of us as far as showing some of the cooler, neater music. They had live music on there before MTV. They had live performances by people who really had musical caliber. Unfortunately, we are still in the wake, in the backwash, of this giant ocean liner called MTV, where you can get a record deal if you're young and thin, which we are not…

And handsome.

Yeah, some of the best bands in the world were some of the ugliest fuckers on the planet.

One of the great things about the Mule is the way you guys, like the Allman Brothers, don't tend to dress up in fancy clothes or costumes onstage. Like Toy Caldwell of the Marshall Tucker Band once said, "We wear the same damn clothes onstage that we are wearing on the bus."

Toy Caldwell is a personality and a musical presence that we all sadly miss—he and his brother both, for that matter. I thought Tommy had a real Berry Oakley type thing going in his playing. He was obviously influenced by Berry, and then he took it to a whole different place. People like that, like the original Marshall Tucker Band, Paul Riddle is a dear friend of mine, he's a good friend of Warren's and Matt's. That guy is a slammin' player. The whole thing that they had going on with that band was great. The songwriting was great, Toy's guitar playing, with the Wes Montgomery thumb-picking, was great. That was a deep, cool thing.

That's one of the things I like about Gov't Mule, is the intense jamming onstage.

About the jamming, I never was a really huge fan of the Grateful Dead. I saw the guys a couple of times, but I always liked things to rock a little harder. I think that bands like Cream and Hot Tuna were overlooked a lot as jam bands, but they had a harder edge.

Tell us how you feel about your old bandmates, the Allman Brothers Band.

Oteil and Derek are dear friends of ours, always have been. We really love Derek, and are proud of what he's doing, too. Jaimoe and Gregg Allman are very dear friends of mine, and will remain so until one of us drops and is planted in the ground. Jaimoe is a wonderful drummer, a wonderful musician that taught me about playing music, a lot about listening to music. It's the same with Gregg. Thank God, he's straightened up. The real Gregg Allman, when he's not screwed up, which these days is all the time, he's a wonderful guy, man. He's a singer's singer. He's the best blues singer that's ever been poured into a white body. He's extremely knowledgeable about people like Little Milton. I knew who Little Milton was, but I'd never been into him. Gregg got me into him, and now we are on his new record (*Welcome to Little Milton*). It was a joy. Once again, I learned tons about music from Gregg and Jaimoe. I learned about writing music with Gregg. And Warren, too. Warren is a great writer.

How did you come to join the Allman Brothers Band in the first place?

Artimus Pyle introduced me to Butch Trucks. Talk about it being a small world. I've been to Jerusalem with Artimus; we have been down some highways together. We were working on an APB record down at Butch's studio which never got released. Warren, Matt, Johnny Neel, and Marty Privette had just finished recording the Dickey Betts Band album there, and then we came in. We were working there when Butch heard me playing and said that they were reforming the Allman Brothers, and he thought I'd be the one for the bass position. Artimus had told him, "Man, he was born to do this gig." So, I went down and auditioned, and got the gig the same day.

Warren and I were casual friends. We had met just prior to that. And you know who introduced me to Warren? Artimus Pyle, once again. But we were in the Brothers, and one night on the bus, we were listening to Cream, and I turned to Warren and said, "You know, man, with the right drummer, we could have a power trio like there hasn't been in thirty years." And he said, "Yeah, with me and you and Matt Abts." So, we went out, we were playing the Greek Theatre, and we went out to the Captain's Cabin to hear Matt play. We did a little jam, and it got reviewed in the paper. Like we were a regular band. They raved about the interplay between people, and everything. With that in mind, we formed, if you will, Gov't Mule, and it turned out so cool, and was so rocking, we started going out on the road in between Allman Brothers gigs. It was like, wow, this is our band. And you know, you don't want to work for somebody else your whole life; you want your own thing. The Brothers had reached a point where the creativity had died way down, and we were feeling like we had a lot of creativity we needed to get out. So, we were on the road with the Black Crowes. We were backstage with Chris Robinson and some of the others, and Chris said, "I hope you guys know that you're poised to happen and you really need to get out and do your own thing." So, we had pretty much already decided, and gave our notice after The Beacon run in 1997. So, we've been together, a little family in a tube, going down the highway for five years now. We just finished our fifth year. But I couldn't ask for two more creative and special musicians to play with.

What can you tell us about the new album you've just finished recording?

It is by far the most eclectic, best-performed, best-written, best-produced album that we've ever done. Once again, Michael Barbiero was in the pilot's seat producing. We are very blessed that we had Ben Harper come in on it. Johnny Neel is on it. We were very lucky that a lot of our friends came in to play on it. What we are trying to do is not dissimilar from what the Beatles or Cream did, where you look in there and George Harrison was playing on a Cream record, like he played on "Badge." But this is the best performance we ever did in the studio.

Here comes the equipment question. What type of bass rig do you use, and what kind of guitars?

I do tend to collect guitars. I use several custom basses that were made for me, but as far as brand names, I tend to play Gibson and Epiphone stuff. I have a lot of the nice, older Thunderbirds, and I've got some of the new ones. And Epiphone, which are guitars made in Korea, that used to be made in America by Gibson. You know, a lot of Fender guitars are made in Korea. They make some really cool guitars. I find myself using the Jack Casady model Epiphone bass, the Gibson Thunderbirds, vintage Gibson EB-1's, EB-2's. They're a really good working-man's guitar. As far as amps, in the studio, I use Ampeg SVT's exclusively. We just finished a tour with the Dave Matthews Band, and I would have to travel in a Lear jet, so I'd find myself taking a Steinburger bass with me. They look a little weird on a big guy like me, but they're a good working tool.

How was the Matthews tour?

Great. It's about time they are getting their due. Dave is the quintessential pop artist. For once, pop doesn't have to have a bad connotation, because the songs are well written, and the guys in his band are great players. Warren and I have known those guys since 1995, when we did the H.O.R.D.E. Tour together. If anything, those guys have gotten even nicer, and they were nice as hell to begin with. It's refreshing to see a group of guys come off the stage that have just made a million dollars, and be nice and cordial, and thankful for what they've got.

That's the same way I see you guys.

One thing I feel about the Mule is that we are there for each other. I'd do the same for them anytime. Sometimes you have to thank your maker that you're in this position, playing great music with good friends. You don't want to ever take for granted that God almighty has put you in the same plane with guys who are dedicated to making good music. I read one time that John McLaughlin said this, about that really fancy double-neck guitar with the design with all of those vines on it. He said the reason he had those was because he felt a musician should be like a vine growing up a tree, where you are constantly evolving upward as a musician, and as a human being, too. I mean, it kind of goes hand in hand.

You can't be a great musician and be a miserable schmuck. I guess you can for a season, but trust me, it'll wear off. You're on this path, and hopefully it's always a path of increased enlightenment and God-consciousness, and you get closer and closer, then one day you leave this tent that we call a body and hopefully go to a better place. You have to, hopefully, become more decent, instead of less so, and become a better player instead of less so, and become more creative, instead of less so.

Rest in Peace, Brother Woody—August 26, 2000.

Matt Abts, Drums

1999

Gov't Mule, Warren Haynes and Allen Woody, should be well-known to Allman Brothers fans for their stint in Southern rock's most famous native sons. In 1989, Haynes became the second replacement for Duane Allman, and Woody filled out the Allman sound on bass. Five years after their debut, the duo joined drummer Matt Abts in the side project Gov't Mule, a band in which the Allman Brothers' influence is apparent but complicated with the psychedelic, bluesy power-trio feel of Cream or Mountain. Gov't Mule debuted in 1995 with a self-titled album, on Sony/Relativity, and then signed to Capricorn Records, where they released the stellar concert recording Live at Roseland Ballroom. *The studio follow-up* Dose *appeared in early 1998, and* Live...with a Little Help from Our Friends, *a recording culled from their marathon New Year's Eve 1998 show in Atlanta, was released this past spring. The Mule has just completed their third studio album, which will be released either late this year, or early 2000. We caught up with drummer Matt Abts during the band's summer concert tour for a few questions.*

MBS: How did you first become interested in playing the drums?

Matt: As a kid, I just kind of gravitated toward the rhythm end of it. Of course, the Beatles were a big part of it. I was interested in it before then, but I didn't get a drum kit until after I saw Ringo on the *Ed Sullivan Show*. So many people say that that grew up during that time frame, that all it took was seeing Ringo. After I saw that, I had a one-track mind. I wanted to do that. Then I got caught up in the whole rock thing of the sixties and early seventies, and of course, once you get interested, you explore all avenues of music.

Did you come from a musical family?

No, not really. My dad played a little ukulele around the house. (Laughs)

I really enjoyed your work on the *Pattern Disruptive* album by the Dickey Betts Band. How did you come to hook up with Betts?

I first met Dickey in the early eighties. During that time, I had moved down to Florida and I was playing with a friend from the Virginia area. My dad was in the Army and we moved around a lot, so I ended up in Virginia. I worked the East Coast right after high school for six or seven years, and we all gravitated toward Florida, where the weather was nicer. (Laughs) So I was playing in Florida with a friend of mine in a Top-40 cover band, and that's where I met Dickey, down in the Sarasota area. Gregg was living down there at the time, too. Dickey used to come into clubs we played in, and we had some sort of jam relationship going. After I moved out of the area, Dickey had a band called BHLT, which was Dickey, Jimmy Hall, Chuck Leavell, and Butch Trucks, during one of the times when the Allman Brothers were broken up. At one point, Butch couldn't make the gig, and Dickey had my phone number, so he called me. I was in Virginia. I ended up touring with them that summer, and working with Dickey from 1984 until '89. We had a number of guitar players, and then Warren was brought in around 1986, and we went on to do some playing. In the meantime, Warren had brought Johnny Neel in. I played with Dickey for about five years through a bunch of different configurations until it ended up with me, Marty Privette on bass, Warren Haynes, Johnny Neel, and Dickey Betts. We did the record. That was the best band, but it only lasted about a year before the Allman Brothers were reunited, and Warren was invited to join them. It was a great learning experience, and I met a lot of people from the whole Allman Brothers family. I had a great time and I enjoyed it very much.

What did you do between the time the Allmans reunited and the time the Mule was formed in 1994?

At that point, I made a conscious move to Los Angeles, to settle down. When I got here, I did the Mick Taylor record. I was also playing with a guy out of Florida named Chris Anderson, and we did a record, just before the Mule did its first record on the Sony/Relativity label. Anderson was a great player. I also did a bunch of side projects. I was living in L.A., but in and out of L.A. a lot.

So how did Gov't Mule come together?

At this point, when Johnny Neel and Warren were invited to join the Allman Brothers Band, it was the end of the Dickey Betts Band. I would see them almost every year when they would play the Greek Theatre. We all remained friends, and I was happy for Warren. It was a great break for him, and it brought him a lot of well-deserved notoriety. I would get up and jam with them, and there was this whole brotherhood thing going on. Talk kept coming back to Allen, who I didn't know at the time, and we talked about doing the trio thing. Warren had this solo project he had been working on since before he was in the Dickey Betts Band, and I knew he had to finish that up. He had a lot of New York players on it, and Chuck Leavell produced it. We all had stuff we needed to get out of our system. So, in early 1994, Warren gave me a call and said that he and Woody had been seriously talking about the trio thing. So, he called me up and formally asked me what I thought about it. Of course, I thought it was a great idea. So, we started scheming at that point. So, the next time the Allmans were in town I took them to a club I had a gig at called the Captain's Cabin in North Hollywood. Just a little rock club where we did a blues jam every Sunday. So that's how the band actually started. We initially went in and said, "This is cool. Let's record it ourselves." So, we went to Telstar Studios in Sarasota where we had all done a bunch of work. It was owned by Bud Snyder, who is the soundman with the Allman Brothers. We recorded on our own with no record company, and then by the end of 1994, we got signed with Sony/Relativity, and that's when we went in to do that first record.

How would you compare playing with Warren and Woody now to playing with them when they were in the Allman Brothers Band?

They were just more stressed out at the time because they were doing double duty. At this point it's all Gov't Mule, so there's no dividing it. At that time, we were just getting started, and it was fine then. Everything turns into what it is supposed to turn into over time, you know? That was a good time, and this is a good time now.

If you could jam with anyone, living or dead, who would it be and why?

Oh, boy, wouldn't it be nice to play behind Jimi Hendrix? I'm thinking to myself, most of these people are dead. (Laughs) But, just in our lifetime, people like Miles Davis, Stevie Ray Vaughan. I have played with some great people, and I'm very thankful for that. But, people living today, wouldn't it be great to play with Clapton? You know, Allen and Warren and I have such a great time, and it's hard when you spend so much time together, although we've never come to blows or anything, or gotten tired of each other, but it's great to play with those guys.

Can you tell us about the new studio album?

It is done. I don't know what to tell you. There was a scheduled release for it this fall but I'm not sure that's going to happen. But it is done and we are really happy with it. We recorded half of it in Muscle Shoals, and half in New Jersey. We spent the first six months of the year working on it. There are twelve songs, most of which nobody has ever heard. It's our best album yet, and our best-sounding. I think more thought went into this album than any yet. Some of the songs are shorter, more concise. We're all very excited about it.

What's next for the band?

We have the live album out this year, and a new studio record ready to go, so we are cocked and loaded. Let's just say, up until the New Year's Eve gig this year, which will also be in Atlanta—it was originally supposed to be the Roxy, but I'm not sure the Roxy will be available—up until that point we are staying really busy. •

Jimmy Herring

2001

Is there anything Jimmy Herring can't do musically? I have personally witnessed his fret-board dexterity at shows by Gov't Mule, John Schofield, the Allman Brothers Band, Aquarium Rescue Unit, Phil Lesh and Friends, and Warren Haynes' all-star Christmas Jam. Back pre-9/11 we caught up with Jimmy via Phil's publicist, J.C. Juanis, for the following insightful interview.

MBS: Let's start by affirming your Southern roots. Where were you born and raised?

Jimmy: Fayetteville, North Carolina. South of Raleigh. Where are you?

Greenville, South Carolina.

We were just down the road from you in Spartanburg with this other band I have called Project Z.

Marshall Tucker territory.

Yeah! In fact, Paul Riddle was going to come down and jam with us, but he had a prior obligation.

He's a great guy.

He really is. Really cool.

I'd like to jump back and ask you a few questions, like when did you first become interested in playing the guitar?

I guess I was about ten. 1972. My brothers always listened to Hendrix, the Allman Brothers, Santana—it was listening to their tunes that made me want to play guitar. Hendrix and the Allman Brothers mainly.

Who are some of the other bands or musicians you listened to as a budding player?

Well, like I say, Hendrix and the Allmans. And from there, I got into Aerosmith, Led Zeppelin—and the Beatles, too, were an influence on me. My brothers had *Sgt. Pepper*, *Revolver*, *The White Album*, —that stuff really stuck in my head. I started getting into instrumental music around 1978. I really got into the Dixie Dregs, Steve Morse. He's probably my biggest influence in terms of making me want to try and make music my life. If you're going to try and play his stuff, you're going to have to do it a lot. I never really could play the Dregs' music the right way. I played it the best I could, and I would woodshed, like, eight hours a day trying to play like him. He was an incredible role model. He pretty much did everything I wanted to do before I knew I wanted to do it. He was from the South, and their music was undeniably Southern music, but it was very sophisticated. Southern rock had gotten the name of being a bunch of rednecks getting drunk all the time. You know, the Lynyrd Skynyrd/Molly Hatchet era—when I was in high school. Then the Dregs came along, and it was like, this is Southern music, but it's very advanced, like classical, like jazz. They had all these diverse influences in their music. They had the country thing. They had this Celtic thing, real Irish-sounding. Through listening to their music, I got introduced to all this other music, like Mahavishnu Orchestra, John McLaughlin, Jan Hammer, and Billy Cobham. Most people heard them before they heard the Dregs, but the Dregs led me to them. And that led me into the whole fusion thing—Return to Forever, Al DeMiola, Stanley Clarke, Lenny White, Chick Corea. I was really into that scene for a while. I couldn't really play like that, but that's what I was aspiring to. And Jeff Beck was a tremendous influence on me. The two albums, *Wired* and *Blow by Blow*.

The Dregs seemed to be the only thing I wanted to listen to for a long time. There were so many things in that music. But I got so into them, and so into Steve Morse's guitar playing that it became a problem for me. I wasn't branching out enough. I started to sound like a little imitation of Steve. People were telling me, "You look like Steve!" (Laughs) I don't know what I was doing. Maybe I was standing like him. I must have been, because people were telling me I looked like him, and I don't look like him at all. It was time for me to start branching out. I started really listening to Coltrane and Miles Davis, Bird and Diz, and all the associated musicians they played with. You could rip off things from them, and you weren't stealing from another guitar player. Getting in Aquarium Rescue Unit was real healthy, because those guys were tracing everything back to its roots. We were listening to Charlie Christian, Django Rhinehart, Wes Montgomery, Monk—a lot of oddball stuff—Sun Ra.

How did the Aquarium Rescue Unit come about—your association with them and Col. Bruce Hampton?

When I first moved to Atlanta, I met Jeff Sipe, the drummer, Apt. Q258. I met him, like, the third day I was in town. Then about a week later, Oteil and Koffi Burbridge had moved into town and were living at Jeff's house. And we formed a band. There was another guitar player named Charlie Williams in the band, too. All of these guys knew of Bruce, but none of 'em were really playing with him except Jeff. He would just play with him one day a week. At some point Oteil started playing with them, and they asked me to come down and sit in one night, so I went down and heard 'em. They played three sets. The first set, I'm just sitting there dying to play with them, and they never asked me up. The second set they never asked me up, and I was thinking, man, I am dying to play! Well, the third set the Colonel asked me to come up and play. I went and got my amp out of the car and sat in. The chemistry was great from the first minute we played together. We knew we had to do something with it. Bruce asked me to join the band the next day, and I said, "Man, there's nothing in the world I'd rather do." See, I played with Oteil and Jeff in another band, but we were playing all-original material and none of us knew how each other played normal music. We had only played this fusion-type music, you know. That music was hard to play. I never knew they liked blues. I thought playing blues would bore them. I loved blues! We discovered stuff about each other. They didn't know that I was a blues fan and that I enjoyed country picking stuff. And I didn't know that they did, so it was pretty interesting. We started playing one night a week at the Little Five Points Pub. And it wasn't about money at all. It was about "everybody hates their life" and this is the one night a week we get to play. We didn't rehearse; we just got up there and played. Then one night Widespread Panic meandered into the club, on a Monday night, 99-cent cover charge or something, and they heard us and said, "Wow, you guys are different. Would you like to come and play with us?" And we said, "Yeah! Thanks!" We had never left Atlanta. Then we started playing Birmingham and other places real close to town. Then Widespread took us on tour with them, and we met Phish, and went on tour with them. And then we met Blues Traveler, and then we met Dave Matthews. So, all these groups, we used to play together all the time. All of those groups are responsible for helping us get the little bit of notoriety that we had. They loved us, and helped us. Like with the H.O.R.D.E. Tour. The people putting on the festival were not in favor of us being there. They just thought we were too weird. So, John Popper and the guys from Widespread just said, "Look. If they don't do it, we don't do it." That's the kind of guys they are.

I just had the pleasure of meeting and interviewing Col. Bruce Hampton. Would you give us your thoughts on this man?

I don't think anybody can sum him up in very few words, because there are so many layers to the man. He's incredible. He made us the musicians we are today, and I'm not talking about the technical stuff. I mean, he tried to get us to get in touch with our essence. He wanted us to know what is really important in music wasn't how fast you could play, or how many chord voicings you knew. Getting in touch with your essence is what's really important. He is a paradox. He can't play, but he can. He can't sing, but he can. He is in touch with that thing that very few musicians are in touch with. He can play himself in any situation, and it's hard to do that. Bruce can look at a fencepost and play it. He can look at a sunset and play it. He can play, you know, a storm. My daughter Cameron was just a little girl when I started playing with Bruce. She's 12 now. He used to say, "Alright. Play Cameron. Play your daughter. Let me hear what she means to you." That was very hard to do; I couldn't do it. Then he took the guitar and said, "Let me show you." And he took the guitar and played what she meant to him. The notes he played had nothing to do with it. He is in touch with his essence, and he can display it, and will. He's an open channel. He can let it come through him. Not many people can do that. Through playing with him, what we mostly learned was how to let go of all our preconceptions about who we are, what we're doing, and why we are doing it. And it's very hard. I can't sit here and tell you that I can do it. But sometimes, if you're open, you can let go of all that, and the best music you've ever played will come through you. And it's not you doing it. He always wanted us to know that it wasn't us doing it. If you're doing it, it's not going to be divine. But you can't just sum the Colonel up in a few words. We did used to call him our Alabama football coach version of Miles Davis. (Laughs) We had many names for him. He's a lot like Miles Davis in a way. He always surrounds himself with interesting musicians. I don't mean interesting like they can play fast. What I mean is, he puts interesting chemistries together. He'll surround himself with people who are totally different from one another, yet they have a chemistry with each other when they play with him. Aquarium Rescue Unit was that way. Now we've grown together through the years, because we have shared an experience together that no one else can understand if they weren't there. Derek Trucks is there. He totally gets it. Bruce has ruined him. When we say he ruined us, we mean it as a compliment. It keeps us from being just like all the other players. There's a lot of good guitar players out there, and you have to have something more. I don't know what it is. But had it not been for Bruce Hampton, I don't think I'd be in the place I am now, getting to play with all of these great musicians.

How did you wind up playing with the Allman Brothers Band, and would you ever do it again?

I loved every second of it, and I would do it again anytime. The way it came about, I had known Derek since he was 11 years old. His manager, Bunky Odom, was a friend of Bruce's and he kept coming around to our shows and saying, "Wait 'til you hear this kid. You'll think you're listening to Duane Allman." We're kind of like, "Yeah, right." But then he came and played a show with us in Chapel Hill, and he put all of us on the floor. His essence was right up front. All the things we had been struggling to find, he already had it! We were just knocked out by him, and our relationship just grew and grew, and we're the best of friends—all of us are. I was on tour with him about two or three years ago when the ARU wasn't playing as much. Butch came to the show one night, and he liked the chemistry that Derek and I had, and he wanted to form a band. He asked if I knew a bass player. I told him I knew the Michael Jordon of bass players, and that was Oteil. So, Butch said let's all get together at this time down in Florida. We'll rent a bed and breakfast and we'll rehearse. And that was Frogwings. That's how I met Butch. Actually, I had played with him once in 1993 when Dickey missed a show and I sat in with them. Not long after Frogwings formed, Warren Haynes and Allen Woody left the Allmans, and they wanted to get me and Oteil to come in. But Dickey was still there, and I knew they needed a slide player. I said, "I'd love to be in the Allman Brothers, don't get me wrong, but I'm not a slide player." I said, "You should get the best slide player in the world, your nephew." At that time, Derek was only 17. They felt like he was too young, or maybe Butch was a little bit concerned about bringing in a family member who was only 17 years old. So, they ended up getting Jack Pearson, who is just an extremely good musician. I love Jack Pearson.

So, with Oteil in the Allmans, one of my best friends was in the Allmans. Then when they got Derek, two of my best friends were in the Allmans. Plus, I had played gigs with Butch and Marc, and I'd played with Jaimoe when the Allman Brothers were broken up back in the mid-eighties. So, I knew everybody in the Allman Brothers except Gregg and Dickey. So, when Dickey didn't play the summer tour, they asked me, I guess because I knew everyone. I felt very lucky to get the call, but I was also very skeptical about doing it. I mean, Dickey is one of the reasons I started playing guitar. It was great, but during the summer, I started talking to Phil Lesh about the band he wanted to start putting together for the next year. I said, "Phil, I don't know what to do. I'm in the Allman Brothers Band." He goes, "I know. That's unbelievable!" He was really happy for me, but he still wanted me to be in his band. Having to choose, I was in a tough spot. My decision was based on many angles. Number one, I played with Phil before I played with the Allman Brothers, and he had mentioned he may want to put together a full-time band someday, and I had told him that I would be interested.

Then the Allmans called me. By the end of the summer, I was real comfortable with the gig. The gig was the easy part. The hoopla surrounding it was tough. I mean, Dickey didn't retire. He didn't leave on his own. He wasn't happy about it. And the guy can still play. He's awesome. It made me feel like I was standing between him and his rightful place, regardless of what their problems together were. That's none of my business. I never asked them about it. Whenever they would start to tell me, I would say, "Please don't tell me about it. I don't want to know." So, I went ahead and took the job with Phil. One reason is, this is Dickey's road that he paved here. All I can do is basically drive up and down the road he paved. With Phil, I could pave my own road, even though we are playing Grateful Dead's music, and even though there are the inevitable comparisons. But both of those gigs were great, for different reasons.

With the Brothers, you get to stand there and swing the bat hard. You get to play loud, and you're playing huge venues. With Phil, it's more about open-ended experimentation and you're not playing that loud. And you're not swinging the bat that hard, because you aren't trying to hit a homerun with Phil. You are playing it totally as a team sport. You know what I mean. With Phil, it's like Dixieland music—three or four guys are playing at the same time. Phil doesn't want you to fall into the thing of you play rhythm for him while he solos, he plays rhythm while you solo—he's not into that scene. He's looking for everybody to open it up, you know. Whereas with the Brothers, it's more like "you swing the bat."

Now, in Phil and Friends, you're not playing just Grateful Dead stuff, right?

Oh, no. Phil's writing new stuff. Warren's writing new stuff. All of us are writing new stuff, really. We haven't started doing everyone's tunes yet, but that is definitely in the plans. Phil is just so open to everything. I mean he is just wide open. The weirder you play, the more he likes it. (Laughs) Which is great. Like I was telling you, with Project Z, that's all about the moment. We don't rehearse. We just go out and play whatever comes to mind. A lot of my favorite stuff that I get to play is in that outlet.

We should get Phil Lesh and Col. Bruce together. It might tilt the Earth on its axis. (Laughing) It might misalign the stars. They're very aware of each other. I talk to Phil about Bruce all the time, because Bruce is one of my biggest musical inspirations. And so is Phil. I'll play something, and Phil will go, "What is that?" (Laughs) And I'll say, "I don't really know."

I'm playing the tree.

(Laughing) Yeah. No, I wish I could play the tree. I can't do it. I can kind of, but Bruce is a master of it.

One day, young grasshopper.

(Laughs) Yeah. That's exactly the way I look at it.

I know you are good friends with Warren and Gov't Mule. We were devastated by the death of Allen Woody last year. I wondered if you could share some special memories of Captain Al.

Oh, man. There are so many. I wouldn't even know where to start. Woody is one of my favorite musicians that I ever played with. One of my favorite memories of him would be when Aquarium Rescue Unit was playing in Gainesville, Florida. They had just gotten through cutting that album at Burt Reynolds' place—was that Seven Turns? I'm not sure. He had finished his tracks and was on his way back to Nashville where he lived. He stopped off in Gainesville. You know, he played mandolin, too. He came and brought his mandolin and a little Marshall amp, and he played that gig with us. He didn't know a single song, but he killed it. It was great. Then he went to Tallahassee the next day and played that gig with us. We hung, and we talked and we listened to music, and we discussed all sorts of philosophies. It was a real treat to have him there.

What are your future projects?

The main thing is this Project Z, other than playing with Phil. Of course, any time the Allman Brothers needed me, I'd be there at the drop of a hat. I know that Warren's going to play the Beacon run with them. It's funny, because I've played shows with the Allman Brothers with Warren and Woody. And with Derek. And then when Derek couldn't make the One for Woody show because of a prior commitment, I played with Warren. And then we did another one at the Warren jam in December.

Project Z is really the outlet I need. So, do the guys on the album. There are no walls. We don't even play songs. We just play. We did an album that should be out soon. It's on Terminus Records here in Atlanta. But that's what I like. There are no compromises. No holds barred. And Hampton used to say all the time, "Freedom can be a prison." But I like it like that, with no song to fall back on. •

Jimmy is now a member of Widespread Panic.

Johnny Neel

2001

A singer, songwriter, masterful keyboard player, producer, and former member of the Allman Brothers Band, Johnny Neel is a consummate musician. In 2001, I sat down with Johnny to learn a little about his life and music.

MBS: Where were you born and raised?

Johnny: I was born and raised in Wilmington, Delaware, and stayed there until age of 30. I shot down to Nashville in 1984.

Everybody is always asking if you were born blind?

No, I was an incubator baby and was put in the oxygen and this burned out my retina. This was back in 1954. They didn't know that much about it then.

Sounds like my friend Rickey Godfrey [formerly of Garfeel Ruff]. Do you know Rickey and Ronnie Godfrey?

Yes, that happened to both of them, too. I do know both of them and we are very good friends. I just used a keyboard of his. He plays in a club near my studio.

How did you first become fascinated with music? Were you really young when you got the bug?

Yes, when I was about six or seven years old. I always had a musical environment. I stared playing with the bongos, then when I went to blind school, everybody was playing the piano, so I had to do the same. Then when I got to be about 12 I made a couple of records on the Richey label up in Delaware and they did pretty well regionally, and I made about nine singles in a band called the Shapes of Soul. I got interested because it sucked me in.

Who are some of your earlier influences?

I think some of my early influences were jazz in the early days and then the Beatles and Motown. Stevie Wonder's album from when he was 12 years old got me rocking, *Fingertips*. Then I started liking the Stones, but when I started looking at piano I did the obvious—Elton John, Billy Joel, Oscar Peterson, Chick Corea. I play jazz pretty good and I have a couple of cuts on Warren Haynes' new album that are pretty jazzy.

A lot of people do not know you have written lots of good songs.

The biggest one was with the Allman Brothers—"Good Clean Fun"—and I wrote 4 or 5 songs on the *Seven Turns* album. Then there was the Dickey Betts album *Pattern Disruptive*—I wrote about six songs on that. Travis Tritt cut a song of mine. I went from the Forrester Sisters, Oak Ridge Boys, John Mayall, to Dorothy Moore, and Malaco artists did some of my R&B stuff. I have just been busy and the last two cuts I did was with Warren Haynes. My new album is out now also.

How did you first hook up with Dickey Betts? That *Pattern Disruptive* album is really great. How did you get in with him?

I had been playing at the Bluebird Café; it is now pretty prominent, but before it was a little joint you know, I did a benefit for him with an organization that he was involved with at the time but then he heard me play a slide synthesizer. I was playing through a Marshall with a wheel on the slide lick. That is how I got involved with him. I worked with him for about two years and then I quit and then he called me to write the album with him. Then I hooked up with Gregg Allman and wrote a song called "Island" with Gregg on *Before the Bullets Fly* and then I got involved in the Allman Brothers Reunion Tour. Then I did *Seven Turns* and then we separated and I went to work for Huey Lewis' people. I enjoyed working with the Allmans.

Why did you leave?

It was just a feeling and I got kind of bored doing the same stuff—nothing to do with them. I wasn't singing enough and I wanted to and it was just time. Sometimes you do not know why things happen the way they do. I like to sing and wanted to do more of it. We are all still good friends and I just saw them up in New York after Allen died.

You are a good singer and you should do as much of that as you can. I have seen you play with Gov't Mule. What that was like?

If you look at it in the historical sense, it was like it was just one guy. I played with Matt Abts in Dickey Betts Band and with Warren in Allmans, and Woody with the Allmans. I fit in pretty good, like a glove thing, you know. It was just magical, to get with Warren. He is so cool, and Woody and Matt, they just had such a good trio going and all I had to do was play a couple of chords. I am fortunate to know that whole family of people and I love them all.

Obviously, we were all knocked for a loop with Allen Woody's untimely death, and I wondered if you had any memory of him you would want to share…?

I remember that he could make me laugh to the point of tears. He could talk about seeing someone walking down the street and make me cry laughing. He was very sensitive and spiritually aware. He was confused about parts of his life as we all are, but overall, he was a good-hearted soul. He and Warren and Matt were such a thing, in Gov't Mule, I just loved it. That is the kind of magic he was about, and it (Allen's passing) kind of messed me up. We all kind of sat back on that one.

I certainly understand. What about Blue Floyd?

That goes back to Woody again, and I think I was the last-minute "good God, we don't have a keyboard guy" thing. (Laughs) I think that Eddie Hersh was supposed to do it but that was some kind of mix-up and then I got the gig, but, man, that was a blast. Playing with Matt and Marc Ford and Berry Oakley, Jr., and me, just the four of us now. We did five weeks in January through February and I do not know where it stands now and what the future of that band is now. If we do anything we may go to Europe. It sort of stopped for the time being. Now I need to push my album.

Tell us about *The Last Word*… Who is in it?

It started out with a bunch of friends of mine. I met Jack Pearson and he was in it. Tim Lofton and Dale Armstrong and me, and then we went through some changes and now a bunch of stuff happened, and now it is a lifelong friend of mine, Don Smith, on drums and this new fellow just came to town a bass player, Andre, and Chris Anderson who used to play with the Outlaws. He is with me. It is just the four of us. We get out there and whip ass. It is a lot funkier than Blue Floyd.

The album *Late Night Breakfast* is very good. Tell me all about it.

The album was something I started on and was a process over a couple of years. I was working on it and then this record company got involved and this producer that got involved I thought I wanted to work with—and then by the time I figured out I didn't want to work with him, it had slowed me down about eight months. Then we went into the Blue Floyd thing and I managed to have enough money to finish it. I don't have a big record deal with it. I sell them on the website. I'm thinking about doing some travel to Europe and make some quick headway, and then parlaying back this way. That's what I am thinking. I'm still trying to put together gigs and keep the band tight. I'm not traveling too far. I have people working in the office and I have a studio that we had people in recording a big band album last week. We have done more jazz, blues, and funk than anything so far.

Col. Bruce Hampton

January 2001

Prior to his untimely passing in 2017, Col. Bruce Hampton had "been there, done that, and got the t-shirt." He was an avid reader, a film buff, a star man, and a musical enigma. From the Hampton Grease Band to the Aquarium Rescue Unit, the Fiji Mariners, and the Code Talkers, Hampton explored musical stylings that blended one part Frank Zappa, two parts Charlie Christian, one part John Lee Hooker, and two parts Captain Beefheart, with more than one pinch of Allman Brothers Band tossed in for flavor. He was a writer, a psychic, a singer, a guitarist, an actor, a pro wrestler, and a filmmaker. But more than all of that, he was the organizational master, and if Derek Trucks, Jimmy Herring, and Oteil Burbridge were young Jedi's, Col. Bruce was their Yoda. No small wonder he was often referred to as "the daddy of us all."

For one of our three interviews, I spoke to Bruce from Montgomery, Alabama, where he was on the road in the middle of a thunderstorm. The cell phone held up nicely, and we were happy to capture this exclusive one-on-one, Zen-like trip into the mind of a true artist's artist—Col. Bruce Hampton.

MBS: It was great seeing you reunited with the Aquarium Rescue Unit at Warren's Christmas Jam last week.

Col. Bruce: Thanks. We had a great time, man.

You live in Atlanta nowadays, right?

I live in Florida and in Atlanta.

Where were you born and raised?

I was born in Knoxville, Tennessee, but I only spent about eight days there. I was raised in Atlanta. My family has been there since about 1820. I have definite Atlanta roots.

Who would you say influenced you musically early on?

Wow. I would say John Lee Hooker, Little Richard, Bobby Bland, B.B. King—when I was still a single digit, at age 8 and 9.

When and how was the Hampton Grease Band formed?

The name came around in 1967. I had played in a band called the Four of Nine (laughs) about 1964 with a guitar player named Harold. Harold was the guitarist in the Grease Band. We were in a high-school band and it just formed into that.

And you ended up signing to Columbia Records for *Music to Eat*?

That was probably the weirdest record I ever made, Michael. (Laughs)

Weird is good. How did that record do for you?

Well, I think it was on the shelves for about six weeks, and they just thought it was too weird and they yanked it. They yanked it pretty quickly.

Didn't the Hampton Grease Band open for some pretty big names? What about Jimi Hendrix?

We played festivals that Jimi was on. We probably opened for the Allman Brothers about twenty times—although they weren't big at the time—and the Grateful Dead, Fleetwood Mac. About every band out there in the late sixties.

But you guys were different. Were you theatrical?

Yeah, in a non-theatrical sense.

One press release said that you used to throw chairs into the audience.

(Laughs) No, but it sounds good.

What about standing on a pizza and singing?

Yeah. That's true. That's hard to do.

But it's art. Nobody said art was easy.

(Laughs) No. Butch Trucks tells the story that the last time he saw me in the sixties, I was eating Interstate 285. That's always been a good one. (Laughs) Fiction is better than truth anyway. I don't know. You can't write anything better than the 2000 election. Nobody would believe the script. It's got about ten more years until it plays out. We needed it bad, for the drama. How long have you had your magazine online? I see it a lot.

In February, it'll be up for two years.

Let me ask you a couple of questions. How did you start it?

I was writing for magazines like *Goldmine, Hittin' the Note,* and *Relix,* and I kind of became the ambassador of Southern music. So, I decided to start a Web magazine dedicated to good Southern music. It just took off from there.

It's great! I just can't believe you found all those old Capricorn bands. You dug 'em up. It's just mind-blowing. Do you ever hear from Dru Lombar?

All the time.

Please tell him I said hello. It's been 25 years since I've seen him.

Will do. After you left Columbia Records, you signed with Frank Zappa's Bizarre/Straight label. Did you do any recording?

We never did any recording, but I knew Frank in the middle and late sixties. He was very much a gentleman to me and everybody around him. I was a nineteen-year-old kid. We did a cameo on *Lumpy Gravy*. Sam Whiteside was with me. He passed away about three months ago. But Frank was just getting started. Moon Unit wasn't even born yet. There was nothing weird about Frank. He was all work and no play. A very serious-minded guy.

And quite a guitar player.

He was a great picker. And he was himself; that's what I dug about him.

Kind of like yourself. There's only one Col. Bruce.

Well, I don't know whether I'm good or bad, but we have a new movie that came out last week. It's about me teaching guitar lessons. It's called *Outside Out*. I did it with the Phish guy, Mike Gordon. It'll start hitting theaters in a month or so. Let me ask you, Michael B., are you a Leo or a Cancer?

Cancer, Aquarius rising. My wife is an astrologer.

(Laughs) You are kidding! Wow! She must be a Pisces.

She's a Gemini, Cancer rising.

Air and water, good match. Which one's the craziest, her or you?

That's hard to say. We are definitely a unique pair.

You sound like a great pair.

Oh, we are. What can I say? (Laughs)
Where are you from originally?

Just 35 miles down the road in Spartanburg. Jill and I have been big fans of Gov't Mule. Would you care to comment on the death of Allen Woody?
I hated to see Allen go, man. That really hurt. He was crazy as a loon. What a great guy. A good spirit.

You wouldn't know anything about *crazy*, now would you?
I'm surrounded by it, and I *am* it.

How did the Aquarium Rescue Unit come to be? Did you put that together?
I had help from everybody. Jeff (Sipe) and I met about 1985, the drummer. He knew Oteil (Burbridge) before, and I met him in '86 and Jimmy in '89. It all kind of just came together. I can't really take credit for it. I'm an organizer, I'm not a leader. I have to give Apt. Q258 a lot of credit, too. The synergy took itself and made itself.

Did Jeff always go by the name Apt. Q258?
He used to be Jeff, now he's Apt. Q258, named after the Prophet Omega. There's a website on that, too, called "Friends Seen and Unseen," and a movie—with Billy Bob Thornton, Marty Stuart, and myself. It's not out yet, but I think the website is up. I'm not sure.

So, are you friends with Billy Bob? I know you were in *Slingblade*.
Yeah. Right.

It took me a while to realize it was you. I didn't recognize Dwight Yoakam either.
We were both honored to be in it.

That was a great movie. Really strange. My kind of flick. It's, like, my favorite movie other than *The Wizard of Oz*. It really was.

What's funny is while we were shooting, all the producers were going, "This one will go straight to video," and I'm sitting there watching the thing and going, "This is one of the greatest films ever made." Not because I was in it—I was just devastated by it. It was amazing. And Billy shot a good four and a half hours, and he had to edit it to two hours and ten minutes or whatever. The other half of the movie is just as good as that. It's a shame the world never got to see it. I think it's out on a director's cut, though. Billy Bob, you know, is obviously a genius, man. He can act, direct, write. He's written two screenplays that are just unbelievable.

There's one that I heard was coming out called *Daddy and Them*, with Andy Griffith and John Prine in it. I'm really looking forward to that one.

He shot that in Little Rock last year, and I think it would be out now, except he released *All the Pretty Horses* with Matt Damon, and that just came out. But *Daddy and Them* is really, really great, man. *All the Pretty Horses* was shot about two years ago, and I remember he had trouble getting the sound on it. I remember we were in the studio with him in the fall with Matt Damon and Billy Bob and Marty Stuart, and I don't know movie stars, man. I thought Matt was the piano player. I'm saying to Matt Damon, one of the best actors around, "Hey, that's good piano-playing." He just looked at me like I was crazy! (Laughs) Then he found out I was the guy in *Slingblade* and it was just double crazy. But Billy Bob's a genius, no question about it. And a wonderful, wonderful man, too. As good as they get.

What made you leave the Aquarium Rescue Unit and later form the Fiji Mariners?

I didn't leave it. I was told by the doctor to take a long break. My blood pressure was, like, three million over three million. It was pretty exhausting. I took about a four-month hiatus. Then I had to do something, so that was thrown together. I never wanted to leave the ARU. We played two gigs together last year, and maybe we'll play some more this year. Personally, they are wonderful people, and you're not going to get any better players. Or tell me who they are, I'd like to hear 'em. (Laughs)

I just saw a video of you and the Unit down in Florida with Allen Woody sitting in on guitar and lap steel.

He came out on the road with us for a while. The best compliment I ever was paid, Allen said, "The Allman Brothers are crazy, but *y'all are for real!*" He said, "Y'all don't have to try!" It was funny as hell. I miss that cat a lot, man.

Tell me what "Zambee" is.

Wow. If you can explain "life and jazz," I'll explain it! In 1974, I met a gentleman who was a sound man, and his name was Zambee. It's an actual person. And he went 250 thousand miles an hour backwards on the Skylab program—1,300 g's backwards, which is impossible. It broke every bone in his body. In 1979 to '80, we tried to open a Zambeeland theme park in Georgia. It was an absurdity, but I actually started getting some momentum. Then in 1980 we had a Zambeeland Orchestra for one gig, dedicated to Zambee. Then Aquarium Rescue Unit came along later, in 1990 or so, and we always praised Zambee, He was our spiritual leader—our mascot, you might say. He's also the world's fastest man, *backwards*. You know Chauncey Gardner, in the movie *Being There?*

That's another one of my all-time favorites.

What's weird as hell is in 1980 when it came out, I went to the theater with him, and I said, "Zambee, that's you!" He looks like him, talks like him, walks like him. Peter Sellers as Chauncey Gardner *is* Zambee. When it finished, I said, "I'm not leaving. I've got to sit through this again. It's a masterpiece." So, we sat. And I noticed the black kid in the movie, and I said, "Who the hell is that black kid?" Seven years later, that black kid in *Being There* turns out to be Oteil Burbridge! He said, "If you see that honky, tell him I'm gonna cut his ass." It was Oteil! The odds of that are 45 billion to one. So, seven years later, I'm sitting there explaining Zambee to him, and he lays it on me that he was in the movie. That's just too crazy.

Oteil had a talk show on NBC called *Stuff*. He was on every Saturday morning. He interviewed people like Kareem Abdul Jabar. He was also a ballet dancer, and did a lot of commercials and movies when he was a teenager. He was a drummer first, and didn't pick up a bass until he was fourteen or fifteen. And you know what's funny? The first gig I hired him, I paid him with a 1976 Dodge Colt. He had no car, so I gave him one. I knew he was a drummer, and I just marveled that this 21-year-old kid was *that good* a drummer. So, I hired him as a drummer. Then he picked up the bass one day, and we all nearly fainted. We said, "Holy... What is that?!" At 21 he was still getting his thing together, but you could still tell he was going to be the Michael Jordan of bass guitar in about three years. All the old-school guys are coming up to me and saying, "Tell that guy to stop playing so much." And I say, "You're not listening. He's not over playing. He's just embellishing everything, and the bass line is always there."

The bass line is there, along with a melody line, and something else, and it works well. Very well. Very jazzy. The melody line is always there. I've played with a thousand bass players, and he is one of the best I've ever played with. His bass line is always there; you've just got to trust him. You just go. Sometimes there is no "one." When him and Jeff get to going, there's no "one." You just have to hang on and go.

I want to do something a bit different, because you are such a renaissance man. In the tradition of great magazines like *Tiger Beat* and *16*, I want to ask you some fan questions. What are your five favorite record albums of all time? Not including Donny Osmond. (Laughing)

Number one, do you have a pencil? (Laughs and spells out name) Krystoff Penderecki *Threnbony to the Victims of Hiroshima*. That's number one. Number two is *Bobby Bland's Greatest Hits*. Number three is anything by Son House. And number four is Ala Akbar Khan. Number five is any records on Crown by John Lee Hooker. Crown or King.

That's pretty interesting. The first album you spoke of, what is that? Is it jazz?

Oh, God, no. It's from the 28th century. If you ever get a chance to hear it, listen. It's the greatest piece of music I've ever heard in my life. Actually, that's how I met Frank Zappa. I was discussing that piece of music. We were in a café, and one of us overheard the other one talking about it, and said, "How did you know that record?" That's sort of how we became friends.

What's the best book you've ever read?

Fear and Loathing in Las Vegas by Hunter S. Thompson and *Commentaries on Living* by Jiddu Krishmanurti.

So, you like Dr. Thompson. He's one of my favorites.

He's the funniest man. I like him better than Mark Twain. I don't like all of them, but *Fear and Loathing* is madness at its height. That's absolutely a masterpiece.

Your all-time favorite TV show?

Without a doubt, the acting, the production, the directing, is *The Andy Griffith Show.* I mean, you can watch that and learn music, and flow, and life more than anything I've ever seen. Those first fifty, there was nothing that could beat 'em. *All in the Family* was second, I believe. But I study Andy Griffith for musical composition, for space and time. They never did a bad episode. There's not one moment out of place on those hundreds of episodes. When you can perfect something like that, it's amazing. To be that "on" all the time, and that good, is scary. I generally hate consistency. I want something to be great for two nights and then horrible for a night. So, consistency worries me. Consistency is a mediocre mind. But it was a symphony for me each time. It was pro wrestling and it was Shakespeare. They nailed it. Whoever the producer and the director were. And the acting was just great every show—Ron Howard, Don Knotts, Andy Griffith—I don't know how they did it. Thank you for that question. I finally get to answer stuff I've always wanted to answer.

Favorite movie of all time?

Oh, wow. *Being There; Brazil; Magnolia; Slingblade; To Kill a Mockingbird*; and *Women in Love.*

What are your hobbies?

That's so great that you asked that, because I go through passions. I probably do them for about ten years, and then never do them again. I started out as a golfer, believe it or not, until I was twenty. I went to school on a golf scholarship. I have played three times in thirty years. I hate it now. I spent so much time as a young man trying to improve it. I played tennis for about ten years, and I don't play it anymore. For the past ten years, I've been into horseracing. I love the Kentucky Derby. I like any kind of racing that lasts less than five minutes and you can tell who's winning. The hundred-yard dash and the 440 in the Olympics are fun. I don't understand stock-car racing. I'm trying to. I'm asking my friends, "When do you cheer?" I mean, I respect their unbelievable skills, but I just don't know when to get excited. I like drag-racing. Other hobbies. I'm just getting back into reading psychology books for the first time in thirty years. I read all of them back in the sixties. I'm reading philosophy again. I really don't know why. (Laughs) Everybody has an opinion.

Describe your favorite meal?

Actually, in May of this year I started on a diet to lose weight, and I stopped eating as many carbohydrates. I went on a low-carbohydrate diet and I dropped about 40 pounds in two months. Since winter's come, I've gained it all back. It's from eating too many carbs. My favorite food, I am proud to say, is corn. It's hard to beat cream corn. What do you like to eat?

If you saw me, you would see that I definitely have my own food issues.

Yeah, but in reverse. You're too thin, right? (Note: Col. Bruce had obviously not seen me in person yet!)

Not exactly. But my favorites are Indian food and Middle Eastern.

Oh, I love Indian food.

What music do you listen to today?

I can't stand any popular stuff. I try to be open, but I turn on the radio today and it makes my epidermis hurt. I mean, what in the world? These kids are getting married at 23… Do they come back at 70 and hear all this noise and say, "Darling, they're playing our song"? I mean, there's no melody. I'm sorry, I just don't get it. It's not that I'm old, it's not a generational thing. It's just awful. I'm listening to Charlie Christian and Django Rhinehart today, and Robert Johnson.

But I'm sure you listen to some of the young bloods today, like Derek Trucks. I know he's your boy.

I talk to Derek about every three days, and he's coming to see me next week. I've been a friend and a fan since he was nine years old. There are a few hopes out there. As long as it's pure, I'll dig it. As long as it's from the heart. There's no bad or good. It took twenty years for people to get Monk. To get John Lee Hooker and B.B. King, it took forever. I saw B.B. King get booed in the early sixties. People didn't appreciate him, and he's one of the best. But I just talked to Derek last night. Derek's it.

To wrap up, what do you have coming up?

On February 2, at Variety Playhouse (Atlanta), we're showing the movie we did with the Phish guy, Mike Gordon, *Outside Out*, and we're playing afterwards. And I'm playing three or four days a week with the Code Talkers. We're about to get a new record company. Capricorn closed last week, ironically. But we should be doing some new stuff soon.

Thanks for your time, Col. Bruce. It's been great. I hope you can visit again soon.

Thank you, Michael. It's been a real pleasure. I am sure we will get to hang out again really soon. I'm planning on playing in your area again soon. •

Col. Bruce Hampton collapsed onstage during his 70th birthday celebration on May 1, 2017, at the Fox Theater in Atlanta, surrounded by friends and loved ones, and doing what he loved the most. He died before they could get him to the hospital. It was so ironic the song was "Turn On Your Love Light," and the last song of the evening.

Charlie Daniels

2017

I have been following the career of Charlie Daniels and his band since 1972. Sometimes it's hard to believe that I heard my first Charlie Daniels Band record some 45 years ago. The thing is, Charlie has only continued to grow as an artist, and at the age of 80 years young, he is still getting out there and rocking the country. In fact, this has been one of Charlie's biggest and busiest years ever, as he was inducted into the Country Music Hall of Fame, released a great new album of cowboy songs, readied his autobiography for publication, and continued to do more than his fair share of charitable works. In this, the ninth interview with Charlie of my career, we spoke about his special year, and his continued success.

MBS: Hi, Charlie. How you doing?
Charlie: Pretty good, son. How are you?

Pretty good. I'm just trying to get my digital recorder to work. This technical stuff is driving me insane.

It always will; I hardly fool with it. If you are over 14 years old you ain't got no business messin' with it anyway.

That's right. I have to use it to record. I was so used to recording interviews all those years on cassette tapes and that was just fine. Now that I am using this digital stuff, it's like things keep going wrong and I get nervous because it comes time to do the interview… Until 5 minutes ago I couldn't get it to work, and now supposedly it is working so that is good. That is all that matters, right?

That's right.

First of all, I want to talk about how great *Nighthawk* is, your latest release—I love it. I love the mix of old cowboy songs and remakes of some of your classics. What made you decide to pay tribute to the cowboys on this album, Charlie?

Michael, I've been getting songs together for this album for…I don't even know how many years. I didn't keep up with when I first started, but it was always in the back of my mind that I was going to do a cowboy album, though. I wanted to do an album of working cowboys songs as opposed to movie cowboy songs.

Oh, yeah.

...and I just kept, when I would find a song I liked, I'd just stick it in the back of my mind and just think, ya know, when I get enough I'll get'er done. So, I finally got enough songs to do an album and it's a tribute to the working cowboy, it's not really a very, you know, commercial sort of album as far as radio airplay or that sort of thing. That really wasn't what we were after. I had a special thought in mind on this record, I wanted to pay tribute to the working cowboys, so I think we managed to do that.

That's great. The working cowboy is just like the American farmer—they are very, very important. But going the other route, just out of curiosity, thinking of the singing cowboys of the old days in the '40s and '50s, I grew up watching them on TV and my mom and dad loved them all. Did you ever watch Roy Rogers and Gene Autry and that stuff?

Every Saturday.

That's nice, man. I remember my mom was all about Gene Autry, my dad liked this guy Hop Along Cassady a lot.

Oh, yeah. For sure. When I was a kid, that is what played in every theater in the South that I knew anything about, in every little town I ever lived in—which was quite a few of 'em over the years. Every Saturday it was Roy Rogers, Gene Autry, Sunset Carson, Bob Steel, "Lash" LaRue...every Saturday.

Yeah. Movies were a lot less expensive then, too, weren't they? That was the good ol' days.

I use to go to the movies for 9 cents.

(Laughing) Nine cents! Not 10 cents but nine cents!

Yeah, 9 cents.

Well, congratulations are in order for your being inducted into the Country Music Hall of Fame. That's very prestigious. And you were inducted alongside Randy Travis and Fred Foster, two other good ones, on

October 16, 2016. What are your thoughts on being inducted into this organization?

Basically, humility and I'm thankful to the good Lord. I have had so many blessings and that's one that I didn't know if it would ever happen, that's the one you can't lobby for, you can't do anything about it because you don't even know who is voting. They keep that pretty much a secret. It's an alternating channel of people who I think serve for three years or something like that, and they get together and vote and decide who's gonna be inducted. You never know anything about it 'til they actually get through the whole voting process and they finally come and tell you. You don't know you are going to be inducted and the night it happened to me, it just—of course, I didn't know it was gonna happen. I went to where I went under false pretenses. I didn't know that's what I was going for. I thought I was going to take a picture and when I found out what it was, Michael, it's pretty overwhelming, to be honest with you about it. It sure was, I don't know any other way to put it, it was… I have had a lot of accolades in my life, I've been blessed with making a living doing something that I thoroughly enjoy doing, and I've had a lot of icing on the cake and awards and special things that have happened to me. But this one was one that I just didn't have any idea. A complete surprise. It just comes out of the clear blue sky and just knocks you to your knees almost, it's that powerful. And still, when I go to the Grand Ole Opry and the announcer is bringing us on, he says, "…a member of the Country Music Hall of Fame," it's like, *What*? You know?

I would imagine so.

It's still a thrill to me to hear somebody say that, to be honest with you, I am not blasé in the furthest stretch of the imagination about that. I'm pretty gushy about it, and I don't think that will ever go away. I think it will always be there. I think I'll always be very humble and very thankful and, really, still to this day pretty surprised about it.

Well, I'm very happy for you. I went on their website and just looked at the list of names that have been inducted and it must be absolutely mind-blowing to be grouped with some of those folks.

There's no doubt about it, it was for me. You know, I've been asked a lot of times since then what I thought about it and how I perceived it and I have yet to be able to completely articulate my thoughts to actually put into words how I felt, because I don't know how to do it. I know it's a special feeling to me on the inside. What I felt when I walked up and Brenda Lee put that medallion around my neck, it just…it's just hard for me to do. I just have not found an adequate way to express it yet, so I'm still kinda zinging on this, buddy.

(Laughing) Yes, sir. The Hall of Fame has the Million Mile Reflections exhibit that has been renewed until September 4th. What kind of things do they have in this exhibit that people can see?

They came out to the house with some of the curators and people in charge of procuring this stuff and putting it together. We just gave them the run of the place—like, "This is where this is stored, this is where that is stored, this is where the pictures are, and this is our stuff hanging on the wall that we've kept." Anything that you want you take it, ya know? Whatever you find that is hanging on the wall, if it's in one of the storage places or whatever, it's yours, just take it. So, we just let them go at it, and they took, Michael, what I consider to be a good cross-section of my personal life and my professional life. They got some stuff in the house…they got something that I was really surprised that they took. I collect walking canes and have for a lot of years, and I have a pretty good collection of 'em. I got a case I store 'em in and it holds a whole bunch of them, and they took that. I never thought about them coming in and taking that cane case. It just never struck me that there would be any interest in that, ya know, or whatever, but some of the things they took kinda surprised me. They took, I guess, what they thought would best show my life, my personal life and my professional life, and I think they did a good job in doing it.

Cool. I Look forward to getting up there to see that. There is so much going on right now for you, the one thing I'm really looking forward to is your book *Never Look at the Empty Seats* that is coming out in October. How long did it take you to write this book?

I've been writing on that thing, Michael, for about 20 years or so, I imagine. But the hard part about the whole thing was I wrote and rewrote and tried to put things in it that were interesting. You can get carried away with your family tree or some part of your career that's not interesting to anybody else, and put a bunch of stuff in it nobody cares about. So, I kinda purged it of that a couple of times and I kept writing, but I could not find a place to pause it or to end it because my career was ongoing. I was still doing things that were interesting, I was still having exciting things happen, and I just couldn't find a place to pause it, and then when I found out I was going to be inducted into the Country Music Hall of Fame, I thought what a great place to pause it.

Yeah.

The next day after I was inducted I sat down and wrote the ending while it was still fresh in my mind. Then I just back-wrote from there to where I was, which I was pretty far along the line. I went back and grabbed the pieces that I had written and put them all together and turned them in and here we go.

Great, and I understand from the website that anybody that is interested can go ahead and pre-order it there through CharlieDaniels.com.

Oh, yeah, yeah. I never realized how into pre-orders and everything that the business has become, and that is one of the things they have really stressed to me is the pre-orders. That way they get it right away. I mean, you pre-order it right off to start with.

Yeah, most of us, you know, that are fans want it the minute it comes out. I'll encourage everybody that's a fan, too, even people that just might not be hardcore fans like I am—they might just be country music or Southern-rock fans, you know—to order it. This is gonna be a great book—I know it's a great story—because you are also a really good storyteller and writer so that helps, too.

Well, I appreciate it, Michael. I am extremely happy about this book coming out. I think it's a great time for it to come out, of course, during my eightieth—actually my eighty-first—year here. I've been wanting to tell this story for a long time and, as I said, I just couldn't find a place to stop it so…we got all that part of it accomplished. It is a thrill. I've had some books out before, but nothing like this; this is my life's story. The other stuff were bits and pieces of this, that, and the other thing—short stories and fiction and stuff. This one is my life's story. This one means a lot to me.

No doubt. Like you said, you just had your eightieth birthday on October 28th of 2016. Congratulations again on that—that's a big deal!

Well, thank you.

It's hard to believe that you're 80 because you look at you onstage, you kinda act like a 30-year-old. It's really cool.

Well, you are very kind.

You played over 100 shows last year…

I tell people I only work three hours a day so I can do this.

(Laughing) Right. No pre-planning at all, right? I was wanting to ask you, is it getting harder to do the touring as you get older, and also, do you have any plans to retire? Please say no.

I will answer the last question first. I don't have any plans to retire until people get to where they don't want to hear me, or I have any kind of a health thing that would be a problem, or God calls me home. As far as retiring, I have made no provisions. I've made no plans or anything about retiring. I just don't have it in my DNA to do that. As far as my creativity is concerned, I'm still writing songs and still doing new things and we are constantly doing something new. I've got enough ideas for albums to last me if I live to 150—I mean, I just never run out of projects. Like the cowboy thing, for instance, back when I was on major record labels and we had to do an album a year, the pressure was on—pretty much, you've *got* to get it done. My recording life is totally different now. I record what I want to, when I want to, and if I want to. So, um, I've just got all kinds of ideas and I'm not bound by any one genre of music I've done, you know? I've done a cowboy album, I've done bluegrass albums, I've done the tribute to Bob Dylan… I've got all kinds of ideas in my mind. Some of these ideas that we are doing now have been around for a long time, we just never had a chance to do 'em. So, I've got enough stuff. You know, somebody said Michelangelo, to accomplish what he had planned, he needed to live to be 150 or something like that. Well, that's kinda the way it is with me. I don't plan on living to be 150, but I think it's great to always have something to do, that's the thing. I think people who lose their vision and have no desire to create and have nothing that excites 'em, I think that's when you would probably lose your interest in living and just sit down in a rocking chair, ya know? I think that is what happens, and that's fine if people want to do that. I am not knocking anybody who wants to retire. I think some people *need* to retire; some people don't do things they love as much as I do, some people have health problems and this that, but with me, it's all about the people. It's all about getting onstage one more time, get out there and entertain people and having people enjoy it, that's my life, that's what I'm all about.

I want to ask about your humanitarian work. Tell us a little bit about the Journey Home Project.

The Journey Home Project is, our overall mission is helping veterans any way we can, but what we started out as and what we feel, what we still try to throw a lot of our resources into is helping our veterans readjust to civilian life. When they come home, especially from war zones. To those of us who are under-initiated in that process, it seems like it would be a pretty simple thing. It'd be like changing jobs to us, moving from one town to another, but it's a lot more involved than that. Of course, it's a case-by-case, person-by-person thing; some people adjust easier than others. But some people, when they come back it's like, it's hard, it's hard to do, especially with the way that our government has treated our vets. Which is another whole story, I don't want to get started on that. They don't really take care of their needs, so I think that we owe our vets an unpayable debt of gratitude and if there is a need we should try to fill it if we can, so that's what this is all about. We've done things like—good gosh Michael—we've helped people get cars, we've helped people get furniture, we've helped people get an education, whatever we are able to do that meets their needs. That's basically what it's all about.

Is the Charlie and Hazel Daniels Veterans and Military Family Center connected to Journey Home, or is that a different program?

No, it is connected to it. In fact, our contributions that were made were from the funds of the Journey Home Project and they decided—I don't know who made the decision, I guess the college people over there—I think maybe the head of the college made the decision to name it after Hazel and myself, which was not part of the bargain. I mean, it was just something that they did; it had nothing to do with the contributions we made in all. But it's up and running, it's state of the art, and we're just tickled to death about it.

Absolutely. Well, are you planning a Volunteer Jam this year again?

We haven't decided yet, Michael. There are a lot of things that come into play here… It's like the availability of the hall, the time that we're able to do it, the feasibility of doing it, what artists we can come up with… We've had a dynamite bunch of artists on here the last couple of times we've done it, and you know you feel like if you're gonna do it, you gotta keep it going, so only if we can come up with a dynamite roster of artists will we do it. We'll just have to wait and see.

Alright, the last question. Do you have any other big plans coming up this year that we didn't touch on?

Gosh, I don't think so. I don't really know of anything that I've got planned. My next big deal is the book coming out. That is gonna take quite a bit of energy with doing the promotions on it and everything. I am gonna have to devote a lot of my time and energy to that, and I basically wouldn't have time to get to any other kind of a major project. I think we are probably gonna have to pretty much stick it out and get that done, 'cause I ain't as young as I used to be so I don't try to do things that I'm not able to do. I used to stay up 24 hours a day if I needed to. I don't do that anymore.

I fully understand.

I block out time for rest. I block out time for doing what I need to do to try and stay as healthy as I can. It's a little more time-consuming doing something than what it used to be, so I imagine we are probably gonna pretty much stick with that for the rest of the year, but you know, don't hold me to that. Something could come up that would grab my attention and we might get into that, but we will see.

Never know when you are going to pull one of those hundreds of ideas out of your head.

You never know when the good Lord is going to throw something your way—well, he doesn't throw things, but when he's gonna bring something your way, you never know—so we'll wait. We will leave that up to him.

Yeah, that's true.

Whatever he wants me to do, I want to do it.

Me, too. Alright, Charlie, I sure appreciate this, buddy.

Well, I appreciate it, Michael. I appreciate your devotion to our brand of music and you've been very faithful to the cause and I appreciate you doing it.

Always, always. Thank you and have a great and blessed day.

Okay, brother. God bless. •

Franklin Wilkie

2015

I have known Spartanburg, South Carolina-based musician Franklin Wilkie since the early 1990s, and have always had a great time talking with him. I conducted several interviews with him back in 1995 for my first book, Carolina Dreams *(Marshall Tucker Entertainment, 1996). I recall meeting him for lunch several times at Garners Natural Café in Spartanburg and recording our conversations about his band Garfeel Ruff and his tenure as bassist for the Marshall Tucker Band following the death of Tommy Caldwell in 1980.*

I recently met him again, and believe it or not, we returned to Garners twenty years later, and their food was still great, and I still enjoyed my time with Frank. Parts of the following interview were done in 1995, and part in 2015. We are proud to present a brief version of Wilkie's long and successful music career, and how it all brought him to Zataban.

MBS: Let's go back a few years. Tell me about the first time you played with Toy Caldwell.

Frank: My first band with Toy Caldwell was called Magar's Madmen. It was a three-piece with Kenny Magar on drums. We were in the seventh grade, and Kenny was in the ninth. We played all instrumentals, no vocals. Right after Kenny, Toy and I met a guy named Jimmy Trout. He had a Falcon station wagon, and played keyboards, which he was always carrying around in that wagon. He was older, and kind of helped us get organized. The band that came out of that was the Ramblers. We had these red and white shirts with a block "R" on the pocket and black pants. We were doing "Green Onions," early instrumental stuff. When that band broke up, we still had those shirts that had an "R" on the pocket, so we had to come up with another band name that started with "R," and that's how we got the Rants.

Since I covered a lot about the Rants in my book, tell me about the next bands you played in.

I was in my second year at Spartanburg Junior College—now Spartanburg Methodist College—when we put together a band called the Puzzle, with George McCorkle's brother, Chuck; David McCutcheon from the Rants; Steve "Smitty" Smith; David Ezell; and Wayne Casasanta. Toy had done the early sign-up with the Marines, and every once in a while, he would come up from Paris Island on weekends and jam with the Puzzle at these different fraternity parties.

Tell me a little about the Toy Factory.

I was let out of the service on a hardship discharge, because my father had cancer. Word had already gotten to Toy that I was home for good. That night, I dropped by to hear the Toy Factory play. Toy went up to Chris Brawley, a friend of Jerry's who was playing bass, and told him his friend that had been in the service was back home, and he'd be playing from now on. He didn't fire him in a mean way, just matter-of-factly. But that was Toy. Friendship was everything to him. Chris went on to start a band called High Cotton, which recorded an excellent record for Mercury Records, produced by Allen Toussaint. I do remember that Chris had a terrible accident with a chainsaw, and lost a couple of fingers on his left hand. He had to quit playing bass, but he took up slide guitar and became one of the best.

Shortly thereafter, Carol Cox joined the band for a while. He came to auditions on Spring Street. He was well trained on piano, so it caused the band to expand its horizons. Doug no longer had to sing all of the songs, and the choice of material was becoming jazzier. Toy Factory was playing Steve Winwood and Traffic tunes, Elton John and John Mayall. They were just beginning to play some originals; "Can't You See" and many of Caldwell's songs were taking form during that time period.

We were booking through Beach Club Promotions, Cecil Corbet. Cecil heard some of our original material and sent us to record in Muscle Shoals. We did some tapes with Barry Beckett, a keyboard player and engineer. I remember him saying the material was good, but he wanted us to leave Toy down there. (Laughs) After all, that's where Duane Allman got his start. Corbet engineered the opening spot for the Toy Factory on the Allman Brothers Band's eastern tour.

Once again, all of this is in *Rebel Yell* (Mercer University Press, 2012) so I will skip through the timeline, past the changeover from Toy Factory to the Marshall Tucker Band, and their years of major success, and past your years in Garfeel Ruff. Then in 1980, Tommy Caldwell was killed and you were asked to join Marshall Tucker. Tell me about that.

It was probably a lot harder on the other guys than it was on me. I guess I was the choice because I knew the material, and I was friends with the band. I had been playing at a club called Cassidy's, and Toy called. He was a little apprehensive, because things had been going pretty good for Garfeel Ruff. We had one album on Capitol Records and we were looking for a new deal with another label. He told me they had decided to continue, and then he said, "If I'm going to have to go up there and play, I can't think of anyone I'd rather look over to my left and see than you." I told him I'd be honored, and he said, "Well, we'll be starting rehearsals in about two weeks. We want to have you up and running in three weeks."

We began rehearsals at Memorial Auditorium in two weeks. I could tell it was real hard on Toy. It was hard on all of them. Songs they had been playing for years and years, and now they were having to rehearse them. They didn't want to rehearse "Fire on the Mountain" or "Can't You See." So, they'd get about halfway through one song and stop.

My first show was at the Warehouse in New Orleans, and it was packed wall to wall. With no air conditioning, the temperature hovered around the 90-degree mark. The band was drenched by the end of the first song. I didn't move a lot; I remained very stationary. But I could feel Tommy there with me.

The second show was at the Astrodome in Houston. I remember Doug coming up behind me shaking his tambourine, and George would come over and play beside me, all making me feel more comfortable. Then I looked behind me and saw this 100x100 screen with the back of my head and my bass on this closed-circuit TV screen. I froze in my tracks and wasn't moving. George came dancing over beside me and said, "C'mon, buddy, you gotta move!"

Paul T. (Riddle) made sure that me and him had connecting rooms. He really helped me through. He'd have a stereo and we'd listen to tunes. He was really an anchor. He reached out to me, and we've become very close over the years because of that.

We had completely finished the *Dedicated* album when Warner Brothers told us they wanted something more pop-oriented to go on the record. They said they were going to push the album to a pop audience, as opposed to the new country that was forming in Nashville. Bad decision. We did the beachy "This Time I Believe." We could have slid right into that movement that was forming where Alabama was breaking ground.

Not long after I joined, we did the Born to Play concert at Spartanburg Memorial Auditorium. I'd been with Marshall Tucker about a year at the time. Garfeel Ruff still owed the bank a lot of money for loans we had taken to buy equipment. So, we did that concert to pay off the loan. We made just enough to pay them off, with the help of MTB, who's rumored appearance packed the house. The Marshall Tucker Band played "This Time I Believe" and "Tell the Blues to Take off the Night" from the new record.

So, you played with Tucker from 1980 until 1984. What did you do after the original band broke up in 1984?

After the original band broke up, we took 1985 off. Then at the end of '85, or the first of '86, Toy called me up and said, "Frank, I think I want to go out again... You want to go out?" I said, "Man, I'd love to." And he said, "Well, I'm gonna call Ronnie Godfrey and Al Pearson and see if they want to play." So, the four of us jumped into that big green truck and took off playing up and down the East coast. We played in Woodstock, Upstate New York—and we played a lot of the ski resorts, too. It was the original Toy Caldwell Band. Cecil Corbett was doing the booking for us, and Bob Morrell, who worked for Cecil, was our road manager. We did that for a couple of years.

That's something I did not know.

Yeah. There was somebody from Macon—I can't remember his name—that really believed in what Toy was doing and he helped a lot. We went in the studio with Paul Hornsby and recorded some songs with John Townsend from the Sanford-Townsend band. It was called the Caldwell-Townsend Project. Those tracks were never released, but I believe Paul has them. There were four tracks—two that John wrote and two that Toy wrote.

Moving fast-forward into the present, tell me a bit about your band, Zataban.

We had the band called Gypsy Souls. That was Big Tez Sherard on drums, Shane Pruitt on guitar, Craig Sorrells on trumpet, Kym McKinnon on guitar, and myself on bass. That band played at the Nu Way every Tuesday night for about seven years. What happened was, all these other bands evolved from Gypsy Souls. When that gig terminated, you had the Craig Sorrells Project, and we started Zataban during that time. Zataban has actually been rehearsing and playing around the area for about five years now. We recorded our first album with Buddy (Strong) at Southeastern Sound. We had about 200 songs, and we narrowed it down to these which we felt best represented the image we were going for. We have been working ever since on our original music record. That song "Dirty Dog" that Kym McKinnon wrote, and Patrick Purnell wrote a couple, and I've got a couple on there—so we've got three writers working on songs for the new record now. We hope to have it out by summer. You know how you look all your life for that band where every song you call out, you say, "Man, I can't wait to play that!" This is that band. I just enjoy every song, every track that we play. We try to carry on that spirit of New Orleans funk, Southern music, second line.

The band sounds great. We wish you continued success with Zataban, and I thank you for your time, as always.

Thank you, Michael. Anytime. •

Stuart Swanlund

2000

Born an "Air Force brat" in Puerto Rico on April 3, 1958, Stuart Swanlund used to sit on his grandmother's porch and listen to his neighbor, Doug Gray, rehearsing with a rock-and-roll band across the street. He was only five years old, and had no way of knowing that one day he'd play alongside Gray.

Back in the early 1980s when I first met and became friends with Stuart, I could tell that he was no ordinary guitar player. He rocked the city of Spartanburg, South Carolina, as a member of many a band, including Lightnin' West and White Wind. When he joined my friends' band, Silver Travis, I got to see him play up close several times a week, and I was always impressed. This guy really had something special. He played with his own style, and it was almost impossible to compare him to any other individual player.

Later that same decade, when he was asked to join the Marshall Tucker Band, I was probably as excited as Stuart. Maybe I was just proud of him. I could think of no other player who deserved the opportunity more. Although he dropped out of the lineup a couple of times for different reasons, he has remained an enduring influence on the sound of the "new" Marshall Tucker Band. His slide, lead, and rhythm guitar work is unique and energetic. His vocals on songs like "Why Can't You Love Me?" (a Stuart original on the Southern Spirit *CD) and "Hillbilly Band" are great.*

When I was out with the band on tour in Hickory, North Carolina, I invited Stuart up to my room. While he enjoyed a Subway sandwich, I asked a few questions about his MTB career.

MBS: A lot of people have wondered how you are doing following the hand surgery last year.

Stuart: Good. It was about a four-hour surgery. They had to do a skin graft. It's pretty ugly, as you can see. They had to cut all of this stuff out. This finger had been bent down for so long, that this joint was frozen. He had to cut up in there into the joint. It still gets a little stiff. But I can play stuff now that I haven't been able to play in years. And I can play it the way I want to. It's doing really good. It'll never be a hundred percent, but it's great.

What caused that, to begin with?

It's called Dupitrin's Contracture. It's a bunch of scar tissue that starts building up in your hands and fingers and starts pulling your fingers down. It's an inherited disease, and I just happened to get it. Only people with ancestors from Northern Europe get this disease. You know, my dad was Swedish-Norwegian, so that's probably where I got it. Nobody in his family had it that I know of.

When did you come to join the Marshall Tucker band?

I was asked to join in 1985 and played for eight years. I left in October 1993 the first time. I just wanted to stay at home and play around Chicagoland and all that good stuff. The second time I was out because of the hand.

What has been the high point of your time with Tucker?

I really enjoyed that tour with Hank Williams, Jr. The "Southern Thunder Tour" in '96 with Charlie Daniels and everybody. That was probably the most fun year I've had with the band. He only did, like, 50 shows a year, but we were on most of them. It was a big production. That was probably one of the high points, I guess. Another high point was when we sang the national anthem at Wrigley Field before a Cubs game. That was in 1993.

What's the most rewarding thing about playing on the road?

I think when the fans enjoy it and like it, that's rewarding.

What's the hardest part?

The traveling. It can wear you down a lot.

I know that there have been some wild times with the MTB. Would you say that you are as wild on the road as you ever were? Or have you calmed down as you've gotten older?

Oh, I've calmed down a whole lot. It's age mostly. I can't party like that anymore. I don't drink at all anymore. I used to have two or three beers before we even started. Now, I'm just not into it.

What about drugs?

Nah. No, thank you.

So, you live in Chicago these days. How do you like it?

I love it. Lots of beautiful women there. My old lady won't care if I say that. She catches me looking all the time. And the food is incredible. So many different things. And the ball park is there. I love Wrigley Field. It's just like going back in time. But I remember one year, we were so busy that I only got to go to one game the whole season. Last year I got to go about 20 times. And there are a lot of good musicians there. Lots of cool blues clubs. It's a happening city, and a pretty clean city to be that big, you know?

What are some of your other favorite cities to play and visit?

I kind of like it out west. It's like a whole different world out there. It's a lot of fun.

Tell me about your fellow bandmates.

Doug is a lot of fun. Real funny. Rusty and Tim I've known forever. Tim and I have been in other bands together. Rusty's a great player.

What about B.B. Borden?

Of course, he played for Mother's Finest, and that was one of my favorite bands.

Wasn't that a great band?

Great! And he's a nice guy. A good, solid drummer. Real funny, too.

David Muse?

He's a good guy. He's a helluva player, too.

What kind of guitar do you play these days?

Fender. Only Fender. I got a Strat and a Tele. Ernie Ball strings. I just picked up a cheaper Telecaster. It's called a Nashville Tele. Instead of having two pickups it has three. It has a Strat pickup in the middle. It's nice. It got a lot of good reviews.

Have you seen the reissued Danelectro guitars?

I love those things. They're not real expensive either. I'd like to have one just to have. They're identical to the original '58 model. The guy at Guitar Center said they play better than the original. Those things are so cool.

Have you ever played onstage with anyone that was a real thrill for you to play with—I mean, besides Doug?

(Laughs) We played one time at Lakewood Amphitheater, and Steve Morse (the Dixie Dreggs/Deep Purple) came out and jammed on "Can't You See?" and just smoked it. That was cool. A lot of fun. I haven't had a chance to jam with a lot of people.

Well, you'll get to jam with me one day...

(Laughs) When I get to jam with Michael Buffalo Smith, that'll be saying something!

What was your favorite Tucker album that you played on?

Southern Spirit. It didn't sound as good as the two after that, but I liked the songs on it. It's probably my favorite one.

What about the original band?

The very first one. I love that. I have the CD at home.

You know, the most successful touring bands these days allow taping at their shows... the Allmans, Widespread Panic, Gov't Mule, Little Feat, and Blues Traveler. And the people trade the tapes.

I've got a 1975 board tape of Little Feat. They did a lot of stuff that was on *Waiting for Columbus*, but it was totally different. It was great.

Do you think the MTB will ever allow taping at shows?

I don't know. Of course, that would be Doug's decision.

Who would you say are your guitar influences?

My biggest was Lowell George. Duane Allman, too. He was incredible. And Bonnie Raitt, she's a good slide player. She plays with a lot of feeling. That's the way Lowell played, too, with a lot of heart. He didn't play it like everybody else. A totally different style.

Do you think there's a chance for a second coming of Marshall Tucker? I mean, I know they've never gone away, but I'm talking about big hit records, stuff like that.

I don't know, but it sure would be nice.

If there was a big Southern rock tour put together, who would you like to play with?

The Allman Brothers. I love that band. And Gregg's solo band. Gregg sold out two shows at the House of Blues. Jimmy Hall was playing with them, too.

Do you like the current Skynyrd band?

Yeah. Hughie Thomasson, Rickey Medlocke, and those. But my favorite player with Skynyrd was Ed King. Great tone.

Did you play on the new MTB album?

I played on two cuts. I played those before my surgery. So, it's been a while. It's really a good album. If it's promoted good, it should do real good.

Well, thanks, Stuart. It's been great seein' you again, buddy. Keep on playin' that hot slide.

Thank you, M.B. Let's stay in touch. You have my new number. •

My dear friend Stuart passed away suddenly on August 4, 2012. He was 54. His passing was covered by everyone from MTV to Rolling Stone. *He would have liked that.*

Tony "Smoke" Heatherly

1999

The first time I ever heard Tony Heatherly play was way back in the seventies when he was playing bass for Mickey Fowler and the Variations. Many years later in 1984, following the breakup of the original Marshall Tucker Band, Heatherly was tapped by Toy Caldwell to play bass in his solo band. Flash-forward a few more years, into the early 21st century, and Tony was hired as bassist for the Marshall Tucker Band. But before he joined Tucker, I sat down with the man we all call "Smoke" at my home in Greenville, South Carolina, in 1999 for a talk about his life and music.

How did you first meet Toy Caldwell?

I first met Toy somewhere around 1973. I was with a group called Mickey Fowler and the Variation Band, and we were playing down in Spartanburg. We were playing a lot of Waylon Jennings and Outlaw music, some Marshall Tucker, too. Well, as much as we could, with Mickey and me singing. I mean, who can copy Doug Gray? I don't even think Michael Bolton could copy Doug Gray. We had just certain songs that we could play by them. But Toy came out to a little club on the Frontage Road off of I-85 that Moon Mullins was running. I remember Moon wanted us to come down there and jam. I kept hearing this sound in the kitchen, and I went in there and it was Toy playing the steel guitar. You know how he was always on fast-forward… He jumped up and shook my hand and said, "I'm Toy Caldwell." Later, he came out to jam and he wanted us to play some old Hank Williams songs, because he wanted to get the feel of that pedal steel guitar. From then on, when they were off the road, we were Toy's chosen band to jam with, and that went on for several years, on up until I left Mickey's band in 1980. We used to play at Big Daddy's here in Greenville. In fact, the first time I met Charlie Daniels, it was at Big Daddy's. They were in town, and Toy brought Charlie over. There we were in this club in Greenville with Toy Caldwell and Charlie Daniels onstage. We had a fiddle player that was really good at the time, from Lyman, named Jimmy Rumsey, and he was up there playing twin fiddles. The Skynyrd boys would come over and jam when they were in town, and bring those backup singers. They were great.

You were a friend of Tommy Caldwell early on, right?

I'll tell you what a great friend Tommy Caldwell was. I was playing with Mickey Fowler and the Variation Band back in the seventies. We were Toy's favorite jam band. When he was off the road, he was with us. Toy was always coming in and jamming with us. He loved to play his steel guitar with us, because we did a lot of the old classic country stuff a lot, too. Anyhow, I met Tommy, and we just hit it off like we'd known each other forever. Naturally, I tried to copy every lick he ever played, because he was one of the greatest bass players ever. His tone and everything was so good, I just tried to carbon copy it. Toy told me one time that I was a champion at that, and that I could copy Tommy as well as anyone he knew. You don't know how good that made me feel. Tommy, bless his heart, would send me, like, a gross of Rotosound bass strings. And you know how expensive those are. He'd send me about twelve packs at a time. He kept me in bass strings for years, up until his death. And one night I was playing at Big Daddy's here in Greenville, and I blew a speaker. Toy got on the phone and called Moon and some of the guys from the crew. It wasn't but about an hour before they were all over there with these drills, taking my speaker out, and put a new one in. I said, "Wait a minute, man. Who do I owe for this?" And they said, "No, man. Tommy told us to go get a speaker out of the warehouse and put it on for you." They looked like a crew for Richard Petty. It was things like that that really blew me away. But nobody had a freer heart than Toy or Tommy. I saw Toy give a kid from Spartanburg a Les Paul guitar, because he wanted to learn to play. He also gave Mickey Fowler one. He gave Jimmy Westmoreland a guitar. I kidded him about it—I said, "Toy, you've given everybody else a guitar but me." He looked at me and said, "Yeah, but, Smoke, I gave you a job!"

How did Toy feel about Doug and Jerry's later version of the Marshall Tucker Band?

There were all these rumors going around that the Toy Caldwell Band was in competition with Doug's version of the Marshall Tucker Band, but that was just untrue. We took up for one another; we were brothers. Toy was real proud of what Doug was doing. We all know that the old version of Marshall Tucker will never happen again. They all contributed their part that made that band what it was. It was a hit machine, as far as I'm concerned. Doug's great vocals, and Toy's writing ability and guitar playing. All of them, like Eubanks with the flute; Paul, a great drummer; McCorkle—all of them. It was just a great band. All of that was just something that came together that was just wonderful. I admired Doug so much for keeping the name going. He has a different version of Marshall Tucker. The main thing is, I think Doug is around my age, and he's keeping 'em rocking. He looks good, and he's got things really happening. I'm really proud of him. I never got to know Doug that well, because back in the old days, they all had their circuit of friends. I had shaken Doug's hand and told him he was great many times, but I never got to just sit down with him like what we're doing now. So, I never got to know him until I joined the millennium a few weeks ago. I e-mailed Doug, and he wrote right back to me.

Did Toy ever say anything about the breakup of the original Marshall Tucker Band?

Basically, what Toy told me was that they had been together for, like, fourteen years, and they had known each other for longer than that. He just felt like he wanted to do something on his own. I think the feeling was mutual. He never told me anything about any animosity. He said they had gone as far as they wanted to go. I don't think they realized that they could have latched onto the new country thing at that time like Alabama did. They wanted to remain rockers. But I don't think they had any idea of how big the young-country thing was going to be. But Toy, even up until the time he died, didn't have much faith in Nashville. So, I think they all just decided to go their separate ways. I don't believe there was any big blow-up or anything.

How did the Toy Caldwell Band operate?

We sat up late and talked all the time. We had that military mentality. We'd be up driving and talking all night. The band was even arranged like that. Toy was the general, I was the captain, and it went down like that. It went down in a military manner.

Tell us a little about the auto accident you and Toy were involved in.

It was the first year I joined the band, 1989. It was Mother's Day. We had a rental car from the airport. We were in a seven-car accident, and we all came out of it without a scratch. Toy was driving. We had just left New Jersey headed for Connecticut. The car we were driving was totaled.

What is the true story behind your leaving the Toy Caldwell Band?

Contrary to what some people have spread around, Toy and I did not have a falling out of any kind. We were best friends right up until the end. There was even a plan for me to return. But I was a walking diabetic, and didn't even know it. I couldn't understand why I kept getting weaker all the time. I mean—you know this, Michael—the road can really take its toll on you anyway, in good health. I saw Toy on Sunday before he died the following Thursday, and he said to me, "Smoke, any time you get ready to come back, just let me know. You know you're my bass player, you're my bandleader, and nothing has changed." Ryan (Ware) was a good bass player, and I'm not taking anything at all away from him. But I did plan on coming back; I just had to get my health together first. I didn't know what was wrong. I was passing out, without even drinking. You just wonder, what's wrong with my system, you know? I wouldn't go to the doctor, and my wife stayed after me to go. One thing Toy and I had in common was that we were both Vietnam veterans. So, I went to the veteran's doctor, finally, in November of '92, and I was told I needed to stay home for a while. Toy died in February. So, Ryan played bass with Toy for about three months. Ryan knew I was going to return, and he knew there would still be a place for him in the organization. That's the way Toy was. Once you were in, you were in. You were there until you got ready to leave. When he signed me on, I had questions about Frank Wilkie. I said, "You and Frank have been friends since kindergarten." He said, "Hey, man, Frank left me. If you sign on with me, the job is yours. As long as we don't have any major problems, we get along and everything, you'll have the job." Toy and I had been like brothers since the early seventies, since the first day I met him.

Ryan is the son of longtime Tucker roadie, "Stump" Ware, right?

Yes. Ryan is a really good boy, and Stump has been a friend of mine for years. They are some fine people.

Is it true that Toy was extremely well-read, and knowledgeable about all sorts of things?

Before we got into a bus type of thing, we'd be up late at night driving, and Toy didn't trust anybody driving but me, and I didn't trust anybody but him. I guess it was a Vietnam buddy thing. But, I've always been a history buff; I am really into the Civil War. We'd be going through the Shenandoah Valley, and we'd always go 81, through Gettysburg. I'd get to talking about it, and I'd say, "Man, Toy. This was a great battle that was fought here in

1863. I think if we had not been so much on the offensive, we may have won this thing." He'd say, "Really? I don't remember too much about the Civil War, Smoke. Tell me some more." I'd tell him, "Wouldn't it be something if we'd be riding down through here and see a ghost cavalry coming through?" I really think I inspired a lot of his songs. He didn't forget a thing. Anything you told him, he remembered, and drew off of it later. He was the type of fella that, if he knew you were into something, it wouldn't take him but about two or three weeks, and he'd be an authority on it. He read all the time. Then he read all these books on the Civil War, and he was telling me things I didn't know. It was amazing. If he knew you liked something, he wanted to learn about it so he could talk with you about it.

Tell us a little about your daughters.

I've got three daughters: Tina, Paula, and Brandy. Tina is 30, and graduated from the University of South Carolina, and she's a pharmacist. Paula is 24, and she's doing very well now. She's still finding her direction. Brandy is 20, and she's a Down's Syndrome child. She's really into music. She loves country music—especially Little Texas. That's why I saw Toy on that Sunday before he died, because I took her to Littlejohn Coliseum in Clemson to see Little Texas opening up for Travis Tritt. I think that God meant for it to be that way. For me to see Toy again. I had not seen him in months. At the time, we were hugging one another, and I was telling him I just needed a little more time to get it together, health-wise. At the time, I didn't know that I was a diabetic, or had high blood pressure, or any of that.

You and Toy both were probably in bad health at the time the album was released. Did you ever talk about it?

Toy was the type of guy, he was always concerned about me and my health—but he was in bad health himself. He had that Marine mentality. Keep going and going until you drop. He needed some medical attention himself. Every time I tried to talk to him about it, he'd get almost blazing mad. He'd say, "You tellin' me I can't do my job? You think I can't do it no more?!" He didn't want to talk about his health. But one time we were playing, and Toy had developed an abscessed tooth. Well, he wouldn't tell anybody what was wrong, but he was getting so ill with Dibby that Dibby was going around borrowing money from everybody to quit and fly home. We finally did get in touch with management there, and they took him in and did a root canal. He was fine after that. But he wouldn't come out and tell anybody he was hurting. I hate to say it, but that might be one of the reasons why he's gone now. He just wouldn't go to the doctor and get something done for himself.

What can you share about February 25, 1993, when you heard of Toy's death?

It was devastating. I was alone. I was running a store down in Anderson, Jimmy Rogers House of Music. I didn't have many customers, so I was alone. I just locked the doors and pulled the blinds. I didn't want to see anybody. I watched it snow for a while. It seemed like it just started snowing when I got the word he was gone. My wife called and asked me if I was alright, and I said, "Yeah. I just don't want to talk to anybody right now. I want to be left alone." I went and got my favorite guitar off of the rack and sat there and played "Can't You See?" I couldn't hardly play for the tears, but it's something you have to get out of your system. I was over at Mark Burrell's house the other night, and he was playing some of the stuff we were getting set to release when he died. I was remembering how excited Toy was about getting the next project going. But it was completely devastating. Charlie Daniels said it best when he said, "There's a great big hole in the world that only Toy could fill."

You worked a lot with Charlie, didn't you?

We did many, many shows with Charlie, and we were all like family. Charlie Hayward, Charlie's bass player, is still my favorite bass player in the world.

What were your favorite songs to play with Toy?

It was always "I Hear the South Calling Me." That one had that same tempo as "Ramblin'." And "This Ol' Cowboy." But Toy always gave me a whole lot of freedom on the bass. He wasn't like a whole lot of guys who write a song and say, "I want it played exactly this way." Any time he'd write a song, he appreciated my input. He'd say, "You're the bass player, man. Here's the chords and here's the melody, you figure it out." That last song, "Why Am I Crying?", he wrote that thing in no time because we needed another song in a pinch. To me, that's one of the greatest songs he wrote. I had some help on the bass part from Rusty McFarland, who was a bass player, too, and the engineer on that album.

What were some of your personal high points playing with Toy Caldwell?

I'd say the high point of my whole career—and I've played professionally for over thirty-one years—was playing bass on the Toy Caldwell album. I mean, that was Toy's only solo project, and that was quite an honor. And to be able to sing a song on the album was a thrill. The ultimate compliment. There couldn't be enough money in the world to take that memory away from me. That was the biggest honor of my life. •

Several years after this interview, Tony was asked to join the Marshall Tucker Band as bassist, recording and touring before retiring. He passed away at home on May 15, 2013, at the age of 63.

Henry Paul

2011

He is the leader and a founding member of the legendary Southern-rock band the Outlaws. He also scored big with his own Henry Paul Band, and as a member of Top-40 country band Blackhawk. Now, Henry Paul is touring and recording with a new set of Outlaws. When we caught up with Henry Paul at his home in Nashville in 2011, we spoke about the current lineup of the Outlaws, the new album, the original band, and Southern rock in general.

MBS: The first question everyone wants me to ask is...what is the status of the new Outlaws album and the band? We have all heard about the challenges you have faced concerning the band name and all. Can you shed some light on that?

Henry: Well, as much as I can. I mean, I am in the middle of a federal lawsuit that has to do with serious legal ramifications concerning trademark issues. So, I'm not at liberty to just discuss it openly and candidly. Let me just summarize where we are at by saying that we have defended ourselves—Monte and I and the other members of the band—in what we consider to be our respectful effort to continue forward with the band the Outlaws, and in Monte's and my case, our right to do that. We have taken this seriously. The idea that we were going to put a band together and continue as the Outlaws, we took that serious. There's a serious musical legacy to live up to and honor. And there's great new music and a new band that deserves a chance to be heard. So, all of that being said, we have in this last year spent a lot of time in that effort—a lot of money, a lot of emotion, a lot of anxiety on accomplishing that goal. It's really difficult to try to explain to someone who's not in my shoes how it feels to get e-mails with federal court hearings on them and to know that there's an entire life's work in the balance. So, for Hughie, and Billy, and Frank, and of course for Monte and I—you know, the five guys that created that band, created that musical personality, and went out on the road and helped to make it a reality—I feel entitled and I feel obligated at the same time to stand my ground and to fight this battle. We have a great band here that cannot only preserve the Outlaws legacy but help it grow. It is not my intention to just see the Outlaws continue; my intention is to see the Outlaws grow. Unfortunately, we've had our hands tied. During the last year, especially. Well, for the two years before that, too. We were always operating in an unknown area. What can you do? What can't you do? Who's calling the shots? Who's in charge? What are the rules? Who's making them up? What the hell are the rules and why are they there? Why are there all the barriers to hold us back and keep us from moving forward? It seems very counterproductive and very destructive and sort of difficult for me to understand and for me to embrace at all. So, we're fighting for our band and our love of this music, and we want to first and foremost create a musical legacy that will embrace the Outlaws' legacy and unite the fanbase. And I want the ugly and untrue things that have been said to finally see the light of day and to wipe the slate clean and to roll up our sleeves and go back to doing what it is we do. And to cut the bullshit of this confrontational and senseless and pointless battle. I think we're getting close. We're very excited about taking these demos I let you hear into the studio and turning them into records.

We look forward to it. Going back now, what would you say were the highlights of your first round with the Outlaws?

You know, being thrust into the major league of rock, from playing arenas to stadiums with the Stones, to Central Park with Jefferson Starship, playing in front of literally hundreds of thousands of people. Being shoved out there and being expected to win these people over. The pressure on the band to succeed was huge. It was great being charged with energy from the audience's positive reaction to your music. It included such social props as bottles of Jack Daniels Black Label whiskey, cowboy boots, cowboy hats—the brotherhood we formed with bands like Charlie Daniels and Marshall Tucker.

The Allman Brothers were a little bit higher up in the feeding chain, so they didn't give back quite so much as Charlie Daniels or Tommy and Toy Caldwell. Tommy, especially, was more gracious and inviting. All of those guys, but Tommy in particular, like we were talking about the other day.

Can you run back over those thoughts on the record?

Sure. We were talking the other day about the band Cowboy. They had a record out, and Marshall Tucker was way out there with a very, very popular record. We were still playing clubs; we had not quite arrived. But when we played with Marshall Tucker… We never played with Cowboy—they sort of evaporated before we got going—but the Tucker band was huge and they embraced us, as did the Charlie Daniels Band. David Corlew, Taz, Tommy Crain, Toy and Tommy Caldwell, Paul Riddle especially, George McCorkle—Jerry Eubanks was more of a jazz guy. He was on a different page sort of, but Jerry was a very nice man, but he seemed a little more intellectual. He was a little more sophisticated. But Tommy was the focal point of that group as the gatekeeper and he set the tone. He was enormously huge in our hearts. I would say Tommy Caldwell and Charlie Daniels were the two biggest influences on me as bandleaders and as cultural icons. They were two people who were worthy of imitation. We had this brotherhood. It was us against the world. It was, "Fuck L.A. Fuck the Eagles." I remember feeling it was us and Tucker and Charlie against L.A., the Eagles, and Linda Ronstadt and Loggins and Messina. It was "The South's Gonna Do It Again" and "Dixie." It was tattoos and the flag and a cultural bonding of like-minded spirits. It was going out on the bill with Tucker or Lynyrd Skynyrd.

But Skynyrd was more punk. A little bit more rock and roll with all the fixin's. The fighting and the swagger. The Tucker band didn't play that game. They were men. They were fuckin' men. They wore United States Marine Corps tattoos. It wasn't like, "We're in a rock band, fuck you." It was, "We're grown men who play the shit out of music." I don't know how much older Tommy was than me, but I was not as grown up as he was. I had not done as much as he had, not only professionally, but his stint in Southeast Asia—I mean, the boy had been all up in it. Grinderswitch was the perineal opening band on all these tours. It was just a cultural extravaganza. Southern rock was sort of born from what all of that was, and the Outlaws were probably the last band to get in on that. I mean, you can say Molly Hatchet, but they were a totally different thing. We didn't share with them what we shared with Tommy and Toy and Charlie. At least I didn't. They came along and enjoyed significant success, and I was respectful of their success. You learn to appreciate someone else's success. But I didn't embrace it musically and culturally like I did Charlie and Tucker.

Well, they were a different kind of band. I always felt Skynyrd and Hatchet were more redneck rockers, drinking and fighting and rocking out garage-style. But the Outlaws, to me—like Charlie and Tucker, and Dickey in the Allman Brothers—were my kind of music. A mix of country and rock with a unique Southern swagger. And it was a real brotherhood.

It was learning by example. If you were embraced by someone like Tommy Caldwell—and of course Toy was the creative core of the band, but Toy was always in fast forward; you had to watch that movie in fast forward. But Tommy was the voice of reason, the methodical calm. I went to Tommy's funeral, and they took this guitar strap of his and laid it over the casket before they lowered it into the ground and it was the end of an era right then and there. I went to Ronnie's funeral, too, and that was the end of an era as well. Very emotional. The last time I saw Ronnie Van Zant alive, I was playing a show with him in Winston-Salem, North Carolina, and he and I were on the bus drinking whiskey together. He was intoxicated and telling me that he was the Prince of Dixie. I was sitting over there drinking and going, "Fuck you. What the fuck is the Prince of Dixie?" He said that Duane Allman was the King and he was the Prince. He had the whole thing figured out. We got back to the hotel and were riding the elevator up and Ronnie and I were just cranked up. We got to the top floor and the door slid open and we came spilling out, and we knocked over one of those ash trays full of sand. It was a scene. Gene Odom was there and he said, "Is everything okay here? Are we cool?" And I said, "Yeah." Ronnie went his way and I went mine and that was the last I saw of him.

The Henry Paul Band came along…unfortunately, Tommy was gone, Tucker was evaporating. Charlie was still in business and we shared that relationship with them. Then Hughie and I reconciled our ongoing relationship of difference to put the Outlaws together in 1983. It was weird Hughie wanted me out of the band in '77 because he wanted to go in more of a rock-and-roll direction, and I was sort of the country-rock guy in the band. And there were conflicts between Billy and I and Hughie, and there wasn't a core that held us together like the Tucker band. So, Hughie thought it was a good idea for me and him to get back together. Billy Jones was already out of the band and on a downward spiral as far as substance abuse. Frank was not in the music business anymore. Monte was spinning his own web. But Hughie and I continued to move forward from '83 to '89 with one album called *Soldier of Fortune*. One odd record. I tried to get us into the modern music scene but it was like a dog chasing his tail. You're either out in front or you're just jerking off. That record had "Cold Harbor" on it, which I am thankful for. It was an odd song for the record, but it turned out to be the best song on the record. And it had "What You Don't Do," which I thought was a good song, and the title track, which was an interesting melodic Hughie Thomasson song. But we couldn't get arrested. We were out there playing clubs for very little money, and it was a great job but it was a labor of love. We started doing things ourselves.

Then in '89 I wanted to come to Nashville. I wanted to take the Outlaws with me but Hughie didn't want to, so I went on my own and ended up forming Blackhawk and had significant success with that band. Then Hughie and I got back together in 2005 and I basically put Chris Anderson in. My job was always to put the band together. I met Chris in a bar in Sarasota and gave him a job. Randy and I played together in Blackhawk. And Dave Robbins and I played together in the Outlaws and he got the keyboard job. And then it was down to Dix and me and Monte and Flame (Hughie). Then when Hughie died, we added Billy Crain, who was perfect for the job. That was huge. I had this idea of consolidating the bands into one—bringing John Coleman into the band—and that worked well. I always thought the two-drummer thing for us was not necessary. It was a great entertainment, but musically, Monte was enough. So, we decided to move forward as the Outlaws, and we would rehearse the songs and I would sing the shit out of them and play the damned dog crap out of them and see if we could win over the faithful. And we were able to do that. It was mostly on the strength of the band's heart.

I still have a strong singing voice. So, I was able to sing his songs with authority and with this enormous, earth-shattering volume. "Ghost Riders in the Sky" is a powerful moment in the show, as is "Hurry Sundown," which Hughie wrote. It is another high point in the show. The band is really, really good. Right now, I think it's important to redefine who we are through the songs. When you are going to write songs for an album for the long-time Outlaws fans that will sit squarely in the musical style of what that band and its musical legacy represents, you are going to have to dig deep. I think we did a good job remaining true to the stylistic issues of the Outlaws. And I think the Henry Paul Band and the Outlaws are the same group, spiritually and stylistically and musically. I think that "Grey Ghost" is just an extension of "Hurry Sundown." So, when Billy and I—with some help from the others—set out to write these songs, we did not wander far off from the path that has been laid down. We're just not going to disrespect the musical legacy that the Outlaws created. We want to write a record that is going to grow but not abandon what we are. That's a little bit of a fine line to walk but I think we've done a pretty good job.

Billy Crain has to be a real asset to the band. He and his brother Tommy have always been great. They always have been. I met them in 1973 and they were amazing then. So that's where we are now. The Outlaws gig these days is a labor of love. There's not a lot of money in it. It's not some fat and sassy rock-and-roll gig where you're making a fortune. I am very acutely aware of the negative crap that went on prior to the band's formation. Most of it has gone away. Some of it may never go away. I'm a busy guy. I don't have time to worry about what a few people are saying on the Internet. I'm going to do what I need to do to make a living. I have enough on my plate. But there are key characters in the drama, especially one, and I am well aware of them. The one guy is just an evil guy. Nobody likes him and everybody ignores him. He spins everything. But I can see where some people said the things they said; I understood the emotion and the perception issues that go into making people feel the way they do.

But long ago and far away before any of those people knew who the Outlaws were, I know how they came to be and what my part in it was. Not only am I entitled to move forward with a band that I was a part of and instrumental in creating, but I have a right to do whatever I want to do and not answer to anybody. It's in my makeup. I'm not interested in playing into the public opinion polls. I don't have time for it. •

Danny Joe Brown

1998

When you talk about Southern-rock legends, one of the names that will always come up will be Danny Joe Brown, the founding lead singer for those bad boys of Southern rock known as Molly Hatchet. Danny—whose rapidly declining health, including a stroke, chronic diabetes, and pancreatic problems, had taken him off the road—spoke with me about the band, the controversy of "Old" vs. "New" Hatchet, and life in general.

MBS: The very first thing I wanted to ask you is, how are you feeling?

Danny: I'm out of the hospital; I'm feeling okay. I'm doing much better than I have been doing lately. I had a big Thanksgiving. My son came down from Jacksonville and spent the weekend with me. I have a one-room condo down here, but it was kind of tough on me. I was in the hospital the day before he got here having a stint replaced in my pancreas. It'll be good for another three months. I have to have one replaced every 8 to 12 weeks.

Well, as I am sure you are already aware, the fans are really thinking about you and keeping you in their prayers.

I want to thank everybody for their prayers, because I think that's the only thing keeping me alive. I believe that with all my heart.

I was glad Riff West left the part on the CD [*Jammin' for Danny Joe Brown*] where you made a public profession of faith in Jesus. Do you consider yourself a Christian?

I am not a *Christian*, but I do believe in Christ, and I thank him for all the time he has given me—especially this time—to express that fact.

I know by now you have heard the *Jammin' for DJB* album. I just wondered what you thought of it...?

Riff sent me copies of it. I tell you what, I really thought it was great. The guys did a great job on that. I want to thank Riff, especially, for the work he did on it. He was a trooper on that whole thing, and I don't think it was a monetary thing. I think Riff did it out of the goodness of his heart.

There was a time a few years back when Riff's mom got really sick. He came to me, and he was real scared. Scared for his mama. And we prayed together.

That's very kind.

Well, she's a good girl. I know it's kind of a funny thing for a couple of guys in Hatchet to fall down on their knees. But we did. And damned if she didn't get better. I think he's always respected me for that.

I understand that you have a good relationship with Riff's mom nowadays.

Yeah, I do. I spoke with her about a week ago or two, when Riff went up to see her. When he found out she has cancer. I told her it was music to my ears to hear her voice.

Going back to the Jammin' for Danny Joe event…what went through your mind as you got back on that stage to sing "Flirtin' with Disaster"?

Oh, man. I couldn't believe everybody was there. And the place was so full, nobody could get in. It was wall to wall. And I'd just gotten out of the hospital. I couldn't walk. I had to be led up on the stage, really. But my brother was there, and my nephew, and they helped me get up there on my stool. I did the best I could. It wasn't good enough, but I did the best I could. It was fun.

Who would you say influenced you the most in the beginning and made you want to be a singer?

I guess, Elvis Presley. Phil Everly. Paul Rodgers. Those are just some of the guys that were influences on me.

I know you were in a band early on with Bobby Ingram called Rum Creek. Did you have any other bands prior to Molly Hatchet?

There was a band called What.

What?

Yep, that's what it was. (Laughs) That's what we named it. That was me and a couple of other boys out of Jacksonville. And then there was Molly Hatchet, which was starting up. Actually, they were already going, and the guys in the What band were getting married and going off to college, so I said, "I've got to go."

You wanted to go on the road.

I had to. There wasn't no making a living in Jacksonville. So, I joined Molly Hatchet. Actually, I went out to audition for them one night and did three Lynyrd Skynyrd songs and got hired.

Is it true Ronnie Van Zant had planned to produce the band?

Yep, he was going to produce the first album. As a matter of fact, Johnny [Van Zant] called me last night. He was at a restaurant where my wife works. She and I haven't been together in about eight years, or something like that. But she was at the restaurant, and talking to Johnny, and she said, "Why don't I call Danny?" And he said, "I'd love to talk to him." And Leon [Wilkeson] wanted my number, so we talked for a few minutes. They sounded good.

Were you friends with Ronnie Van Zant?

Well, I knew Ronnie. The first time I ever met Ronnie I nearly got into a fight with him.

I have heard that he was a fighter.

He was a helluva fighter. Not just a fighter, but a *helluva* fighter. That boy could whip some ass. (Laughs) I drank a couple of tallboys and got into a fight. My best friend actually fought him. I picked up Gary Rossington and put him up on the stage so he didn't get into it. But Pee Wee, my friend, got into a fight with Ronnie, and they duked it out on the dance floor. It was at a church dance, believe it or not. (Laughs) St. Andrew's church dance in Jacksonville.

A perfect place for a fight.

Wasn't it? After two tallboys at the age of 14 it was.

I was reading the history of the band, and it said that by 1979, you guys were playing 250 shows a year. How did you do that and maintain your sanity?

Who maintained their sanity? (Laughs) I think that was the beginning of the end right there. The new album was to me the best we ever sounded. But we were running like dogs. Like greyhounds.

Describe for us your feelings about the members in your original band.

Oh, my God. [Pause] Well, I had three guitar players who were absolutely and totally different in sound. And I don't think anybody could drive a set of drums harder than Bruce Crump. And it took Steve Holland leaving before John Galvin came in. John was the best keyboard player that I've ever worked with. Ever. And I've worked with all of them, as far as Southern keyboard players go. He's the best I've ever heard. And when I left Molly Hatchet, because of my diabetes, and my pancreas and all that crap, John sent me a tape from Detroit and told me if I ever decided to do something else, to please consider him. He sent me a tape that was gospel and country. That's what made me decide to put back together a band. And I knew immediately that Bobby [Ingram] was going to be my lead guitar player. Besides John being the best keyboard player I ever worked with, Bobby was the best guitar player I ever worked with. I felt he was the best, and I still do, to this day.

After you did the Danny Joe Brown Band thing, how did you come to rejoin Hatchet?

Well, it was one of those things where they came out with *Beatin' the Odds,* and I came out with my solo thing, and their album sales fell off. I mean, just dropped off. We were a platinum act before that. But when my solo album came out, I didn't do but a couple of hundred thousand records. And they dropped off from platinum back down to gold. And it took them a long time to get back up to platinum. And they realized we weren't going anywhere separated. The company didn't push my record, and they didn't back Hatchet. And I remember going to the bathroom with the president of the record label. He said, "Danny, you guys have to get back together." I remember looking over at him, and he was in one urinal and I was in the other. (Laughs) Anyway, we decided right there in the bathroom that we would get back together. And that's the truth.

It has to be. You couldn't make up a story that good.

That's the fact, Jack. Michael, I couldn't make this stuff up. (Laughs)

What else are you going to talk about while you are peeing?

(Laughs) Right! What else are you going to talk about while you are peeing? Jimmy had to go. He's a great singer and a lovely man, and I love him to death. And thank God he was on this album, the *Jammin' for DJB* record. He can sing his ass off. I ain't never heard anybody sing "Mississippi

Queen" better in my life. I think I about wore out my tape in that spot, because I play it so much.

Well, that is certainly a compliment coming from a singer of your caliber. Now, in 1985 you say Steve Holland left the band and Bobby Ingram came in. Why did Steve leave?

Steve was absolutely insane, that's why he left. I've seen Steve Holland eat cornflakes, pouring beer on them. I love him to death, don't get me wrong. Ain't nobody can play "Gator Country" like Steve. Even though Banner Thomas wrote it. Banner had a dream one night on the bus, and came out of his bunk one morning with that written down on paper. I couldn't believe it. How did he do that? I don't know.

We may never know. It's an eternal mystery.

An eternal mystery. (Laughs) Like the *X-Files*.

Hey, don't talk about my favorite TV show!

It's mine, too, man! I love it. I was just watching it last night!

Is it true that you chose Phil McCormack to be your successor in Molly Hatchet?

Yes, I did. Phil is a good guy. I suggested Phil, and I endorse Phil.

Danny, there has been so much controversy on the Internet regarding the current band and the original one. What are your feelings on the current Molly Hatchet?

Well, I don't know the current Molly Hatchet. I don't know who's playing.

I don't know the names of all of the band members, except for Bobby and Phil.

Bobby and Phil are fine. As long as they keep John Galvin on the stage, they'll be in the clear. But Mack Crawford is really good. I'm not sure he's still with them. He's played with everybody. He's one of the best drummers I've ever worked with. As for the band being called "Molly Hatchet," Bobby doesn't have any right to that name at all. The only right Bobby has to the name Molly Hatchet is the right I gave him. That's all he's got. I think he should call it "the Bobby Ingram Band." *Damn* sure ain't Molly Hatchet. And you can underline "damn."

What do you think about other bands like the Southern Rock Allstars playing the old Hatchet tunes?

Well, Dave Hlubek *is* Molly Hatchet. Dave Hlubek started Molly Hatchet. He could *be* Molly Hatchet if he wants to be. But Bobby Ingram didn't start Molly Hatchet, so he can't be Molly Hatchet. He was brought in by me, and that's all Bobby will ever be. I hate that, but that's the truth.

What would you say have been some of the high points in your career?

Selling out the Spectrum in Philadelphia twice in one week. Selling out Madison Square Garden. Playing with the Who in front of 180,000 people. Being on tour with the Outlaws. That was one of the greatest tours I ever had. For me, anyway. I don't know what everybody else thinks.

Did you guys ever tour with Lynyrd Skynyrd?

Well, Skynyrd was always scared of us. We always tried to tour with them, but they didn't want to. It would have been fun. But they would have had their ass handed to 'em back then. We tried to get 'em, but they got away from us.

What message would you like to give your fans on the Internet?

Just tell them to keep me in their prayers. And keep Riff and Riff's mama in their prayers. And keep Southern rock alive as long as they can. And thanks for all of their help. I love 'em all. •

Danny Joe Brown passed away on March 10, 2005.

Dave Hlubek

2001

Dave Hlubek needs no introduction to fans of Southern rock. As the co-founder of Molly Hatchet, as well as one of her most prolific songwriters, Hlubek scorched across the fretboard on hits like "Dreams," "Flirtin' with Disaster," "Beatin the Odds," "Gator Country," and so many others. When we sat down with Dave in 2001, he was a part of Southern rock's premier super group, the Southern Rock Allstars. We caught up with Dave in between recording sessions for the new SRA album and endless tour dates for a few questions and answers.

MBS: Dave, who were your earliest musical influences?

Dave: The Beatles, all the groups from the British Invasion—I was fascinated by that. I loved Cream, anything by Clapton, the Doors. Early Hendrix stuff blew me away. Pretty much anything loud would do.

How did you first come to form Molly Hatchet?

It was after having a long line of local bands in the Jacksonville area. After so many years of playing in all the different clubs, I happened to meet Steve Holland at a local music store called Paula's Music in downtown Jax.

He had just moved from Virginia Beach to Florida, and I heard this voice behind me saying, "That guitar really sucks." I turned around and asked who he was and he said, "I'm Steve Holland! Wanna start a band?" We started rehearsing that very afternoon, and that band is what went on to become Molly Hatchet.

Tell us about your relationships with the original band members, especially Danny Joe.

I think the relationships between the original band members and myself are really good considering all the things we've been through, and put ourselves through, over the years. We are all on speaking terms and we all love and respect each other. I'm proud to know all of 'em. We conquered the world together and that's not a bad thing!

As far as Danny Joe goes, I see him as often as I can and try to give him all my support. He is my friend.

What is your favorite Molly Hatchet album? Favorite songs to play?

Flirtin' with Disaster for the album. Anything on the first and second albums. *Take No Prisoners* was my least favorite. I got real lazy in my songwriting, the band was lazy overall, and I think the album reflects that. We were not focused.

What kind of guitar and amp rig do you use, and is it the same as what you used in the Hatchet band?

Back in the Hatchet days I used Peavey Mace amps. I use a Line Six Axe 2X12 rig with SRA. As for guitars, I'm using the Hamer equivalent of a Paul Reed Smith. I was using Stratocasters, but Jay won't let me anymore!

What are your fondest memories of playing with Hatchet?

Touring Europe together, selling out the hometown coliseum, getting our gold and platinum awards. Just sharing our lives together—there were good and bad times. Sometimes it's counterproductive living too close together.

Tell us about Riff West.

The best. Just an all-around great guy. When I grow up, I wanna be just like him.

Your thoughts on the Jammin' for DJB event? How did it feel to play beside Danny again?

It was very, very emotional. I was not sure how I would feel until the night of the show when everyone came together. It was one tearful night, but it felt great playing with the guys again.

What is Southern rock?

Southern rock is one part Jack Daniels, one part Wild Turkey, one part stupidity, and 72 hours of pain.

What's your idea of a "perfect day or evening" off the road?

TV!

What are your 5 all-time favorite albums?

1. Pink Floyd: *Dark Side of the Moon*
2. Anything by Cream

3. Gino Vanelli: *Brother to Brother*
4. Jimi Hendrix: *Are You Experienced?*
5. Spirit: *12 Dreams of Dr. Sardonicus*

What about movies?
I got lots of 'em!

Books?
What? Me, read?

Tell us about the Southern Rock Allstars and elaborate a little on each of your bandmates.

Okay—to quote a phrase from *Animal House*, "They are all special in their own unique way." They are a great bunch of players and I have a great time touring with them. Good friends! Being in the SRA organization, I have been given a second chance at a career that I thought was over with, a lot because of my own doing. Making it simple, the SRA is not a babysitting service and refuses to be so.

Jay Johnson: One of the most talented performers I've ever worked with onstage. In the studio as a producer he's able to extract performances out of me I never thought I could do, challenging—*daring*—me to do better. He's a great father. He's got one of the smartest 9-year-old kids, who is actually pretty tolerant of me. On the flip side of that coin, Jay's got one of the most wicked right crosses. He hits like an anvil and then moments later is one of the most compassionate people you'd ever meet. Believe me, I know! A real snappy dresser.

And Jakson Spires?

You know him, you love him, you gotta have him! He's been a better friend to me than I will ever be to him. I've known him a lifetime and consider myself the richer for it. Sweet man, great songwriter, great performer.

And Charles Hart?

What can you say about a man that knows *something* about *everything*? And if he does not know something about a particular subject, he'll talk about it anyway. Seriously, he's a real hardworking, in-your-face country boy that doesn't ask for anything that he's not willing to work for. He expects everyone around him to work just as hard to achieve the same goal, and there's something to be said about that. One hell of a good bass player.

How do you feel about the new SRA album?

I absolutely love it. The teamwork, the songwriting, the performances blow away the first SRA album. It's gonna surprise a lot of people, and I'm proud to be on it.

Who are some of your favorite people that you have jammed with in Southern rock?

Dan Toler, Gregg Allman, Dickey Betts, Dru Lombar, Allen Collins, Jeff Carlisi, Don Barnes, Henry Paul, Tommy and Billy Crain, so many! The list goes on and on.

Who would you like to jam with in a perfect world?

I would like to be onstage one time with Eric Clapton, Jeff Beck, and Jimmy Page.

Back to Hatchet. Your thoughts on the current version of the band with Bobby and Phil?

The best way that I can answer this question after much thought is this:

What was once is not now, and what was once is not meant for now. It is a different time, and a different group of people. It is a new administration. That's the best I can do. I don't want to give it any more lip service because I think that it is time to stop all the backbiting and mudslinging. It serves no purpose.

What sign are you? When were you born?

Virgo. August 28, 1951.

What advice would you offer to kids aspiring to become rock-and-rollers for a living?

It's kinda difficult for me to give advice in this new millennium, me not being a product of the new. I don't think that you can take a shortcut to paying your dues, though many folks seem to give it one helluva shot. The new pop-rock is just designed for money- making, and when you get to be a certain age, you're out. But that's not to take anything away from the hardworking musicians out there trying to make their mark, who are willing to work hard to achieve it.

Any other words of wisdom, Dave?

You haven't forgotten who you're talking to, have ya? Words of wisdom? On a serious note, all I can pass on is just be grateful for every day you have, because there are no guarantees. •

John Galvin

2002

John Galvin joined Molly Hatchet in 1983 as their first-ever keyboard player, a position he still holds today. My 2002 interview with Galvin was a treat. I found him to be not only an extremely talented keyboard player, but also a highly intelligent and fun conversationalist. He remains a true friend to this day, and one of the finest piano players in rock and roll.

MBS: John, were you an original member of Molly Hatchet?

John: I am not an original member of Molly Hatchet, per se; however, I am the original keyboard player. I was called in to play some keyboard parts on the *No Guts, No Glory* album in 1983, which was just after Danny Joe rejoined Molly Hatchet. There was some talk at that point of them pulling me into the band, but nothing was concrete. After the album was complete, and the band was on the road, they played here in Detroit with Sammy Hagar, at Cobo Hall. I remember going down there and waking Dave up on the bus out in front of the venue, and a few minutes later Sammy came on the bus and was trying to rouse Dave also. After the show that night, Danny Joe and Steve Holland came to my house for a little late-night party, and Steve said, "Wanna be in the band? You can take my place, I've had enough." Well, of course he didn't have to ask me twice, and after that tour, I was called to be a full-time member of Molly Hatchet, at which time we went into rehearsals for a new album, *The Deed Is Done.* I also must add that on the first couple MH albums, session-man Jai Winding played keys on a few tracks, but was not in the band.

What was it like when you first joined the band?

When I first joined the band, it was so overwhelming. The crowds were bigger, the venues were bigger, we were treated like kings. I felt like, "Am I really getting paid for this?" It was really like a nonstop vacation with all expenses paid, and spending money to boot. Kind of like a rolling party with your friends. The only real downside was having to leave my family at home, although there were times they could join us on the road. It was hard not to go home and say, "I did this and this, and went here and there," because I didn't want them to feel left out, so I had to suppress some of that… "Yeah, it was pretty rough out there. Pretty much stayed in my room with the door locked." That kind of thing. But the band really made me feel like part of the family right from the get-go. It was an experience I wish everyone could share at least once.

What were some of the highlights of being in the band with Danny Joe?

It was just a thrill being onstage with all my heroes, and playing behind Danny Joe. He had something that few front-men have. We did some videos back then that were a real kick. It was kind of funny to see these video girls come in in the morning, and you wouldn't recognize them; they all looked like they just crawled out of bed, but as soon as the makeup people got through with them, BAM! Instant supermodels! The transformation was incredible. It was a lot of fun getting to act a little in the videos, but unfortunately, they never got much, if any, airplay, and MTV pretty much refused to play them. They considered us a "classic" act. But all in all, it was an enlightening experience. Traveling in a luxury tour bus was also very cool, because as a teenager, I was into custom vans, and did some custom painting, so the bus was like an extension of that.

At times, we could be a hell-raising band, some members more than others. I think that would have to fall into Danny and Dave's lap. They were the hardcore party men, the ones that would take the most risks, and hang with the riskiest of people. Bruce was into health and bodybuilding, and kind of lived in his own bubble. He would prepare all his own food, and rarely ate in a restaurant with the band, and only drank bottled water. There was a time in Iowa, at a ballroom, that Bruce and Danny got into a fistfight offstage, right before the encore. I still have no idea what it was about, but soon after, they settled their dispute. Incidents like that were not unusual, but the band had pretty much settled down by the time I joined. Of course, we have always had a strong biker following, so it was not unusual to see the Hells Angels, Outlaws, Banditos, or any other bike club at our shows and occasionally onstage with us. They have been with us from the beginning, all over the world, and we welcome them wherever we go. Everyone in the band, at one time or another, has partied with the best of them, and rarely passed on an invitation to join in.

Tell me about Danny Joe Brown.

Danny Joe and I used to room together frequently. First off, I have to say, if it wasn't for Danny, I wouldn't have been in Molly Hatchet. He is very generous, very kind, and would give anyone the shirt off his back. He was the most non-materialistic person in the band and pretty much lived for the moment. He frequently read the Bible, and treated everyone that came his way with respect. He has a good-ol'-boy persona that's almost Elvis-like. He was a "yes, ma'am/yes, sir" kind of guy that appealed to both young and old. He would have made a great actor. He definitely had an aura, and when he entered a room he commanded attention. The women wanted him and the men wanted to be like him. He is a very likeable guy, but his image created problems for him. People saw him drink onstage, so they wanted to drink with him, and bring him liquor as gifts, and buy him drinks, and I think it just got away from him. Now he's having some serious health issues as a result, and I know it wasn't part of the plan, but it's something we all have to face, and learn from it.

Back in the '80s, we had this bus driver by the name of Joe "Bear" MacIntire. He looked just like Willie Nelson, and everywhere we went, people thought he was. He even had the braids, the beard, the whole nine yards, and I think he even played off that a little. Anyway, we were on our way from Georgia up to New Jersey, I think, and everyone was asleep on the bus, when Joe Bear stopped at a truck stop for fuel and coffee. Danny usually had a habit of calling his wife whenever we stopped, and for some reason he woke up and got off the bus to find a payphone. Joe Bear was in the truck stop and unaware that Danny was off the bus calling home from a payphone across the parking lot. After paying for the fuel, Joe hopped in the bus and resumed the trip, unknowing that Danny was gone. In the meantime, Danny finished his call and started back to the bus, not realizing it had left. Now, you have to picture this: here's a guy with nothing on but a pair of shorts, no ID, no money, except the phone change, with a little Jim Beam buzz going, trying to explain to people that he's Molly Hatchet's singer, and needs to get to New Jersey. Meanwhile, the next day we arrive at our destination, when everyone realizes, "Where's Danny?" Suddenly, out of nowhere, Danny appears with a big grin. He had borrowed a shirt from a trucker, called our manager at home, who got him a flight, had a state trooper rush him to the airport, and actually beat us to New Jersey! So, ends the saga of the missing vocalist.

How is Danny doing now?

I haven't talked to Danny since around Christmastime, and I'm really not sure how he's doing at this point.

Tell us about "Big Dave" Hlubek, and the other original members.

Dave was the showman. He was the spark that would turn a lead into a flash-fire. Along with Danny, I think he brought a certain "toughness" to the band, and a look that defined Southern rock. Together, they were unstoppable. Dave also had a great gift for doing interviews laced with wit, sarcasm, and pride. Later on, though, I sensed a certain competition within the band for the "top" spot; that, I think, created a certain edge.

Duane Roland was the unsung hero, and really was more of a family guy, but you couldn't tell by looking. He was less flashy, but more precision, and did a lot of his leads in one take in the studio. I had the pleasure of staying at Duane's house in Jacksonville when I first joined the band. He had a bad hip, which he ended up having replaced, and I think it prevented him from running around onstage too much.

Bruce Crump, also very family-oriented, had a style all his own, and would blow your mind onstage with some new drum-fills he would throw in. A great drummer, and a great guy. Very disciplined in his diet and health issues.

Riff West was the bass player when I came into the band. Riff and I were very close, and pretty much hung out together, later to be joined by Bobby Ingram. We dubbed ourselves the "3 Amigos," because the three of us were the ones that would go exploring in every city, and pretty much were the most compatible. We partied a little lighter than the rest, and would be off to find another adventure at every turn. The rest of the band would be sleeping off hangovers or nights on the town, but we didn't realize at the time that they had already done what we were doing many times over, so they opted to relax. Riff was a super guy and organizes many charitable events for animals and the Humane Society, as well as the Jammin' for DJB benefit. We still keep in contact occasionally.

Did you work with Jimmy Farrar?

I never had the chance to meet Jimmy Farrar, or even hear him live. We were busy with the Danny Joe Brown Band during that period, of which Bobby and myself were members. However, I do own *Beatin' the Odds* and *Take No Prisoners*—and, Jimmy, *you rock!!!*

What are your favorite Molly Hatchet records?

My favorite Hatchet records actually are the first of each lineup. I love the first album with "Dreams," and I prefer *Devil's Canyon* over the last two. I thought the music was more diverse, the songwriting more hook-laden, and I liked the production better. A close second would be *Lightning Strikes Twice*. Now for my least favorite, *Double Trouble Live*, not due to the playing, because the playing smoked, but the production didn't. It was produced by our former manager, at his home, who really had no business producing such an important record, our last record with Epic. The band did such a great job, only to be ruined by bad production and a God-awful jacket. Of course, this is just my opinion. The photos did not capture what the band was about in any way, shape, or form. However, we are about to change all that, with our new and improved live album coming out this year. I have not heard any final mixes yet, but I did hear it, the night we played it afterwards, and it ripped!

What are your favorite songs to perform live?

Playing live is always the biggest thrill of being with the band, and I would have to say that "Dreams" is my all-time favorite to play live, along with "Fall of the Peacemaker," "The Journey," "Tatanka," and "Devil's Canyon."

Any comments on the "old Hatchet vs. new Hatchet" thing?

Over the last few years there has been a lot of controversy over the "old band" vs. the "new band." I was fortunate enough to be a part of both versions, and I have to say that I had an equally great time in both bands. When I joined the original band, everything was new and exciting, and I was playing with people that were my musical heroes, that I had seen in concert many times before I ever met them. To be a part of that was a gift that can't be compared. That band started it all, wrote the hits that went platinum, and whether or not they are still onstage as a band, they will always live in our hearts as Molly Hatchet. The "new" version of the band, which a lot of people think just happened overnight, in fact was an evolvement of sorts that happened over years. Members would come and go, as early as 1980, when Danny first left the band. It was never the same since.

The new version, in my opinion, has picked up where *Flirtin' with Disaster* left off. It feels fresh again, the songwriting is back on track, and it is self-sufficient. The internal struggles within the band are gone, and music is now the number-one priority. Bobby has singlehandedly transformed a band that had one foot in the grave, and gave it new life. Why he chose to use the Molly Hatchet moniker, I don't know. It could have been called anything, because I don't think it sounds exactly like the other band, but maybe what the band would have sounded like today. I think it's a definite progression for the better. The only hurdle we haven't seemed to jump is selling records. Radio won't touch the band, and neither will MTV. The stores are slowly building stock of our latest CDs, but distribution has been minimal. I think once we overcome these obstacles, we'll be on our way, because the music speaks for itself.

Tell me about what you did between the time the original band broke up and the time you came back in.

During the time the original band split up (1990) and the new band formed (1995), I went back to Detroit and started gigging in a local band. In 1994 I was divorced from Pam, my wife of 17 years, and was in a situation that I'm sure some of the guys out there have dealt with called "child support." I had to get a better (non-musical) paying job with insurance, and fell into a good job with a local furniture store that was not only a union job, but offered an assortment of benefits. I had been with the company a couple of years when I got the call from Bobby to play on a new MH record. He said, "If you like it, you can go back on the road with us and be a family again." I did the record, but unfortunately my bills were overwhelming, and I couldn't go on the road and make it. I did as many shows as I could until Bobby called one day and said, "Look, we gotta get someone out here to play your parts," so they brought in Tim Donovan, a fine Florida keyboardist to fill my spots on the road. Thanks, Tim. In the meantime, a turn of events happened in 1999: my ex-wife awarded me custody of my kids, and house. So now I'm raising my kids and taking care of the house, and still doing the day job. However, I still play as many shows as I can, mainly throughout the summer, especially in the Michigan/Ohio/Indiana areas, and wherever I'm needed elsewhere. Also, I still gig locally here in Detroit to keep up the chops. I also try to do the European tours in the winter.

Speaking of Europe, the band has a great following in Germany. Tell me about that.

Germany is like our second home now, thanks to Rainer Hansel and the people at SPV. We go there every year to record and tour, and we've been there so much that we pretty much know our way around, especially the Hamburg area. The fans in Germany are wonderful, and some of them we take with us from show to show.

Who are your favorite bands to tour or share a bill with?

We've done shows with so many, it's hard to pick a favorite—but 38 Special is always fun, Nazareth, Blue Oyster Cult, Saxon, and of course the great Charlie Daniels Band! No matter who we play with, we always have a great time. The more, the merrier!

I hear you have a diverse taste in music. Who do you like?

People have always criticized my taste in music, but I listen to a very diverse variety of music ranging from New Age to metal to industrial, and everything in between. I'm also into trippy, or psychedelic, music that can take me somewhere without the hassle of drug use. I like Monster Magnet a lot, and got a chance to meet Dave Wyndorf, the vocalist, on the ferry from London to France last year. I recently went to see Rob Zombie—what an awesome production! Another cool band is the Genetorturers from Tampa. I never miss their show when they come here. Another band called Down is cool, kind of Black Sabbath with a little Southern rock mixed in. On a lighter note, there's a cool band called Gomez I like. The Church from Australia, Gino Vannelli, the new Raul Malo album...Dread Zeppelin is a hilarious act to catch if you can.

Tell me about Bobby Ingram, the bandleader.

Bobby Ingram has a heart of gold. He is very driven to make the band a success, and is ambitious beyond anyone I know of. He knows what he wants and how to get it. As a guitar player, he ranks with the best. He can play whatever you want him to play, and then some. And he gets the tone from hell without even trying!

How did you first become interested in music?

I grew up in Cleveland, Ohio, until the fourth grade. During that time, my parents discovered that I had a knack for singing and picking out songs on my aunt's piano in her bar, so they bought an old upright piano, which I took to immediately. So, when I was 6, they set me up with lessons, starting with musical theory, at the Cleveland Institute of Music, under the direction of instructor Lillian Husak. My mother would take me by train to the opposite side of town for a half-hour lesson every week. This went on a few years until we moved to Lima, Ohio, where my parents grew up. I then studied piano with Don Hurless, a local jazz and classical legend. This went on until I was 18, for a total of 12 years. At that point I was tired of lessons and wanted to play to make money. I would start by playing at the Allen Co. Fair, for Porters Music store. They would pay me 25 dollars to play for a few hours to attract business to their booth. From there I landed a full-time gig, playing organ music at a roller rink. That lasted 4 years, during which some nights I played piano in a Sweden House restaurant. From there I hooked up with a group back in Cleveland that were on a label, called Damnation of Adam Blessing. They had broken up and were reforming a new band, and at that time were very big regionally. Then I hooked up with a Detroit-based country duo, Bob Hammond and Irene Dalton. It was my first real introduction to playing in bars, country music, and the big city. We would play in Ontario, over the bridge, for a while, then here in Detroit in some of the roughest places you could imagine. I've seen people shot, beaten, stabbed—you name it. It was a wakeup call to the real world.

Then I was offered a house gig at a nicer club called Grant's Lounge, and played with Kelly Hall for 8 years. During that time, I went to see Molly Hatchet a few times and became a big fan. That is when I met 38 Special, and kept in touch with Donnie Van Zant. He was going to try to get me a gig with his brother's band, Austen Nichols, the future Johnny Van Zant Band, but thought they were really too young for me. One day he told me he heard that Danny Joe left Molly Hatchet and was starting a project, but didn't know how to reach him, so a friend of mine saw Bee Jay Recording studio on the *Flirtin'* album and we called it, and lo and behold, Hatchet was in there recording with Jimmy Farrar. We talked to their road manager and he told me how to get in touch with Danny, and sure enough he answered the phone. I sent him a tape and photo and was hired on the spot and had to leave for Jacksonville right away for rehearsal. I loaded up my van and drove straight through to Florida, to a parking lot, and called for someone to come lead me the rest of the way. Soon a car pulled up, and it was Bobby Ingram. He took me to Danny's mother's apartment, where I took a nap, then later we went to the rehearsal hall. I ended up being there 6 months, with no money. We had roadies that would "find" us food from the convenience store across the street. Occasionally, Danny would take us to Red Lobster. Then one day we had enough material for an album and started looking at producers. We chose Glynn Johns of the Who, Clapton, and Led Zeppelin fame. All of a sudden, we were in the Bahamas at Compass Point Studios doing our album and the rest is history. When the DJB band split up, I went back home and played with Kelly Hall again, until 1984, when I got the call to join Molly. In 1990, when the old version of Molly split up, I went home to play with a country band called Coalition at the All-Around Lounge, in Taylor, Michigan, where I now reside.

Do you have any side projects going on at this time?

I don't have any side projects in the works; however, I am working on putting a small studio in my house and hope to record some stuff in the next year or so. I am playing locally here and there, right now as a duo with an extraordinary singer, Don Burton.

Tell us about Phil and the rest of the current band.

First, I have to say that I love Phil McCormack. He is an excellent singer, entertainer, and is the perfect person to carry the torch for Danny. Anyone who knows Phil will attest, he is very funny, will talk your ear off, and would do anything for anyone. Phil kicks ass on- and offstage. It is a highlight playing with the band at anytime, anywhere. Russell, Shawn, Bobby, Jerry—whom I haven't met yet—and Tim, they're all the best there is. And I can't forget Mac, Brian and Andy, and Sean, all troopers in the highest sense. They don't come any better.

What has been the biggest rush for you with the "new" band?

Playing Caesar's Palace, in Lake Tahoe, was a big thrill. That place is like the epitome of entertainment. To see your name on that sign was unforgettable. Going to Germany and running the streets of Hamburg every year is a thrill. Meeting the bands I grew up listening to, such as Ten Years After, Gregg Allman, Ted Nugent, Chuck Negron of Three Dog Night, Lynyrd Skynyrd, Stevie Ray Vaughan…the list goes on and on. To share the stage with those greats is a treasure.

Thanks for your time, John.

Thanks, Michael, and all the Hatchet fans worldwide! •

Duane Roland

2006

When Duane Roland died at the age of 53 on June 19, 2006, he was right in the middle of a major comeback as a member of Gator Country, reuniting him with other founding and former members of Molly Hatchet in a band that was truly on the verge of greatness. They had recorded an excellent cover of "Oh Atlanta" and were working on a full-length album.

As a founding member of Molly Hatchet, Duane Roland brought a massive amount of talent to the three-guitar lineup that became Hatchet's signature sound. A few years ago, when Dave Hlubek left the Southern Rock Allstars, Roland stepped up to the plate to knock it out of the park. Then last year, he suffered one of the hardest blows anyone can suffer when his wife passed away.

Roland picked himself up, dusted himself off, and did what he did best—played guitar with Gator Country. We started this interview the first week in June and never had a chance to complete it. We are printing what we have, as a tribute and insight into a true Southern-rock guitar giant.

MBS: Tell us a little about where you were born and raised.

Duane: I was born in Jeffersonville, Indiana, near Louisville, Kentucky. We moved to Florida when I was seven years old.

Was there a lot of music in your family?

Oh, yes, definitely. My mother was a concert pianist. My dad played guitar some.

Who was your biggest musical inspiration early on?

There are a lot of guitar players that inspired me, but my favorite was, and is, Eric Clapton.

How did you initially hook up with the guys in Molly Hatchet?

I was working on putting a band together with Banner and Bruce, but that didn't work out. They joined Dave and Steve, and then Danny. At this point, I was in another band called the Ball Brothers Band. Dave didn't show up for one of Hatchet's gigs and Banner called me to fill in so they could get paid for the night. They and their management were thinking about going to three guitar players, so one night they came down from Macon to hear me play and after that I was asked to join.

How did you come to leave the band?

We were only planning to take a year off. But that changed. There was a lot of corporate b.s. going on that's best left unsaid.

What is your favorite Hatchet album?

I really loved the second album. It's usually pretty easy to come up with a debut album because everybody in the band has been writing for years. The sophomore effort is usually the one that tells the tale, and I think we proved ourselves.

What was it like to be a member of the Southern Rock Allstars?

I had forgotten how much fun it was playing music with really great musicians. It woke up an old rock beast in me. I loved playing guitar with Jay. Charles is a fantastic bass player, and Jakson—*damn*—Jakson, what a powerhouse! I miss that man every day. And it was great to once again stand behind the greatest singer I've ever played with, Jimmy Farrar.

Which brings us up to Gator Country. Once again you are playing with Jimmy, and many of the original Molly Hatchet members. How does that feel?

I tell ya, Michael, it's great. You heard the single, right?

Yeah, you sent it to me. A great cover of the old Bad Company song "Oh Atlanta." It's awesome.

Thanks, man. We are not really trying to sound like the old Molly Hatchet, although we certainly tip our hat to that music in a big way. But we have all matured a lot since those days, and we have a lot of music in us we want to let out. We are just getting started.

I was sad to hear of the death of your wife last year. Are you doing okay with that?

The best I can, man. It was one of the hardest punches I've ever had. All of the deaths lately have been really hard, but to lose your soul-mate is the worst of all. I just take it a day at a time, you know. But there will always be a part of me missing.

I fully understand. I want to talk a little about the current Molly Hatchet band with Bobby Ingram and get your thoughts on that.

Oh, sure. No problem. Michael, can we finish up the interview next week? I have to run. Would that be okay?

Sure it will, Duane. I'll call you back. Thanks, bro. •

Less than a week later, Duane Roland was dead from natural causes. I was honored to be the last journalist to interview him, even though we never finished our conversation. Godspeed, Duane. To the rest of Gator Country and Molly Hatchet, all our best wishes. Keep the music alive, fellas. I'm sure Duane would want that.

Riff West

2000

Prior to joining Molly Hatchet in the 1980s, Ralph "Riff" West, Jr. of Sanford, Florida, spent time as a member of the band White Witch. Then in the '90s he played for boogie rockers Foghat as well as a group of former Molly Hatchet members known as Gator Country. We met for the following in-person interview, and I feel like that initial meeting formed the bedrock for a lifetime of friendship. Sadly, Riff's life was cut short when he died on November 19, 2014, after a lengthy illness following a car accident in which an air bag deployed, damaging his head and chest.

Back in 2000, Riff was in high spirits, and the more we delved into the discussion of music, the more excited he seemed to get.

MBS: Tell us a little about where you were born and raised.

Riff: I was born in Texas, and grew up just about everywhere. My dad moved every two years; he was a 30-year naval officer. I moved constantly.

When did you first become interested in music as a possible career?

The Beatles on *Ed Sullivan*. Like everybody else. And all I ever wanted to be was just a bass player. I never wanted to be one of those guys that played everything. I just picked the McCartney instrument, and that's all I ever wanted to play. That's my style. I never wanted to do a whole bunch of different styles. I'm not a Flea, or that type of player.

So, you keep your clothes on?

(Laughing) Yes! I keep my clothes on. I wear more than a sock, yes. But I grew up mostly on English rock and, you know, Buffalo Springfield and Poco, stuff like that. Of course, the Beatles, the Stones, the Kinks, Steely Dan.

Can you tell us about some of the first bands that you played in?

I started a band called Angel years ago, and then went right to White Witch, Molly Hatchet, and then Foghat. Those are basically the only bands I've been in.

We've received several requests for a story on White Witch.

We just lost our singer recently, Ronnie Goedert. He died about a month ago. If you want to do a story, I'll gladly help you on it. It was one of the best times of my entire life. It was the age of innocence. We were young and crazy and having a good time.

When did you join Molly Hatchet?

In 1981 when Banner (Thomas) left. I spent a year with Jimmy (Farrar). We did the whole *Take No Prisoners* tour. I joined right after that album. Then Danny Joe (Brown) came back. Molly Hatchet did break up in 1990. I stayed with them through their last show in 1990. There actually was a final tour, and a final concert.

With Danny Joe Brown?

Yes, with the original band. We played somewhere in Ohio with Meatloaf, and all of our old friends and old crew came out. That was it. We were taking a break, and were going to get off the road for a year or so. There was really no intention of the band actually breaking up. We just wanted a break. During that time, we figured out we didn't all want to go back out, but Danny did want to go back out. We didn't have any problem with that whatsoever. He went back out as "Danny Joe Brown of Molly Hatchet." It wasn't Molly Hatchet. He had Bobby Ingram in his band at the time. Bobby did play with Molly Hatchet there at the end, but he was a hired sideman. He had his own band, China Sky, and was on Polydor Records, so he couldn't be in both bands with two different record companies, so he was a hired side-guy. He was unable to sign with Molly Hatchet because of the other contract. Eventually the management licensed the name to Danny and Bobby. They were partners at the time. None of us wanted to go back out, and as long as Danny was in the band, we were fine. We were all for it.

And after a couple of years, around 1993, Danny left, and Bobby became the leader of the band. I admire Bobby for what he has done for ten years. He's kept the name going. I don't have anything at all against Bobby Ingram; he was one of my best friends at one time. I don't begrudge him for trying to keep the name going, for making a living for himself, but I don't agree with it. We always wanted Danny Joe to be the singer of Molly Hatchet when the name was licensed. We always thought it was going to be Bobby and Danny, not just Bobby. But I don't hold grudges; it's just not worth it.

What is Danny Joe Brown really like?

From this day until the day I die, I will say Danny is one of my best friends. He's a meathead! I call him that all the time. He knows it. But he would do anything in the world for you. Danny could never beat his demons, you know, the alcohol—he knows that. And being a diabetic, that's a lethal combination. I've known those guys for years, even before they got a record deal or anything. And I'll tell you a story. My mom has been incredibly sick for years. I was already out of the band and in Foghat, and Danny would always ask me how my mom was doing. My mom always thought Danny was like Charles Bronson, the neatest little guy in the world. Danny knew my mom was dying at one time, and luckily, she didn't die, and Danny grabbed me and prayed for my mom. Another time he called my mom and prayed with her without me knowing it. For me, my parents are my best buds. I knew right then if Danny ever needed my help, I'd be there for him. So even though Danny can be a meathead—he's had a lot of problems, he's got a temper, he's done things we wish he didn't do, and he's done things that *he* wished he didn't do—he's still a great guy. And I'll do anything in the world for him.

How's Danny's health now?

It's really bad. He's in and out of the ICU constantly. That's another reason I had a couple of "mock" CDs made up, so he could see and hear it. Even though we'll start taking orders soon, it's going to take five weeks for me to have the actual CDs in my hand. And I would be mortified if this thing took so long that—

That he died. I fully understand. I am doing a CD right now that is a tribute to a friend who is dying of cancer (Bobby Lowell), and I am pushing to get it out so that he can see and hear it. Let's talk about *Jammin' for DJB*. Besides the CD, you are doing a video, right?

We are. That is more loopholes than I could ever imagine. But we are working on it.

Who else played at that benefit? Wasn't Pat Travers there?

Pat was there. Pat's my neighbor. Captain Beyond re-formed and played. Artimus Pyle, the Southern Rock Allstars, Charlie Hargrett. At the end, we all came back out and did an acapella version of "Free Bird." It was a great time, and between the two shows, this one and the one in Macon that Bruce Brookshire organized, we basically helped Danny make a down-payment on a condo. Now Danny lives by himself. He has a nurse come in, but he doesn't have to live with his mom or in a nursing home. He has his own crib. If anybody knows Danny and doesn't want to help him, I find that pathetic. We're going to help him.

When will the CD be out?

It should be out around Thanksgiving. We could have been finished a little earlier, but the record company that did *Live at the Agora,* Phoenix Gems, and our manager, Pat Armstrong, asked me to hold off about three months. So, what you have is basically the same band twenty years later, although we are not Molly Hatchet, we're the Dixie Jam Band. Bobby legally has the name "Molly Hatchet" and we don't claim to be Hatchet. This is just a CD with all of the original members. And Duane Roland, who did not play at the benefit due to legal reasons, came in and put tracks down, overdubbed.

So, do portions of the profits from the CD go to Danny Joe?

It all goes to Danny. We are a non-profit. Everything goes toward helping Danny, whether it's the huge medical bills, or whatever. Danny can't work. He can't go out on the road. So, anything we can do. He's Danny Joe Brown. He's our bud. He'd do the same for me. He'd do it for you.

How did it feel when you first reunited with your old friends to play?

It was great. We rehearsed the night before, and it was magic. I'd been playing phone tag with everybody for about eight months because we had a schedule and it got cancelled. So we all knew the songs and the order we were going to play them. I made tapes up and sent them to everybody. Basically, everybody did their homework and we just came in here and ran through everything. It was just incredible. At the last minute, Jay Johnson from the Southern Rock Allstars filled in for Duane. We didn't know until the morning of the show whether Duane could legally do it or not. It got to be such a legal hassle, and we couldn't stand the chance of losing the whole show any longer, and Duane knew that. We talked it over. Sometimes you have to make compromises in order to do things.

Something else I wanted to touch on was your involvement with Foghat. When were you with them?

Right after I got out of Molly Hatchet, I got the call from Lonesome Dave. Actually, right after Hatchet broke up in 1990, our entire crew went with Foghat reunited, including our road manager and everybody, our techs, bus driver. Our road manager had said, "Man, Riff, you've got to be in this band! Nobody smokes, nobody drinks, they're all vegetarians. They're all like you!"

So, Lonesome Dave knew me and called me up to invite me to do the western tour with them. I said, "Yeah!" So, I stayed with them a while, and they were going to have some pictures taken, and Dave said, "Do you want to have your picture taken with us? Do you want to join the band?" I said, "Yeah!"

I miss Lonesome Dave a lot. Out of all the bad people in this business, he was one of the good guys. He was a dear friend and I really miss him. He was one of the nicest people. He renewed my faith in music. After ten years with Hatchet and seeing all the bull that went down, I was really burned out with it. I was ready to get off the road. But just getting with those guys was great. Dave was the kind of guy who would deliver the same show at a little tiny club for 40 people that he would do at Madison Square Garden for 10,000 people. They loved playing. They went out because it was fun. They didn't need the money; they just wanted to play. I just grinned every night. When they put all four of the original Savoy Brown guys back together, I came off the road to begin my benefit work. But Dave was one of the good guys.

Tell me a little about the *Animal Magnetism* CD you produced. Is it still available?

It sure is. It's something I always wanted to do. I do animal benefits every year for the Orlando Humane Society. I've been doing it for about fifteen years. And I had wanted to do a solo album for the animals. I had been working on it, and I am pretty vain, but not *that* vain. I couldn't call it *Riff West & Friends* after I got all these people! It turned into a compilation album. I felt so silly even sticking my name in there! (Laughs) Who is this Riff West guy? I just called everybody. Linda Ronstadt, Edgar Winter… For some of the songs I flew people in, and some of the times I went to them. And we had Linda McCartney.

What's next for you?

I still have a band together called Riff West & Friends. All I do is benefit work. I just sing, and we do some White Witch stuff, some Hatchet stuff, and some Foghat stuff. That's it. Just having a good time. All I ask everybody is to keep rocking and rolling, and pray for Danny Joe. Not just Danny, but pray for anybody that needs good thoughts. We all have people we need to help out. Don't wait until it's too late. •

Ralph E. "Riff" West, Jr., 64, of Sanford, Florida, passed away on November 19, 2014, after a lengthy illness due to a car accident.

Bruce Brookshire

2001

One of the hardest-working bands in the lexicon of Southern rock during the seventies and eighties was Doc Holliday. Oddly, Doc tends to be repeatedly overlooked by authors and writers chronicling the history of the genre. Fact is, they are just as deserving of inclusion as their fellow brothers of the road. Sporting an impressive catalog of recordings on A&M Records, and a legacy that continues to evolve even today, Doc Holliday still creates tight, funky Southern-rock music.

At the helm until recently has been Warner Robins, Georgia's own Bruce Brookshire, a talented singer, songwriter, guitarist, and Episcopal priest. A couple of years ago, Doc member Eddie Stone took over as bandleader when Brookshire retired from the band to work more with his church.

Back in 2001, we spoke with Bruce about his band, their upcoming new album, and his strong Christian beliefs.

MBS: Where were you born and raised?

Bruce: I was born in Colorado Springs, Colorado, but I was raised on an Air Force base in Germany called Spangdahlem. I moved to Georgia in 1969.

Who were your earliest musical influences?

My first records were by Peter, Paul & Mary. But my earliest influence, like so many of my generation, was the Beatles.

Were you from a musical family?

Yes, my father played blues harmonica and loved Josh White, Mahalia Jackson, and many of the artists from his sons' record collections, like the Righteous Brothers and Steve Winwood. My mom was quite musical. She sang in church choirs, in musicals, and had a jazz radio show in college. I remember my parents doing "House of the Rising Sun" for me when I was about 10, Dad playing harp and singing and Mom singing.

Were you exposed to Christian music as a child as well as secular?

I was exposed to all forms of music as a child. I saw the Vienna Boys Choir live. I listened to classical music like "Peer Gynt." Buck Owens used to perform regularly at our base. The Everly Brothers appeared there. And anyone from England at that time caught my attention. I also used to listen to German rock bands like the Lords, and Dave Dee on German radio. I saw Jimi Hendrix at Cincinnati Gardens in 1968, and Taj Mahal "live" that same year. Taj was a very big influence on me in my teen years, as was Peter Green, my absolute guitar hero at the time.

Tell us a little about how Doc Holliday was formed, and a bit about your recording history.

In the summer of 1971, my brother Bob and I formed a blues band called Roundhouse. My brother plays guitar, piano, and harmonica. Eight years later, Roundhouse, with different members (my brother had gone on to play with Johnny Taylor, Clarence Carter, ZZ Hill, Solomon Burke, and other R&B artists), began to get hot and attracted some attention from Molly Hatchet manager Pat Armstrong. Later on, we found the guys that managed a band called Nantucket, Bill Cain and Jet Matthews. We liked them, and they managed to get us a record deal with A&M in 1980.

We went in the studio for our first LP, *Doc Holliday*, with Tom Allom, the guy who produced Judas Priest and Pat Travers, which was how we knew him. He did a fabulous job of making us sound like a world-class band. He's a class act all the way. Our second album, *Rides Again*, was produced by David Anderle, who worked at A&M and was a fan of the band. He later became head of the label. He was a very laid-back and supportive producer. Not a Tom Allom, David was more of a "vibes" man. He just sort of sat there and bobbed his head along to the music, and he would stop us every now and then and suggest something. Tom gets in there with both hands and works a band. So, different styles, but great results either way. *Rides Again* was pretty successful worldwide and helped to get us a fair amount of European attention.

Our third album was recorded in Munich, Germany, and produced by Mack, a guy who produced ELO, Queen, Billy Squier, lots of superstar bands. Mack scared us and intimidated us a little, but we were pretty strung out on drugs, so he did what he could. We intentionally tried to combine techno music with Southern rock, and we failed miserably. That album went cardboard—not gold or platinum. We lost our record deal, our house and tour bus, our equipment, everything. Techno was raging in 1983 and a drugged-out Southern band was not big business.

We broke up for about a year and a half, and got Doc Holliday back together for another LP in 1986, *Danger Zone*. We were trying to remember how to play rock and roll with that one. In 1988, we recorded *Song for the Outlaw* for a Paris-based label and toured Europe.

In the '90s we found a manager who was our partner and friend, Dave Hulme, a British guy, and we did an album for a German label called *Son of the Morning Star*. We were beginning to remember how to play rock and roll by that time.

Next came album number seven, *Legacy*, which was a good representation of the band's live sound. It took us that many years to get back on track, since the crash of 1983. That's Doc history in a big ol' nutshell....

What years was Doc at their peak, and what are some of the fondest memories you have of those days?

It peaked in the '80s the first time at Madison Square Garden with Black Sabbath. Ronnie Dio is a gentleman and a good friend. He got us there. Lots of gigs were good: dates with April Wine, Loverboy, Charlie Daniels, Pat Travers. I'll tell you, though, some of the best shows we ever did were as a package with Nantucket, our good friends and brothers from North Carolina. That is and was a great band. It peaked again in the '90s with festival shows in England, Scandinavia, and Germany. We played the Marquee in London in the '90s a few times—that was a kick. The way we look at it, it's always peaking. We are just fortunate to have been at it for so long and made good friends, and stayed good friends.

What are the differences between touring in the '70s and touring now?

Now we are not drug addicts and alcoholics. We can have a couple of beers with our friends, maybe listen to some music, read our Bibles, and pretty much remember everything that went on each night of a tour. That's an improvement, I'd say.

Tell me a little about that great Travis Wammack tune you guys recorded and how that came about...

As many Southern bands did, we did some sessions early on in Muscle Shoals. We were at Broadway Studio, and Travis came in with a 45 that had the song "Keep On Running" on it. He told us to try it out and see if we liked it. He doesn't remember this, but I'm sure he met a lot of young bands. We loved the tune, started playing it at all our shows, and recorded it on the first A&M LP, which sold quite a few. It has become a signature song for us.

Is Doc Holliday a full-time gig now, or do you just do reunion shows with the band?

Music is full time for me, Daniel Bud, and Cadillac. Our music ministry is very important, with *The Damascus Road* CD, but all shows are top priority when they are on.

Tell us about Doc Holliday's European market and audience.

It is very special to us. It's what has kept the band going for so long. There are European fans that still appreciate and support this music. It's not quite the same at home, I'm afraid.

Tell us a little about these Southern rock bands in Europe… Lizard is awesome!

Well, there are quite a few good European Southern bands, but Lizard is the best one without a doubt. Georg Bayer, Lizard's lead singer, is my brother. Our families are very close—our kids, wives, friends, everything. It seems that European bands, especially German bands, take a lot of pride in Southern music and heritage. The Allmans are very important. Skynyrd, too. Southern music is an art form that finds appreciation everywhere.

Let's talk about the new Doc Holliday CD. Tell me everything. The fans want to know.

The new CD is called *A Better Road*. It chronicles our past and our present. There are five newly recorded tracks on it, and five tracks recorded in the '80s, produced by Tom Allom, that have never been released before. I think it's a pretty good CD. The new tracks were recorded at my studio. The old tracks were recorded in Orlando at Bee Jay, which no longer exists. I think it's a good follow-up to *Legacy*. The mastering was done by Michael Hauff in Germany. He did a great job pulling it all together.

I absolutely love your gospel release, *Damascus Road*. Tell us about how and when you gave your heart to the Lord, and how it has affected your life. Also, how you came to record this beautiful CD…

I think *The Damascus Road* is the CD that I was always meant to record. My mom died in 1990, bringing me to God through her experience in growing to meet Him face to face. She led me to the place where I could open my eyes and experience God in a personal way. She led me to the people of God, the Body of Christ, and they helped along the way. Mentors like Marian and Obie Waldhauer, Bob Dunbar and Lee Harris, and spiritual directors like Dennis Smart and Bob Gibson—to name just a few—helped to make me the Christian I am today.

Do you think there is a growth overall in people coming to know God, or a decline?

A growth, definitely. Definitely. Look around… Jesus and prayer are more a part of our culture now than in any time in my memory.

There are several Southern rockers who proudly proclaim their Christianity. Have you worked with Charlie Daniels, Barry Lee Harwood, Billy Crain, Larry Howard, or any of the others in a gospel setting?

Larry is a good friend. Charlie is an acquaintance. We recently went to Memphis for the One Festival, and the Cornerstone Festival as the backup band for Larry. It was a blast, and I'm looking forward to working with him a lot more. He is an inspiration. I knew him "when," and he knew me "when," so it's a kick to get together now. We pray a lot more together now than we ever did, that's for sure!

Let's talk music. When you listen to music, who do you listen to?

If I can grow up to be John Michael Talbot or Michael Card, I will be happy. I listen to those two far and away more than anyone else. I listen to Yellowjackets, a great jazz band. I listen to Gypsy Kings, a great, great guitar band. And Keb Mo's blues reminds me of Taj Mahal. I listen to some new rock stuff on the radio, and some oldies radio, too. Not much new country.

If you could offer one piece of advice to a fan who wants to be a "rock star"—or, at least, a working musician—in 2001, what would it be?

Those are two very different things. Work at your instrument or your voice if you want to be a professional musician. If you want to be a "rock star," you had better be very good-looking, find a well-connected manager, and prepare yourself to be miserable.

What are the immediate plans of Bruce Brookshire the solo artist and Doc Holliday the band?

God is our CEO. Wherever He leads, we will try to ascertain His will and follow. Please join us in prayer, that we will always keep His standards as our goal, and we will not be led by our own egos. That's such a tough thing for a performer. Our prayer partners are our lifelines. Please join. •

Eddie Stone

1999

Eddie Stone spent many years playing keyboard and guitar for the Southern-rock band Doc Holliday, a band he took the reins of following the retirement of bandleader Bruce Brookshire.

When we sat down with him in 1999, the Warner Robins, Georgia, native was embarking on a solo career with a great new CD, Right Tonight, *and performing with an excellent band as Eddie Stone and the Soul Shakers. We met up with Eddie in Macon, where he kindly agreed to an exclusive interview.*

MBS: How did you first become interested in playing music, and what was the first instrument you played?

Eddie: My grandmother and my dad both play. My dad played steel guitar. He played with Raleigh Puckett and Gibb Tanner, who were the first two people in the Country Music Hall of Fame. There's an alternative group called Gibb Tanner & The Skillet Lickers, but they are the third generation from the original Skillet Lickers. My grandmother played ukulele, and I used to strum around on it. I didn't realize that was the seed that was being planted. Then I saw the Beatles on *The Ed Sullivan Show*—their first appearance. I looked at it, saw the look of horror on my parents' faces, and said, "That's what I'm gonna do."

It's amazing how many people I talk to cite the Beatles as a major influence toward becoming a musician.

(Laughs) Yeah, Elvis played the guitar, too, but he didn't get the girl when he was playing the guitar. The Beatles got the girls when they played guitar. I really think that's what made me say, "I want to do that." They were on three weeks in a row and I saw all three weeks. I was not going to miss it.

Tell us about some of your early bands, prior to Doc Holliday.

I guess the very first band I played in was Bolder. I guess I played in one other band. But Bruce Brookshire, from Doc Holliday, and I went to high school together. We started playing together at a very young age.

So, you guys were from Macon, right?

Warner Robins, which is right below Macon. I think Bruce was 13 or 14 when I met him. I was a couple of years older. He was different, and I liked that. He wasn't playing the same stuff everybody else was. We kind of clicked. We didn't actually form the band until after I was getting out of the Army. That was around 1973. I was, in fact, the last person drafted in the state of Georgia. I came home on leave about a year before I was to get out of the service, and Bruce and I started playing. I was dying to play. We opened for Wet Willie down in Albany, Georgia. The band was called Roundhouse at the time.

When did you guys become Doc Holliday?

We signed with A&M Records in 1979. Somebody up in Canada had the name "Roundhouse" trademarked. At the time, I was heavily into this *Time-Life* book series on the Old West. I read that the original Doc Holliday was from the state of Georgia. I thought, how cool would that be? I brought it up to the rest of the guys in the band, because we had to change our name. We had three names. I remember two of them: Doc Holliday and Rebel Gray. We had some notoriety in our home town, with a demo tape that was number two or three on their rotation. So, after we signed with A&M, we had a radio interview and let the listeners vote for our name. "Doc Holliday" won out overwhelmingly.

How long did you guys play together, and when did the band break up?

We were Roundhouse, from the summer of '71—like I said, I wasn't in the band for two years—we became Doc Holliday in '79, and our first album came out in 1980. Somebody said Southern rock was dead in the early eighties. We went to Germany to do our third album, *Modern Medicine*. A lot of pure Doc fans don't care for that record. It had a lot of new sounds on it. It was produced by Mac, the guy who produced Queen and Billy Squier. We actually had a vision at the time of taking Southern rock to this place. Nobody wanted to buy it, until about three years later when ZZ Top did the same thing. They were much cooler than we were. (Laughs) Billy is the epitome of cool. When Reverend Billy said it was cool to do that, it was. Not to say that they were jumping on something we had done. They just had the same idea. The world just wasn't ready for a bunch of redneck Southern rockers to do what we did. I still think it's a good record. We did that, and then in about '85, I think—Bruce can help us on this—we decided we were going to do something different. Then in about '87, we missed it, and re-formed. At one time we had three guitar players and two keyboard players. The guy that plays keyboards in my band, Tony Cooper, was playing in Doc Holliday for a while. We had a different drummer. At one time, Rick Skelton, who was an original member of Doc, rejoined the band. We did the album *Danger Zone*. I left the band again for a while. Then in '88, Europe came knockin'. They said, "Southern rock didn't die over here." We didn't know that. A&M didn't let us know about that. We had a bunch of airplay, a bunch of sales, and a bunch of fans over there. We re-formed again and started going to Europe, opening for Blackfoot and hordes of other bands…Faith No More, different bands. We saw that we had a huge following over there. Then in 1990 I left the band again. The Gulf War was coming; it was harder to get over there and tour. It was dangerous. You know Cinderella was supposed to be on the Pan Am jet that went down. That's scary. I bailed out. They went to Europe a few more times without me, then we started doing the reunions with the original guys and the new guys. I started writing songs. I went to a diaper factory. That'll humble you. So, I started writing to cope with the factory job. I'll always be indebted to them for that; they spurred something in me. So, I've got kind of the best of both worlds. I've got my own band, which contains some great players, and the Doc reunions.

When did you form the new band?

About a year ago. I had already recorded most of the new CD, and was singing at a big club in Macon called Whiskey River, which was a country/Southern rock club. I was fronting the band, but I got to miss the thrill of having my own band. A house gig is kind of a strange thing. A "hush-and-make-your-money" type of thing. I can't do that. I go onstage for the jugular vein every night. We were having big shows every night, opening for Charlie Daniels, Terry Clarke, Marshall Tucker… I was seeing all my old buddies, and they were saying, "What are you doing here? Why aren't you out on the road doing your thing?" So, I put a band together. I called up my old buddies. I asked Herman Nixon, who was the original drummer for Doc Holliday (and played for three years with Toy Caldwell), and Tony Cooper. Herman is the best drummer you could play with. Jaimoe has self-proclaimed that Herman is the only guy who can play his and Butch's drum parts on Allman songs at the same time. He's the only guy Toy Caldwell said that can match the finesse of Paul Riddle, with the soul of an R&B

drummer. And Ken Wynn plays guitar with me. I've got a new bass player, Skip Slaughter. He co-produced and engineered my album. What a hot band. I'm so proud of it.

How are things in Europe? I've seen your CD review in *Bands of Dixie* magazine out of France.

With your help with the CD, and the Doc Holliday notoriety, things are looking real good for us in Europe. We're hoping for a late-spring or early-summer tour. My buddies in Skynyrd are going to be over there, and I've got some folks working on trying to get me on some of the dates. I've spoken with Al Nally, who is Rickey Medlocke's manager, and he's heard my CD, and he likes the fact that there are some good hooks in there.

The album is full of hooks, even the covers. Your John Fogerty cover is great.

I wanted that Fogerty thing to come off like George Jones meets AC/DC. I played rhythm guitar on that with Mike Causey from Stillwater. And then Rob Walker, also of Stillwater, came in and did the harmony leads. That's three slammin' guitars going on.

Who are some of your musical influences, and who do you like to listen to these days?

Influences, obviously the Beatles. Merle Haggard, George Jones, Buck Owens, Black Sabbath, Jon Lord, Bobby Whitlock. Man, when I used to live in an apartment, I'm convinced that the guy next door thought there were 13 people living next door. I'd get up in the morning with George Strait, and by noon, Metallica was playing. When we toured with Black Sabbath, I was in heaven. We did the *Mob Rules* tour.

With Ozzy?

No, Ronnie James Dio was singing then.

He's awesome.

Let me tell you, that elf ain't nothin' but bad! And we toured with April Wine, and I have to say, they influenced me, too. We did the Ghost Riders Tour with the Outlaws. That was our first major tour. It was great. Hughie and Freddie Salem were huge musical influences. Rickey and Blackfoot. Skynyrd. Oh, God. Growin' up around Gregg (Allman)—I mean,

Gregg gets a lot of negative press, and he shouldn't. I've had moments alone with Gregg on the road when he didn't have to be "Gregg Allman." He's one of the greatest guys in the world.

When I interviewed him last year, he was great.

Oh, yeah. Obviously, the Allman Brothers are one of my greatest influences.

What was it like around Macon and Warner Robins during the late '60s until the late '70s during the days of Capricorn Records?

During the mid-'70s, there was a club in Macon called Uncle Sam's that Phil Walden owned. They had a lot of big bands in there, but it was also a playground for Capricorn artists. We were the house band out there. Stillwater was the house band and we were the house band. We rotated out. That's one thing that made the music scene in Macon so hard to do. They could go out to Uncle Sam's and pay a dollar or two cover charge, and see $300,000 worth of entertainment onstage. They'd all come out to have their beverage of choice and party. The equipment was there. I called it the Wet Tucker Brothers. You'd see Jimmy Hall jamming with Toy and Tommy Caldwell. Or Jaimoe, or Gregg or whoever. One night on my B-3, there was Gregg Allman on one manual, and Bobby Whitlock on the next manual. And Toy and Dickey and Martin Mull up there playing. My brother was Bobby Whitlock's road manager during the Capricorn years. So, I got to go in and witness some of the sessions. Bobby had great people playing with him. Dru Lombar from Grinderswitch was a man who influenced me. They were so good. They took us out on the road with them. Great guys—Joe Dan Petty, Dru Lumbar, Larry Howard, Rickey Burnett, Steven Miller—they showed us how to be something better than a bar cover band. I'd go down to the studio, and the Brothers would be finishing at night and Bobby would be starting in the daytime. Or Skynyrd was doing *Gimmie Back My Bullets,* and Bobby Whitlock was recording during the daytime. I saw some incredible things happen in this city. We took it for granted back then. Everybody played on everybody else's album. If you'll notice, my new CD was done that way. It was done in that building, so the vibe was there. I tried so hard to capture the Macon thing on my CD. Everybody I called up was so gracious, and they all agreed to play. Jimmy Hall wanted to play, but we had scheduling problems. Same with Larry Howard. I haven't seen that brotherhood in a long time. I'd love to see a return to that.

My friends in Europe tell me that you have lots of fans over there. Not only as Doc, but solo. Do you have any message for them?

I want to tell all my buddies in Europe, look over your shoulder, 'cause I'm coming. •

Dennis Winters

2001

When I was editing GRITZ magazine, *there was one question that was asked time and time again: What ever happened to the Winters Brothers Band? The answer was always, "Nothing happened to 'em! They are still rocking and rolling."*

When I spoke with Dennis Winters in 2001, the band had just released a new CD called Southern Rockers, *and they even have their own television show. We caught up with Dennis Winters by phone from the Winters Brothers' farm in Nolensville, Tennessee, for an update on one of the South's finest bands.*

MBS: Where are you guys from and where do you live now?

Dennis: Donnie and I were born in South Florida not too far from the Everglade Swamp and moved into the hills of Tennessee when we were about 3 or 4 years old. We have lived in Middle Tennessee ever since. I live in the hills between Nolensville and Franklin, Tennessee, and Donnie lives on the outskirts of Nashville in Bellevue, Tennessee. The entire band is currently located in Middle Tennessee.

How did you and your brother first become interested in playing music? Who were some early influences?

We are third-generation musicians. My grandfather had a group called "Pop Winters and the Southern Strollers," and my father, Don Winters, is a solo artist and also worked with Marty Robbins for 23 years as part of the trio, up until Marty's death. Growing up backstage at the Grand Ole Opry in the late '50s and '60s influenced us a lot. My Uncle Zack Tucker always played music and we always had family get-togethers where we would pick. As we got older, we were more influenced by rock bands of the '60s.

When was the Winters Brothers Band formed? Maybe give a little history of the band…

We lived in a smokehouse converted into a bunk room while raising cattle for Marty Robbins on his farm near Franklin, Tennessee. You might say we were sharecroppers. That's where the initial Winters Brothers Band came to be. We also wrote songs for Marty Robbins.

Did you ever have people confusing you with Edgar and Johnny Winter?

Yes, it still happens. They were much more famous than we were. The only difference in our name is the "s" and a lot of people don't catch it. They never toured as "The Winter Brothers," only as "Johnny & Edgar Together." A promoter was going to book a show with the Winter Brothers Band with Johnny and Edgar, but decided that it would be too confusing for the fans. It doesn't really bother us, as we are big fans of theirs, and it comes with the territory. No one has ever been disappointed after hearing us.

How many albums did you guys record?

Actually, we have recorded four albums and one with our father, Don Winters. *The Winters Brothers Band* was our first, on ATCO/Atlantic Records; *Coast to Coast,* also on Atlantic; *Keep On Running* on Star Track Records; and the latest release on SouthStar Records, *Southern Rockers.* The release which featured our father is called *Yodeling King* on Star Track Records.

Tell us some of your favorite memories of the recording studio.

When we recorded the first two albums at Capricorn Studios in Macon, Georgia, there was always somebody dropping by. There was a rehearsal room in the front, so we were always running into someone from the Allman Brothers, Charlie Daniels, or Marshall Tucker, which was very exciting. One day while in session, we were able to take a day off to go out to visit Dickey Betts at the Allman Brothers Farm near High Falls, Georgia. For Thanksgiving, we took our families to the home of Paul Hornsby for dinner. That was a special treat for all of us.

The worst show we ever had was wonderful, because we had the opportunities to open for some of our greatest heroes. When we toured with Skynyrd, Ronnie would come back to the dressing room before the show each night with a bottle of Jack Daniels and a bottle of champagne. He'd always say, "A little something for the brothers." On occasion, he would ask us to come out to jam with them. The Marshall Tucker Band would do the same, but the most memorable was a show at Boston Gardens… Toy came out and played steel with us. Jerry played sax, and then they had us come out on their last song. I believe it was "Will the Circle Be Unbroken?" and we sang with Doug. Charlie, Taz, and Tommy Crain would jam with us regularly. Once in New York City, Charlie bought us some amps for our dressing room. Dickey Betts would also show up at our pre-jam parties to jam with us in Nashville. Memories like these, you never forget! There are plenty of stories, maybe one day…

Who were some of the bands you toured with and opened for?

We toured with Lynyrd Skynyrd, the Allman Brothers Band, the Charlie Daniels Band, the Marshall Tucker Band, Bob Seger, Outlaws, Grinderswitch, Stillwater, Blackfoot, Wet Willie, Molly Hatchet, 38 Special, Pure Prairie League, Firefall, Sea Level, Dixie Dregs, Atlanta Rhythm Section, Elvin Bishop, and Delbert McClinton, just to name a few.

Did you guys ever play the Volunteer Jam?

Yes, on ten to twelve Volunteer Jams, when they were held in Nashville. We were featured on two of the Volunteer Jam albums, *Volunteer Jam III & IV* and *Volunteer Jam VI* on Epic Records.

Between your '70s Southern-rock stardom and this great new record, what did you guys do?

When the Southern-rock scene started to fade, work dropped off dramatically. We had to pay the bills, so we went to work doing what we could in order to take care of our families. Donnie got into construction and I started driving tractor-trailers and buses for Waylon Jennings, Oak Ridge Boys, and others. Even did a weekend run for Charlie up to West Virginia and Jersey. All the time, trying to keep the band doing as many shows as feasible.

Then, I wound up in a car wreck in December 1993 and suffered a broken neck, closed head injuries, and a few other things that kept me from being able to work. Shortly after, Donnie was knocked off a 15-foot wall by a forklift, landing on concrete, causing him to crush both ankles and heels from the fall.

My wife drove me over to his house to help care for him during his rehabilitation, while I was still being rehabilitated. Man, it was the funniest thing you ever did see, the blind leading the blind. We have both since recovered from these injuries.

Tell us a little about the TV show.

We've been taping the TV show for five years. It's a local show that airs in Nashville, Davidson County, Tennessee, on CATV Channel 19. It airs several times per week. We film approximately once a month and tape 3 to 4 shows at a time. Many friends have appeared on our show…Taz, Sid Yokham and his children, Sydney and Tucker, and a lot of local talent from this area. We like to give newcomers a break.

We have a great time with this show. We also film our Southern Summer Jam each year, which is held on our farm outside of Nashville. When people ask me about the show, I tell them it's a cross between *Hee Haw*, Grateful Dead, and *Wayne's World* all mixed up together. Our producers, Sammy and Betsy Thompson, are to be credited with giving us this opportunity.

Tell us a little about the album. George Clinton mixed and engineered it—I doubt that it's the same guy from Parliament-Funkadelic, right? (Laughs)

Correct. George Clinton is a well-known engineer in Nashville at Bayou Studios where this new release was recorded, originally from Muscle Shoals, Alabama. He's a real pro and it was a pleasure and an honor to be able to work with him. He really helped us to get our sound together, and we are looking forward to working with him in the future.

About the CD, you might say that David Corlew inspired us to do another Southern-rock project. Donnie and I decided he was right, the time was right, and we wanted to produce it ourselves. We knew we wanted to record some of the songs from our first album live, so we decided on "Smoky Mountain Log Cabin Jones," "Sang Her Love Songs," "Misty Mountain Morning," and "I Can't Help It." They were recorded in Nashville on November 27, 1999.

I had written most of the newer songs while on vacation with my family two years ago. Donnie and I really enjoyed producing and recording this CD. The title of our new CD is *Southern Rockers*, named primarily by the suggestion of our bass player, Ron "Rad" Dunn and myself. The concept comes from the reflection of the words and music of all the musicians that helped to inspire the "art" of Southern rock.

You write a lot of good songs. Describe your process. Do you come up with a title first, a melody? Just how do you do it?

Everybody does it different. I personally just wait until something pops in my head. I never know when it will come or where it will come from. I don't actually ever sit down and try to write, and I never write a song down until I am at the point of recording. I figure if I can't remember it all in my head, it's not a strong enough song.

Donnie writes differently, but when we write together, we will sit down to work on it.

Who's in your band, and are they the same guys that were in it before?

Three of the original five are still active members: Donnie, myself, and David "Spig" Davis on keyboards. I think that he is one of the most talented piano and B-3 organ players that has ever played Southern rock. Ron Dunn is on bass. He is an original member, but as a guitar technician. He moved into the bass spot 15 years ago and does a fabulous job of pumping it out. Our newest member is Fred Satterfield, longtime drummer for the Oak Ridge Boys. Fred goes back about ten years when I was driving for the boys. He was familiar with our music then and told me several times that he would love to jam with us. As fate would have it, Fred left the boys to pursue other career opportunities; we crossed paths again and united for this project. In addition to the band, we now have three inspiring backup vocalists—Casey, Cody, and Carly Winters—which are also featured on our TV show occasionally. We call them "the Southern Belles." I'm not honking my own horn, but listen to this CD. These guys are hot, and a force to be reckoned with.

Any European dates? Lots of Winters Brothers fans over there!

Nothing on the books as of yet. One of our main goals is to set a tour in Europe for all of our friends who have been so supportive over the years. We receive tons of e-mail daily from all of our friends in Europe. It's quite rewarding.

What's next for the band?

There are several projects in the works, a tour or two, or three. Our next CD will be a concept that leans toward the western/Southern-rock vein. We have lots of surprises in store. We're also working on the re-release of earlier albums on CD. So, cinch up your saddle and buckle up your spurs!

Devon Allman

2013

When we first spoke with Devon Allman, he had just come off the road with his band Honeytribe, and was preparing to spend some time with his wife and new baby. When he decided to get back out there and play, he pulled out all the stops, performing as a member of Royal Southern Brotherhood and recording his first-ever solo album, Turquoise. *In 2013 we spoke again with Devon about the Brotherhood, Rock Legends Cruise, his uncle Duane, and his hot new solo album.*

MBS: Devon, you've got so many great things going on, so many different projects, so many good things, I want to talk about all of them. The first thing I want to ask is that you tell our listeners about Royal Southern Brotherhood—who's in the band, how you guys formed the group, etc.

Devon: Royal Southern Brotherhood came together last year. The band was born in New Orleans, Louisiana, and really born out of a conversation about what it would be like to have a Neville and an Allman in the same band. You've got two very storied names in music from the South, and we went for it. It was something, from my perspective. Anything can look good on paper, but you have to give it a shot to see if it's legit—see if it's the real thing. It became a legitimate entity in my eyes really quick. We just gelled from hour one. We're really lucky to be joined by Mike Zito, who is a blues music award winner; Charlie Wooten, a legendary bass player from down South; and Yonrico Scott, who played with Derek Trucks for 15 years. The Neville in question is Cyril Neville. He's been in the Meters. He's been in the Neville Brothers. He's a Grammy winner. He's a Svengali, a guru of the percussion, one of the most soulful singers I've ever had the pleasure of listening to. So, we came out last year, put a record out, toured about 20 countries. We're actually going to Australia in a couple of weeks for the first time—we're pretty excited about that. So, it's been one of those "hit-the-ground-running" things. It's kind of crazy to think about how two short years ago it wasn't even a thought, and now it's out there doing things worldwide. So, we're very blessed that it came together quickly.

We had the pleasure of having Cyril on our KUDZOO Radio program several months ago. He was so much fun to talk to, like you said; he's also an

immense talent. I'm a big fan of everybody in that band. I mean, Yonrico—oh, my God…what a drummer!

It's very serendipitous how we all came together, but I believe things like that happen for a reason. As "New-Age-y" as that may sound, I think it's very interesting how those seeds were planted all those years ago without us even knowing. Mike Tito and I, for example, worked at Guitar Center together in 1999. That was a long time ago. To be in a band together, to be with a Neville and touring the world—it's pretty surreal.

Who produced the new record and where was it recorded?

It was recorded outside Lafayette, Louisiana, at a place called Dockside Studios, which is a pretty cool studio. It's got a built-in housing environment so you go and make your record, and hang on the porch, and they have amazing trees and a river that goes out back. It's like the ultimate getaway. B.B. King made a record there. Derek Trucks. We were really lucky to have that place for a week and make that record. We were really flying by the seat of our pants, recording very quickly—but it wasn't rushed. It was just flowing out of us. We were lucky to have the legendary Jim Gaines do the record. He's done Steve Miller, Stevie Ray Vaughan, and Santana, and his discography is about as stellar as you can get. He had his hands on songs that shaped listeners' lives. He's an astute gentleman and he became like an uncle to me. We were very, very fortunate to work with Jim Gaines on it.

Yeah, he's one of the best. The album seems to be doing really well, and I wondered if you could update us on how things are going for the band Royal Southern Brotherhood before we shift gears.

Yes, absolutely. I think it was about a month into the first Royal Southern Brotherhood tour…I had such a strong affinity for what was happening, I pulled everyone aside and said, "Hey, man, are you digging this?" The idea, initially, was that when we have time away from our solo careers, we get to do this Royal thing and go play in the summer, and go play the festivals. And the idea quickly became, this really is the priority, and so let's go out and run this and when we have time away from this, we'll do the solo stuff. And you never know. We may revert back to the other way and maybe only do Royal in the summers. But for right now we're still establishing the brand and, as far as what's on tap for the rest of this year, it's a crazy one. We've got a live record coming out in May. It's recorded in Germany, recorded right at the height of the European tour where we were firing on all cylinders. So, we're excited about that. That's going to be a live CD/DVD combo set coming out in May. We'll be on tour all year, coast to coast in America. We'll be going to Europe four different times, and we'll be going to Australia for the first time in a couple of weeks.

Oh, my! Australia. That's one place I've always wanted to go. Man, just get on a plane for 24 hours and you'll be there. (Laughs)

Yeah, I just found out my flight from Dallas to Sydney is officially the longest non-stop flight in the world, so I think I'll be pounding out an entire season of *Breaking Bad* on the plane.

Why not? Heck, yeah.

Gotta do something, man.

I went on the Rock Legends II Cruise and enjoyed seeing you there with all 48 of your bands (laughs), and I was sitting with a group of people when the Brotherhood played… It was during the day out by the pool, and everyone was like, "Wow! That band is amazing!" And it's funny that a lot of people don't know who's in band. And I said, "Yeah, that's Devon Allman. He's that guy's son—I can't remember that guy…" Nah, I'm just kidding. "…and that's one of the Neville Brothers." Everyone was digging it. It was awesome-sounding. I always like asking people I interview how they enjoyed playing on the pool deck, because most people get blown away by the crosswinds, but I don't know if it was doing that during the afternoon as much.

I don't know, at this point in my career, I gotta tell you, if you have electricity and a checkbook, bro, I'm there.

That's what they used to say about Chuck Berry.

I mean that in the best possible way. If the finances are there and the electricity is open, let's go play two, three hours. At this point, I've found myself in crazy places, from barns, to the fiftieth floor of skyscrapers, to the top deck of cruise ships, to beer cellars in Germany underground—you name it. I've played in the weirdest shit, but I don't mind. I love to play so I'll play anywhere.

Have you done a lot of cruises?

I've wanted to go on them for the longest time, and lately my fanbase has been rallying towards certain cruise operators, for me to be included.

You know, many years went by before I was finally asked, and now they're kind of popping out of the woodwork. I really like the idea of a working vacation. What I like about those cruises is you really don't have the separation from the audience. I think the separation from the audience is important in a theater setting, which, for the show, is better. But for something like a cruise, having that notion that you're all in it together, and you might pass by an artist that you really dig in a buffet line, and that's really very cool. And it's just as cool for me to maybe run into one of my heroes, like Pat Travers or Paul Rodgers, getting a cup of soup—so I'm every bit as much of a fan as I am part of the entertainment when I do those.

It is very cool. Everywhere you turn you're running into someone. Yeah, the second group I wanted to ask about is a little group called Honeytribe. Give us a little update about Devon Allman's Honeytribe.

I just put out my first solo record. Back a couple weeks ago it debuted at #5 on the Billboard Blues Chart—it's doing real well. So, in order for me to do that, I had to put Honeytribe on hold. I've been running that band since 1999 and it's kind of time for me to shake things up a bit. I've pulled away from the Honeytribe brand this year and struck out on my own and started doing the solo thing. Honeytribe is something that I could form back up. If there's time to get back out there with that brand and that band, I will, but right now it's a good time in my career to give to Royal and explore the solo side of things.

Speaking of *Turquoise*—outstanding album, by the way…*outstanding*—tell us about the song "Homesick."

"Homesick." That was the first tune I wrote for *Turquoise.* I wrote it in New York City probably about a year ago and, obviously, I was homesick. Not to be redundant, but when you're out there, you kind of dream of doing this your whole career and then you find yourself right in the middle of it. It's not a complaining song; it's just a yearning, a longing. I had been gone from home for, like, 45 days straight, and all I wanted to do was see my son and cook my own food and sleep in my own bed, you know? So it's kind of that "be-careful-what-you-wish-for" thing. Anything in life that's a wonderful thing, like having a career in music, is a bit of a blessing; it also comes with a bit of a price. So, this song sort of explores that.

So, why now? Why do a solo album at this point in your career?

Well, I did a couple songs on the Royal Southern Brotherhood album that were a bit of a departure for me. The Honeytribe formula was one that was really based on dynamics. We go from a soft whisper to kind of kicking you in the teeth—really born on dynamics. And I really wanted some songs that didn't have dynamics. I really wanted some three-chord tunes that kind of get caught in a groove, that were really the same at the beginning and the end. I used Tom Petty or the Rolling Stones as kind of an example for the blueprint. And, I don't know, once I wrote a couple of songs that were on the Royal record, that's more the kind of speed of things I want to go after. So, I really thought it would be a good point in my career to take that more mellow vibe and magnify it—make a whole record like it. So, I did. It's been kind of a coming-of-age thing for me.

Another track I really like is "When I Left Home." Can you tell us a little bit about that one?

You know, that song was really meant to be kind of for the fans that I already do have that don't know my whole story. And then for fans that are just coming along late in the game, kind of getting them caught up. The idea was to lyrically represent the last couple decades of my life. It talks about, literally, the day that I left home and left school and left the girl that I loved to go try to have a career in music. This was 20 years ago. It's definitely a reflective look. It talks about living in Memphis and playing on Sunset Strip, flying up to New York City to hang out with my dad to learn the business. It really manages to squeeze two decades into one song.

***Turquoise* was produced by Jim Gaines. I'm a big fan of Gaines—always have been—and I wanted to ask what it's like for you, personally, working with Jim…?**

Well, it's wild because, in my head, he's a rock star. I'm enamored with this man. I am enamored with his discography, but when you get in a room with him, and it's just you and Jim and an acoustic guitar, and you're mapping out your songs with him, he doesn't have any air of bullshit. He's just a real cat and he knows how to really pull out the strengths in your abilities and the strengths of the song. So, you forget all about his discography, and forget this guy worked with Stevie Ray Vaughn, and you forget all this stuff and dive into your work. And he's the football coach. You have the asshole one, and he's the cool one that you wish you had. And he really became like an uncle to me. I love the man dearly. At age 70, he's still producing records that are really badass.

Also, on this album you had some really cool friends dropping by to play. You had Jim Dickenson's sons, the guys from North Mississippi All-stars. Tell us a bit about the various people who play on the album with you.

Well, the core of the record is recorded with the trio—myself, Yonrico Scott from Royal Southern Brotherhood, and then Mr. Miles Weeks on the bass. So, we had a good time laying that down. That was in an old cottage in southern Tennessee. That was a real homey environment but I did want some guests on it, so I reserved a couple days in Ardent Studios in Memphis. And I got the lovely Samantha Fish to come down and do the duet. We remade the Tom Petty/Stevie Nicks classic "Stop Draggin' My Heart Around." And Luther Dickenson (son of Jim Dickenson) came down and played some slide on "When I Left Home" and just really killed it. We enjoyed talking about guitars and our crazy dads. Ron Holloway—amazing saxophone player. He played with Warren Haynes, Dizzy Gillespie…he's a dear friend and he came down and played sax on a cut. There's a hotshot band out of Memphis called Lucero, and their Hammond B3 organ player came down and played four or five songs on the record. He's just an animal in the studio—super efficient—so I'm a lucky man. I'm lucky that, not only do I have some friends in the industry that support what I'm doing and are into it and want to be involved, but every damn one of them is absolutely world-class. I am really happy to have them on *Turquoise*. I think the record is a good collection of songs, but I think their performances really take it to a real sweet level.

One thing I wanted to ask you about, before I forget, is… I understand you played a gig down in Macon and you played Uncle Duane's Les Paul Goldtop. Was it for the whole show?

Yeah, that was craziness. The vibe that was dripping off that guitar was palpable. I mean, it was just intense. I'd played the guitar before but I never got to play a whole show with it. It was like a dream come true. He was someone, really, I wish I knew. I feel like I know him through his body of work he left behind, but to hold his guitar all night was really a tender moment.

I would have given anything to have seen that, because I've heard from so many of my friends who played that guitar during the 2009 Beacon Run—where you played it...Susan Tedeschi, Eric Clapton, Tommy Talton—and they were all saying the same thing: it's got some kind of mojo on it.

Absolutely, it does.

I can only imagine. Yeah, everybody loved Duane. When you talk about Southern music, Southern rock, and all that, nine times out of ten his name comes up, followed by Ronnie Van Zant. It's gotta be cool to be Duane's nephew.

You know, to be honest, I don't sit around and dwell on it, because I need to keep my head in the game, but every once in a while I'll have one of those little "oh, shit" moments when I'm, like, "Wow, yeah, I am..."

And Daddy being Gregg is not a bad thing either.

No. Hell, no. But really, if I sat around and thought about who my dad and my uncle are, it'd probably send me to the funny farm. I've got my own songs to write, my own jams to play, my own guitar to play. And at the end of the day, I want to leave something for my son. Life isn't this straight line—you're born, you go down this line, and then you die. Life is a figure eight. And my son is the next one to pass this off to, whether it's music or just a way of life, a way of life and of handling life. I gotta do what I do for him.

How old is your son, Devon?

The kid's going to be 13 in two weeks.

Thirteen! Wow. So he's getting on the guitar already?

Yeah, he plays some guitar here and there and he's an avid piano player. He's been playing it for four years. He's very accomplished at piano. We'll see how it goes. We don't want to pressure the guy. If the bug bites him hard enough to want to do it, it's obviously there for him. He's in Nashville.

What's his name, Devon?

His name is Orion, like the constellation. Orion Gregory, named after his grandfather.

Oh, what a cool name that is.

He's a cool young man. I'm very proud to be his father.

Well, alright. Let's kind of wrap up. Tell me what's coming up next for you. You've got so many things going on, but what's coming up in the immediate future?

Well, I'm going to be touring all year with Royal Southern Brotherhood. We've got a bunch of trips to Europe and a trip to Australia. I've just been appointed to the Board of Directors for the National Blues Museum, which is opening in St. Louis at the end of next year, and you know, hammers and nails come popping out in a couple of months. The building is secured, 90 percent of the funds are secured, so it's all happening. It's all a real deal. It's not a concept; it's a reality. So, I'm going to be involved in helping to pick artifacts and helping to design exhibits.

What else?

Hey, man, my calendar's full. If I am gonna come and wax your car, you're going to have to fit me in for 2015 or '16, 'cause I am busy, bro. But I welcome it, and it's a blessing.

I read your posts on Twitter all the time. I love to see the updates on there.

Well, the way I see it, when I was a kid, if I could have had this fancy little handheld device and it would have told me what Zeppelin was doing that day, or told me what Paul McCartney was doing in the studio today, I would have flipped out.

Me, too.

So, to have that technology now and not connect to the fans is a crime.

Yeah, really. And it's amazing that some of the real stars—actors and such—they actually post their own stuff on Twitter.

I think that's just so cool that we can read these kinds of things.

I agree with that. I'm quite a bit older than you. I sound like my own father when I say, "I can't believe they're doing that kind of thing," but it's crazy. (Laughs)

It's good. It brings everyone along for the ride.

Well, Devon, thank you for your time. And thank you for the good music. I know we're only going to get more and more from you. I hope that we can see you in concert real soon. You put out a lot of good vibes and we appreciate it, and all of your fans do, too.

I thank you, Buffalo, for all the coverage and support through the years, and it's nice to see we're here talking again three years later, and things are up and things are moving. I owe that to the fans and the listeners. The tour continues and I would love to see everybody out there. •

Patterson Hood

2003

In the early 21st century, the Drive-By Truckers came blazing out of Athens, Georgia, a combination Southern rock/jam band with the fire of the early Rolling Stones and the Southern "thang" of Lynyrd Skynyrd. I caught up with guitarist and singer Patterson Hood in 2003 for a conversation about the band, their music, and the future.

MBS: Where were you born and raised?

Patterson: Up in Muscle Shoals, Alabama, and lived there for about 28 years and have been in Athens, Georgia, for about 9 years. I also lived in Memphis for a while and Auburn, Alabama, for a while, but I look at Athens as my home. It is amazing all the music here and the clubs here are supportive of what the bands are trying to do. You get bonus points for being more original.

I was hanging out down there when the B-52's were getting started, and REM and all that. Then came the Widespread phenomena. Are they still there?

Oh, yeah. They are inspirational and have set up their business and ties there and are very honest people.

What was it like growing up in Muscle Shoals with your dad (David Hood) being one of the rhythm section of the Swampers? You must have been exposed to some great music early on.

It was so cool, and the record collection Dad had was the big thing. He was gone a lot and busy doing what it took to do all of that. I didn't really get to see a lot of it firsthand and didn't get to hang out at the studio at that time. It was not in the cards for me to do that, but I did get a lot of time to raid his record collection and got turned on to some great music and a musical education at a much younger age than most people, and I guess that was the biggest impact that was made. I saw them doing things that I dreamed of someday doing and it never occurred to me that I wouldn't be able to do it, too. I didn't bother very much with school and studying and that was a bone of contention with me and my family, and I stayed in trouble a lot over my grades. I think a lot of it was that I saw Dad as a musician, not using his college education, and thought, "I won't need one either." It never occurred to me that I might not make it, or that I would be pushing 40 and not really have any choice but to do what I have done. Now that it is all working out okay, I guess it is all good, but I would be lying if I didn't admit that there were times when I felt like I might have really fucked up. Sort of around the second divorce you are thinking, is this really worth it? It tends to make you question those things.

What were two or three things that really pop out in your mind from your dad's record collection that, when you played them on the turntable, you thought were great?

I became a Neil Young fan at a very early age and became a huge Todd Rundgren fan, and still am. I am particularly a fan of one of his records more than a fan of him in general. The record he really got right was *Something, Anything,* and that is definitely one of my "desert-island" records.

Did you hear *A Wizard, A True Star*?

Yeah, I just found that record in the past five years.

Oh, that is a great example of artistic creativity, and not that many bands these days are coming up with something totally original like David Bowie and Todd Rundgren. What else in the record collection pops out that had a definite influence on you?

I am a big Curtis Mayfield fan. He was a big influence, and then when the punk-rock thing happened, I got heavily into that and was a huge Clash fan, Elvis Costello, and a huge Bruce Springsteen fan. I didn't get that from Dad, or the punk rock from him. He didn't get that. I had a friend that ran a record store and she turned me onto Springsteen, and I was a huge fan of him as a teenager. Around the time of *Darkness on the Edge of Town* and *Nebraska.*

That sounds like me because I got turned onto Springsteen and Kate Bush at the same time. What drew you to Springsteen, lyrics or attitude?

I think it was lyrics more than anything. I just really related. Like the *Darkness on the Edge of Town* era, and he was almost like a preacher role but his church was rock. I think that I bought into that as a teenager and related to that—and I was not particularly religious, although everyone needs something to believe in. He kind of preached the words that I bought into. Probably rock, for me, did play that role in what a lot of people get out of religion or whatever. I was a miserable teenager and couldn't get the first-choice girl, or second- or even third-choice girl I liked, and felt like a misfit wherever I was. But when I went to the rock show everything made sense to me, and when I grew up I wanted to be the one that was up there. Luckily I have been able to do that—maybe on a much smaller scale than I imaged at 15, but you know, it was really cool. About one year ago we opened for Widespread Panic—actually, it was the only time we ever opened for them—and it happened to be at the Huntsville Civic Center. That was the place I went to all the concerts I saw as a teenager, and that was a dream come true on that stage. An amazing experience.

Tell me a little bit about when and how the Drive-By Truckers band was formed. How did you come up with the name?

I don't even know about the name. It was kind of a joke but it was catchy, and we wanted something that didn't necessarily pigeonhole us into any one thing. I don't know if that really works on that level or not. In 1995 I thought of it, and I didn't know I would still be doing this with this band and still have that name that many years later. It does get the job done. A name is important and is a tough thing. I actually had the name before I had the band. It's kind of like half the battle to find a name that doesn't suck and one that no one else has, as far as you can tell. You had better hold onto it.

You have to be pretty eclectic nowadays to find a name that has not been used.

You have to go so far out there just to have something no one else has. Mike Cooley, who is in this band with me, we have played for 18 years together now—and this sort of answers the other part of your question—we had a band for six years called Adam's House Cat, and that to me is not a name that you would think anyone else would have. And it's not that great of a name, but I know of about two other bands using the same name. I met one of the guys in one of those bands. Our band was the oldest of the bands but it is really hard to find a name that someone else has not thought of.

Your drummer played with some of my friends here in Greenville in a band called the Dog Killers. Did you know about that?

Yeah, he's told me about them.

We were buddies and I used to write about them a lot. He's a great drummer.

He *is* a great drummer and we are blessed to have him in the band. He is not the original drummer. Matt Lane played on the first two records we made, and Brad (Morgan) joined about the time we finished the second record and has been a joy to play with. He is a personal asset to the band even if he was not such a great drummer.

Where did you come up with the idea for *Southern Rock Opera*?

About a year before the Drive-By Truckers even started, this guy Earl Hicks, a longtime friend of mine of 12 to 13 years, had just moved to Athens, and we were going back to North Alabama to pick up a truckload of stuff. And we didn't even have a radio in this truck, so over the course of our drinking-and-driving conversation, we ended up talking about writing this screenplay loosely based on the stories and mythology surrounding the Skynyrd story. Similar to what Cameron Crowe did with *Almost Famous*, using a fictional band to tell the stories of all the stuff he had seen. It was a composite character of all these different bands that he interviewed during those years growing up. That's kind of comparable to that but this was in 1995. That is how it started out, and we would meet and work on an outline on this screenplay idea, and he later became our producer and I got busy with the band. He produced *Pizza Deliverance* and *Alabama Asswhoopin'*, and he was going to produce *Southern Rock Opera*, and the bass player that we had set to join the band fell through at the last minute and he ended up joining the band. That is kind of the way things have gone, where we start off doing one thing and it kind of bleeds into something else.

Is it true that when you guys got ready to put that record out, you got your financing from fans or friends?

Yeah, we borrowed money from fans more than friends. I knew 3 or 4 of the people personally and a couple I have been friends with for many years, but some of them I have never met yet in person other than trading e-mails or something. We were making the thing, and everybody we had talked to about it said that it was a bad idea and we were crazy and that it wouldn't work, and we knew better than to try to get financing to make the thing and we had to come up with money any way we could. Then we would go out on tour and we all slept on the floors to try to get some money together any way we could. We would use that for recording. Then once we had this thing recorded, we thought that we could find someone to put it out and we went out and shopped it. Then we heard to play down "rock opera" and play down the "Southern thing," too, and basically redo the whole thing. We literally got one true offer to put it out, and it was such a terrible offer and it would have bankrupted our band if we had taken that deal. We didn't have any other ideas of what to do, and we put our word out that we had this record and what our situation was, and if it was ever going to come out we would need some help. Then people just came out of everywhere. And we were much more obscure at that time, but had been out on the road for years and had built a following so people just came out and offered us money to loan for it. But we told them that they need not use their savings, but we were as good a bet as the stock market and it is money that you feel good about investing. And we told them we would pay people back with interest and put it out the way we wanted to, and Lost Highway picked it up and re-released it about one year later and here we are.

Playing with Skynyrd, did you hear any reaction from them?

They were very nice, but it is not really their cup of tea. My fear was that they would hate it or be angry about it but that didn't happen. I don't suspect that they sat around the tour bus listening to it, and it is probably a little creepy to them. In retrospect—and I didn't think about that aspect then—we were just trying to make this record, but it is kind of creepy having some people that don't know you write these things about your band's personal tragedy. I am not 100-percent comfortable about that myself, but that is what we did. We can maintain all day long that our story is fictional, but we definitely drew from their story and made no bones about it, and so I am sure it is a little weird for them. They have never been anything but nice and they have never publicly commented on the record, but we have opened the show for them on occasion and Gary Rossington came backstage and met the band and was very supportive and nice and all of that. So I am very happy about that.

Did most of the songs on your new album come from personal experiences?

Yeah, it was very much inspired by the bullshit that happened around the time we made *Southern Rock Opera*. I got divorced and another member of the band got divorced, and another member of the band managed to stay together and that was no small feat in its own right because we spent so much time on the road. Everyone pushed their personal lives beyond the breaking point. Some people will listen to the album and get something totally different out of it, though. None of the songs are tied to what inspired them, and I think that they can hold up on their own just as songs that someone can listen to and get their own story out of and because of. I have not been delving too deep into these songs as to what they mean and I would like them to stand on their own that way. Definitely it was a very trying time that almost destroyed the band itself. We somehow managed to keep it together and come out the other side and now we are doing pretty good. We are getting along well and playing good shows and all of that, but it was definitely a tough time that we went through before the making of this record. By the time we actually made the record we had a great time making it. The songs themselves are kind of dark and sad, but we went into the studio and had a great time making it.

It is a good one and I wish you the best of luck with that one. I am still turning people onto the *Southern Rock Opera* and I personally think it is great Southern mythology. Forget *Tommy*. Let's do something Southern.

I am not a *Tommy* fan either, nor am I a rock-opera fan. That was really part of the equation that it was a rock opera done by people that don't like those things. Even the title itself was a little bit tongue-in-cheek, and if some people want to walk away from it thinking of it as a rock opera, that's fine. Or if someone wants to think of it as making fun of that, that's fine, too.

Not just with the rock-opera aspect, but you can take it so many different ways. I can see that. I have had people e-mail me and say that that is almost sacrilegious towards Ronnie Van Zant and all this, and I respond that, no, it is not. But the larger percentage of people will remark on how creative it is and that it is representative of a tribute to the Southern culture.

How can anyone feel that it is sacrilegious to Ronnie Van Zant?

Oh, the Beta Max guillotine.

That whole aspect of it was a tribute to Ronnie's dark sense of humor and I became a Skynyrd fan at a rather late age, and people have said that I probably grew up hating them. That is not true. It was not "my thing." I was in junior high school when the plane went down and had at that time three of their records and loved them. I bought *Street Survivors* the day it came out and that was the day before the plane crash happened. I did legitimately really like them and their music, but at that time the Lynyrd Skynyrd as we knew and loved them was over. Now they are out touring and doing what they do now and that is great and I wish them the best on all of that, but during those years I was in high school, there was no Lynyrd Skynyrd. It was the Rossington Collins Band, which I actually felt was kind of underrated and I felt those records were better than what they got credit for, but again people couldn't get past the fact that it wasn't Skynyrd. In their own right those are pretty cool records and even the second was better than it has been given credit for. I liked *Pine Box* particularly. But around that time I was listening to other things and doing other things and the whole "Free Bird" thing was overplayed on the radio and made you run from it, and you couldn't help but run from it. Then in my 30s I went back and rediscovered it all and I realized how cool and overplayed and underrated it all was. The aspect of Ronnie's irreverent sense of humor is more irreverent than anything in our record. The line "Oak tree, you're in my way" is the exact inspiration for us naming the band in our rock opera that; it was that exact sense of humor. After they were martyred and canonized and all of that from the plane crash, they all took on these larger-than-life personas and a lot of their fans after that kind of missed that aspect of it. Once you are killed in a tragedy, you become so much larger than life and the human aspect is forgotten. They were very much a human band. That was the beauty of it and that's the part that I connected with and made me become a fan as a grown man who was way older than the people who were buying their records pre-plane crash out there. I was apprehensive that they may have felt we were making fun of them or something and nothing could be farther from the truth, and there is not an ounce of that anywhere in our band and we wanted it to be truer to the ideal and vision was and at the same time if you listen to the record there is no misunderstanding that the love is in it.

Oh, I totally heard the love in it when I first listened, and sure, there is some dark humor in it but nobody was better at that than Ronnie. All that about Neil Young, and they were both good friends.

Oh, right, and I have always been a Neil Young fan because he always had this sense of humor in those dark songs of his and to be honest *Southern Man* is a funny song. I didn't agree with some aspects of it. In my memories of where I grew up nobody was being tied to a tree and whipped that I ever saw but the song was not written without humor. He has a great, twisted sense of humor.

(Laughs) He is another artist people either love or hate, but I just love his voice and his weird guitar style. He is just all over the place. I could pick up some of that influence in the Truckers.

Oh, in my guitar playing I am very influenced by him. Out of the four of us I have the most noticeable Neil Young and Rossington influence. I play the Rossington role in the three-guitar attack that we used for the rock opera. Not any one of us plays like the one we represented, but we did play those roles and what type of guitar player that you bring into the thing. I played the slower more melodic solos which were pretty comparable, and I am not a fraction as good of a guitar player as Gary Rossington in my wildest dreams, but that is what I was shooting for on those songs. Cooley played the psychotic lead guitar player, as Allen Collins was and I don't mean personally, but in the approach. Rob was extremely technical and extremely talented technically in every other way, and Steve Gaines was the one he related to. Ironically enough, Jason's favorite guitar player was Ed King in Skynyrd and he has always been the big Ed King fan and that's the one he related to and we did the reverse Skynyrd on our influences.

(Laughs) That's cool. You guys did a run over in Europe, and I was getting e-mail from people and heard from one guy who wrote that you stayed at his house over there and it just thrilled him. What was the experience like for you over there?

It's incredible over there and the people are so passionate about the music they love. They get into it in such a detailed way that the American artists just don't. It's like any other generalization there are certainly as many exceptions as there are rules. You may meet someone that speaks broken English and you wonder, how does he pick up on this stuff, but he can sit there and tell us these miniscule details of something we did or said in a song that nobody outside of the immediate family would know about. They study it and it is really amazing to go over and play for them. The American audiences either like it or not and it doesn't go very far beyond that except for a few diehards. But look at their press over there. There is not a mainstream magazine in American that can compete with *Mojo* or *Uncut*, the better European magazines. Their level of writing and commitment to it and the size of their pieces are unbelievable. I read a piece in *Uncut* where they did a 20-page spread on Neil Young's three records that get the least talked about by the American press. You never hear the other two records of that period talked about in American press and they did this huge story. That was my favorite Neil Young era and it was a big deal to me and I thoroughly enjoyed reading that piece. There are smaller publications like *GRITZ* and *No Depression* that are writing more detailed coverage and *Harp* is another one that is coming along. But you know *Rolling Stone* is not going to commit in the way of a long story to anything that is not fluffy and mainstream at this point in time.

Yeah, and that is what is so sad, because I have lots of the early *Rolling Stone* magazines and they used to do page after page on something—oh, you know, Delaney and Bonnie and other things that are so interesting to me...

Whereas now they have someone to edit and cut it down to manageable size. *No Depression* had this article called "Little Miss Corn Shucks," and to do something like that and a piece that long on something that has not been in print since 1962 is remarkable. It is pretty damn cool. There are no mainstream magazines going to take that kind of chance. I am a businessman and understand how that works because we have lost some money at times trying to follow our hearts around.

That's the thing with *GRITZ*..., I am hoping to make this a big thing, and so far I am doing this from the heart and I feel like someday it will pay off. I feel like there is a big-enough audience.

Have y'all done a feature on Slobberbone? They are amazing. There is another band from Denton, Texas, called Centromatic, and they are not Southern rock by any stretch of the imagination but they are Southerners. They are a fantastic band breaking some cool ground, and they have put out eight records independently and have another one coming out this fall and it is by far their best record yet. Keep an eye out for that band. They are worthy of talking about and talking to. •

Charlie Starr

2016

The interview you are about to read has been a long time comin'. I first saw Blackberry Smoke around the turn of the century at the old Handlebar club in Greenville, South Carolina. At that time, they had a relatively small but appreciative audience. The crowds today are still appreciative, probably more so, but small does not enter into the conversation. The band continues to "spread the Smoke" all over the world, and have performed with everyone from George Jones to ZZ Top, and headlining countless shows to sold out venues all over this great land of ours.

So, after seeing Charlie Starr do his thing for the first time back in 2000, I immediately made plans to interview him for my then magazine, GRITZ. *Of course, the stars never lined up, and I moved on to other bands.*

A few years back my friend Scott Greene started telling me about the band and how they were the greatest thing since Gov't Mule. I started inhaling the Smoke and quickly rekindled my early love for the band. By now, we had started KUDZOO Magazine *and the* KUDZOO Radio Hour. *So back in 2012 some friends helped to put me in touch with Charlie Starr, and I scheduled him as a guest on the radio show. Now, the only real mistake I made was about ten minutes into the show. I had Charlie on the line, and had all my questions ready. Suddenly, the phone lines lit up, and I started taking calls. Well, sir, that was all it took. The night was mostly a non-stop string of callers that wanted to speak to Charlie about how much they loved his music, or just loved him. It was our second-highest-rated show ever, the first being our interview with Billy Bob Thornton.*

Which brings us to the now. When I met Charlie backstage in Atlanta at their recent "homecoming" show, I finally had a chance to give him my contact info and tell him I really wanted to make him our cover boy. With some help from Eric and Trish Almy, the interview was on.

I enjoyed my conversation with the Starr-man more than any in recent history, and learned quite a lot about him as well as the rest of the band. So here it is, submitted for your approval…our exclusive conversation with the guitar-slinging rocker himself, Charlie Starr.

MBS: You guys seem to be on the road all the time. How many days a year are you actually gigging?

Charlie: Well, it varies but we have done up to 250. Usually it's somewhere between 200 and 250, but this year we're easing up a little. We've got a couple of big trips, one to Australia and then another run in Europe. So, I don't know, everybody's kind of like, let's take a breath, you know? The Holding All the Roses tour was pretty long. And it continues…we're doing some short runs here at the beginning of February and we're doing that Sirius XM Cruise with Steve Earle and Lucinda Williams and the Mavericks and—

Oh, the outlaw country thing?

Yeah. So, I think that this year we actually had a meeting for the first time in a long time, and we were like, "Let's take a…not a breather…but let's slow it down a little." And everybody was just kind of like, "Whew!" The last two years have been great but it's just been a large workload, you know.

I was going to ask you about playing… I know you played in Europe a good bit and y'all are getting ready to go back, right?

Yeah, we'll be going back again in June.

And you are going to Australia. Will that be your first time in Australia?

It will, yeah. We're going at the end of March to play the Byron Bay Blues Fest, which is a huge festival down there.

Yeah, and Byron Bay is the most beautiful place on the planet.

That's what I've heard.

I mean, I only know that because of the DVD that was sent to me years ago by my buddy Max who lives there. I'd love to visit there, but you know, it costs a little bit of money to go to the other side of the world. (Laughs) Maybe one day. Have you guys ever gone to Japan?

No, and we actually have talked about that—not only Japan, but South America, because we have a lot of fans in South America. You find that out thanks to the Internet. You get hit up on the Facebook page by a lot of people from different countries and they let you know, "Hey! You've got a fanbase here—come on!" You know, I was talking to an Australian journalist yesterday and they were like, "Why is it taking so long for you to get here?"

I'm like, "You know, that's not a real easy trip to make with a band and crew, so it's not like we've been putting it off. It's quite an undertaking." Plus, you don't want to go there and just play one show. That would not be worth it. So, you have to book a tour, you know. You don't just "drop by" Australia. (Laughs)

Very true. Well, a lot of us are all excited about these shows in the South coming up in the next couple of weeks. Of course, Asheville and then back to Atlanta for three nights. What's it like for y'all playing your hometown?

It's great and it's great that the shows have been successful, you know, the last several years. We've sold out most every Atlanta show we've played and it's just great. It can be stressful because everybody's family comes, you know. (Laughs) You saw it back there when we met. It was a zoo backstage.

Or right in front of the stage as well! I ended up towards the front of the stage in Atlanta, and I thought I was going to die. My buddy Scott had rather stand there than anywhere, but I guess I'm just too old for that now.

(Laughs) Man, I've never been one to do that. Never.

I just can't.

I had a girlfriend, years ago, when I was in my early twenties. This was the one and only time I've ever seen the Stones. It was the *Voodoo Lounge* tour. I think that was in, like, '93 or '94. She wanted to go down—well, she wanted to *sneak* down. We had pretty good seats anyway and I was like, "No! I want to sit right here and enjoy the show." I don't want to get down there where I can't move or, you know—I'm not one to go jump into the pit. I never have been. Maybe that's why I wanted to be onstage instead of in the pit.

Yeah, see, that's my preference. I'd much rather be the guy onstage, or even in the wings or backstage, rather than in the crowd. I can't take it anymore. I'm too old.

I'm liable to get a little claustrophobic, too. (Both laugh.)

So, were you born and raised in Atlanta?

No, I was born in Lynette, Alabama, which is just about 12 miles north of Auburn. Chambers County. It's 82 miles, or something like that, south of Atlanta. Down I-85.

Growing up, when I got into my teen years, I was playing in bars and VFWs and stuff like that around Lynette and you had to play covers, you know? And when I got out of high school I thought, "Well, I wanna go where you can form a band and write your own stuff." And Atlanta was the closest place. And I had a bunch of other friends who were taking off before I did, maybe a couple of years older. So that was like a dream. I thought, "Yeah, I'm gonna graduate from high school and get out of here. Move to Atlanta."

Well, yeah. I'm interested in guitar, too, because I play myself. At what age did you start playing guitar, and who would you say were your earliest musical influences—I mean, not just guitar, but overall?

Well, my first influence on guitar was my dad. He was a bluegrass guitar player. And he bought me my first little cheap guitar when I was six, because I think he got tired of me banging his around, you know? I've always wanted to play. As soon as I was big enough to grab one, I wanted to play it. He would play it for me all the time. He would sit and play and sing old traditional songs, you know? He was a very religious man, too, so he sang a lot of gospel, and he taught me a lot of those songs on the guitar. He was my first influence, you know. He taught me the "cowboy chords," the three chords—G, C, and D—that you need to play a song. The chords that you need to play a song successfully. And then I was always surrounded by that. My grandmother's brothers were in a gospel quartet called the Suwannee River Boys. They formed in 1939, I think.

I remember them. I used to be a gospel DJ. I remember hearing them.

Okay, yeah. That's Buford and Merle Abner, my great uncles. So, music was always around, you know. And, that's what we did—we gathered around the piano and played and sang, and then when I got to be a little older, like 11 or 12, my mother and father were divorced so I split time between my mom and dad. Here's my dad and my grandmother with gospel music and bluegrass traditional-type songs, you know. The standards that I was learning. And then my mom liked the Stones and the Beatles and Bob Dylan. It's funny, when I got a little older and I bought an electric guitar and I had friends, they didn't like bluegrass or country music; they liked Led

Zeppelin. So, I started, especially with the Stones—specifically with the Stones—with "Honky Tonk Women." I remember thinking, "Okay, I understand this now. I'm starting to see a correlation between what I've been taught—this traditional Southern music—and then what they were doing. 'Cause "Honky Tonk Women" really is a country song, you know?

It is. Yeah.

I mean, I get goosebumps just talking about it. All of a sudden it was like everything was illuminated, you know. I'm like, "Wait a minute. I'm starting to get that rock-and-roll music comes from this." And then, I didn't have really any friends to share that kind of information with—that is, anyone who would care. You know what I mean?

Yeah.

And thanks to the Stones and Bob Dylan, I started digging into the blues and got into Robert Johnson and Charlie Patton and Son House and Mississippi Fred McDowell and Mississippi John Hurt. Because they were such champions of that music.

True.

They carried the flag for Muddy Waters and Howlin' Wolf and Jimmy Reed and were proud to let the world know that these are the real heroes. But at the same time, I got into Led Zeppelin and Black Sabbath and Aerosmith. I wanted to rock, you know—I wanted to play loud! (Both laugh.) My entire musical life has been trying to balance all of that, I think.

I fully get it. Did you listen to any of the Southern-rock bands when you were growing up?

I did. I was just telling a friend the other day that I heard the Allman Brothers very early on. You know, before you got old enough to really care about buying your own records or cassettes, it was the radio. The radio is what I heard most, and whatever my mom was listening to. And so I got great doses of especially Skynyrd and the Allman Brothers on the radio, and that sort of gets into your fabric, you know, the fabric of your being, and it never goes away. Growing up in the South, you get it daily. And I remember obviously loving the radio hits, the Skynyrd radio hits, and I had a friend back when I was about 11 years old, and I actually bought my first electric guitar from him. But he had Lynyrd Skynyrd's *Second Helping*, the album.

Of course, I had heard "Sweet Home Alabama" and I had probably heard "Call Me the Breeze" and "Needle and the Spoon." I'm sure they were all being played on the radio at that time. But I remember the first time I heard the "Ballad of Curtis Loew," and there again, I was like, "Okay, this is the same stuff." It's the same. This is like traditional country music; it's very roots-y. It's coming from that same place, you know, that Bill Monroe was kind of coming from.

Really. Yep.

And it blew me away. I was like, "I gotta have this." So that started it. I think I might have gotten the Allman Brothers Band's *At Fillmore East* around the same time. I've still got that copy. But for a little while, I put that away. I was like, "I don't really…" You know, I've heard this, I've experienced this. I know "Gimme Three Steps" back to front. I don't need to… It's like, okay, now I really love Little Feat. You know, I'd go through these phases.

Yeah, I think we all do, really.

Yeah.

I am fortunate to have been dubbed the "Ambassador of Southern Rock," which is quite an honor, but by the same token, there's times I tell people, "If I never have to play 'Gimme Three Steps' again in a show, it'll be alright with me." It just gets to the point where, like you say, you've done it so much.

Yeah, well…

I've got a list of 50 songs I never want to sing or play again.

Yeah. Well, I got to a certain age where, you know, in the early years—when I was 11, 12, maybe up to 18—I grew tired of the music that you hear all the time. I remember back then thinking, "I don't care if I never hear a song off *Dark Side of the Moon* again—because it was played so much on rock radio. Then after a while when you get older, you start to hear with different ears.

Exactly.

I remember I was about 19, maybe, and I was playing in a cover band and we were going to learn "Workin' for MCA," and I'd never played that on the guitar before. I sat down with it and was like, "Wow! I'm hearing this again for the first time!" All the parts…

Right. Kind of complex.

Yeah, the way that Skynyrd put them together—just beautiful. Like the three guitar players all playing something pretty much completely different from one another and not stepping on the others' toes.

Yeah.

The bass and drums were perfectly put together. I think for a time, back at that point, I really could say I loved Skynyrd more than I did the Brothers. Because I felt like these songs are crafted in a way that the Brothers didn't do as much. They were more about the free-form, open kind of jam, you know. Their songs were looser and Skynyrd's were not. I mean, there's beauty in it all. I love 'em all for different reasons.

Yeah, and one thing you said 'while ago made me think, too, man. It's like, as we get to a certain age—I mean, I was a voracious reader growing up, especially of music biographies and music magazines and all that—but once you learn about the old blues players and also the old hillbilly and country players and how that all blended to make rock and roll, once you know that and you go back and you listen to Lynyrd Skynyrd or something like that, you can see the influence of the old blues men. You can see the influence of the old country artists, even way back before Hank Williams, all the old-time music people. That's what makes it exciting for me, Charlie. I don't know about you, but it does for me. Once you start learning and, like you said, hearing it with new ears. That's a great way of putting it, by the way. Connecting the dots excites me.

Well, I had a couple of good friends that were a lot older than me. When I was in my teens, they turned me on to a lot of music. I had a good friend in LaGrange, Georgia; he would make me mix tapes of stuff. I didn't have the Internet so I couldn't readily just go on a website and buy a Skynyrd bootleg. He was a guy that had all that stuff. Another guy named Wildman Steve down in Auburn, Alabama…

Oh, I know him. I love his Internet radio show.

Yep. I got stuff from him, too. And from those older guys, I would hear stuff like, "This is Skynyrd from Chattanooga in 1975. It's the best live show that ever got recorded." And my friend Billy would say stuff like, "You know that Skynyrd were really influenced by Free and Cream." Back then, I was like, "Oh, really? Okay." Well, I need to hear some Free and some Cream." Then I got that and I was like, "Oh, I get it! Okay, I hear that." So, I had some good teachers, you know. Those dudes know…they saw that I was the little nerdy kid that wanted to soak it all up, and they helped me.

That is awesome. Sharing their musical knowledge was cool. I wanted to ask you to tell me a little about each of your bandmates.

Oh, well, we've been together for fifteen years or so, and Paul (Jackson) is, uh, the other guitar player. I've known him the longest. We met just out of high school and he is just a sweetheart of a guy, you know. Just big-hearted, happy, big smiles. We all love what we do. I think he may love it the most. But he just…he's a happy guy.

Yeah. He has fun onstage, I can tell that.

He does. He just loves every minute of it. You don't see him in a bad mood often.

That's good.

Brandon (Still), the piano player, he's the newest member. Brandon's a real sweet guy, too. He's real happy just like Paul. He's a real student of music. He's a jazz guy. He loves it. I'm a bit of a jazz nerd, too. I kind of go in for the Toy Caldwell thing sometimes, that cornbread jazz thing. Brandon really knows a lot. Like, if I write a song and it has a weird chord in it, I can say, "What's this, Brandon?" And he'll tell me exactly.

Oh, wow!

Yeah. "That's an F-non-diminished…," you know, blah, blah, blah…

Yeah. (Laughing)

The Turner Brothers (Richard and Brit), they have always played music together, being brothers. They're the closest brothers I've ever seen. They never fight, which is weird. (Laughs) Sometimes I want 'em to. (Laughs) If you get in an argument with one of 'em, you're basically in an argument with both of 'em, which is just like, "That's not fair! Fight with one another and get it out of your system!" (Both laugh.) But anyway, no, I love 'em. They're a good bunch of traveling companions. That's necessary to be in a touring band; you gotta be able to get along. We all fight, of course, and we want to ring each other's necks sometimes, but you know, that happens with every band. It's like being married to four other dudes all the time.

Oh, yeah. Well...that paints a picture.

Yeah. It's not a pretty one. (Laughs)

(Laughing) I was just gonna say, one thing I've always loved about bands like yours is your obvious appreciation for the road crew. Because I think that—and I'm sure you agree—that you can be a great band but without a great road crew.

Yeah. True.

I wanted to see if you would say a little bit about your crew guys...?

They're great. They never complain. They're obviously the hardest-working bunch. They're first in, last to leave, and we've got dedicated guys. We've had, you know, people come and go. That happens in all bands. Right now we've got a really solid team and we appreciate all the work that they do, of course. We couldn't do it without 'em and we try and make 'em as happy as we can. It's all about trying to pay people fairly and treat 'em fairly and take care of 'em. Don't let 'em get treated like shit, you know. That's a very important part of the business. We don't have a large crew; we just have five crew guys including the driver. So, we all travel on one bus.

And they set up the equipment, run the sound, tear it down...that's a lot of work.

It is. They work hard.

I know you guys...most all of you have got families. How do you manage to balance being on the road so much with home life and do it successfully? I know for some of the bands that I've spoken with in the past, it didn't work out well. But you guys seem to have a pretty good grip on it.

Well, I think it's an important thing with wives to balance it all out. For my wife, I was doing this when I met her so that makes it a little easier to swallow. Being gone so long is still hard, you know, especially when your kids start coming along. I've got two sons. My youngest is two, but I'm lucky. I can only speak for myself, really, on this but I'm lucky to have a very supportive wife, and she loves the music—always has—and she never questions the amount of time that we're gone. She knows that it pays the bills, you know.

Yeah, it's a job.

Of course, we all get bummed out, you know. I'm not coming home for three weeks and that's hard, but it just causes you to make the most of the time that you have when you are at home.

Yeah, for sure. One thing I've noticed from the 7 billion Blackberry Smoke videos on YouTube is that you've managed to either sit in with or have sit in with your band some pretty great guys. I was watching one this morning with Billy Gibbons and you guys together. Without playing favorites or anything, who are some folks that you personally really enjoyed jamming with?

Well, Billy of course, and George Jones. You know, we recorded the song "Yesterday's Wine" with George and Jamey Johnson. And then, as if that wasn't good enough or cool enough, you know, enough of a dream come true… I was telling my wife the other day—Well, before I say that, we were passing through Nashville, we were on tour, and George was playing his last show—what turned out to be his last show at the Ryman. And our management and his management were friendly and they said, "Well, hey, do you want Charlie and Jamie Johnson to come and do 'Yesterday's Wine' at the show?" And they said, "Absolutely!" So, we were like, okay, let's swing through Nashville, so there we go. Well, Jamie couldn't make it. He had to go to Miami or something, I don't remember. So, I thought, "Well, okay, maybe next time." But they said, "No, go and do it. It'll be just the two of you." So, I got to do a duet with George Jones at the Ryman.

Oh, my goodness gracious.

And I told my wife, I was like, "I can't believe that!" I mean, I've got the memory, you know, seared into my brain but I still really can't believe it. That I stood up there next to that man and sang that song.

It is amazing.

Yeah, it's amazing, so definitely I would say my absolute favorite experience was singing with George Jones.

Oh, yeah. Be kind of hard to top.

I love playing, I love playing with Warren Haynes. I've gotten to play with him a few times now.

That's just great. Great guy, too.

Yeah. Rich and Chris Robinson, those guys, it's always great to sit in with them. Rickey Medlocke and Gary (Rossington). We've done jams together. We did Rickey's All Star Jam on the Skynyrd cruise the last few years and got to play with those guys. I got to play through Gary's amp. And just two years ago, or maybe three, Gary and Dale renewed their wedding vows on the cruise in front of everyone up on the deck. And I was asked to play guitar. Gary wanted to hear some slide guitar as they walked down the aisle. So, I played "Amazing Grace" on the guitar all by myself. I was so nervous, it was crazy! Because here they are, Dale's got on a wedding dress and Gary's got a tux on, and he walked up onstage and walked over—I was over in the corner—he walked over and gave me a great big kiss on the cheek. (Laughing) That's another huge one. I mean, if you had told me that I would have been given the opportunity to do something like that when I was a kid, I would have said you were crazy.

Wow! Yeah, I would have loved to have heard that version of the song, though.

Well, it was…

I'm sure it was amazing.

It was weird, too, because he said, "I want to hear some slide. Play some." I didn't tell him I had planned to do "Amazing Grace"—they just wanted to hear something sweet, you know. Then after the "I do's" I think Gary wanted to hear, like, some blues, like some Elmore James, so that's what I did, but I did it at the wrong time. Well, he turned around to me and said, "Do it!" (Both laughing) And the preacher wasn't ready yet, so it was funny. I think my whole band laughed out loud, and I was like, "I'm just doing what Gary Rossington asked me to do!"

Yeah, exactly. What else you gonna do?

Yeah. What was I going to do? Say no?

Well, that is cool, man…that is something I didn't know. I like that. You know *Holding All the Roses* was voted #1 Album of 2015 in *KUDZOO*.

I've really enjoyed that album a lot. Do you have any particularly favorite songs from that one that you still enjoy singing and playing?

I enjoy playing 'em all still. I really like "Rock and Roll Again." It's just a good-feelin' song. My son loves that one. He's two. That's the only one he likes, so… (Both laugh.) I feel like it must be a good one 'cause that's the only one he likes. That and the title track are my two favorites. "No Way Back to Eden."

Oh, yeah, that's good, too! I forgot about that.

Because it's probably the most laid-back song we've ever recorded, I would say. It's got that…it's kind of a groovy thing, you know.

Oh, yeah. Man, I like "Whippoorwill" a lot, too. That's a beautiful song.

Well, thank you.

Man, yeah, I guess I'm just a fan.

I don't know, I really can't pick a favorite.

Yeah. I can understand that.

Yeah, "Holding All the Roses" has got some power live, too, and I really enjoy that. I don't know. I'm wrapped up right now in my brain with new ones. We just finished the basic tracks on a new album.

That's my next question. Boy, you're psychic!

Yep.

I wanted to see what you can tell us about the new album. Are there any songs that you're already getting excited about that you've come up with?

All of 'em! (Both laugh.) There's a couple in particular, though, that I'm just over the moon about it, it's so good. We actually played one last night in Nashville at Music City Roots. It's a dirty little blues thing called "What Comes Naturally." I actually wrote that song a long time ago. It just kind of laid around. I never really did anything with it. I forgot about it, actually.

Yeah.

And then one day I was like, "Oh, yeah," and so we revved it back up. But there's one called "Free on the Wings" that I really like a lot. It's a Macon, Georgia-sounding kind of tune.

Ah, yeah. My kind of music.

It's kind of Capricorn-esqe. (Laughing) And then another one that I wrote with a good friend of mine, Travis Meadows. He and I have written several songs over the years and we wrote a new one called "The Good Life." For my part of the lyrics, I was singing about my dad. And I think he understood that so he probably was singing about his dad or his granddad, too, so…

Ah, yeah.

It's going to be a good one.

Is that a slower song? Kind of a ballad, or…

It is. It's a country song. I would say that it's a stone-cold country song.

(Laughs) Well, that's one good thing about Blackberry Smoke…you guys can tackle country or hard rock or whatever, blues, anything. That's my favorite kind of band.

There's a couple songs on it that are definitely, as of right now, the heaviest two songs we've ever recorded. You know I get…not complaints, but I get comments from fans sometimes that I think they don't quite get it.

Yeah.

Because they'll say, "I like it when y'all are heavy!" And I'm like, "Well, okay, that's cool. I like to be heavy, too. But there's a time and a place, you know. We're not a metal band." You know, there's a weird misnomer in my opinion about a lot of bands, that people call 'em "Southern-rock bands," but they're not! They're metal bands. I'm like, this is not…who am I to define Southern rock? I know what it means to me. That's all.

Yeah, there's really not a definition. I've been asked that a thousand times.

Yeah, right.

It's more like an attitude than anything.

Somebody, when *The Whippoorwill* album came out, I remember talking to a guy at a show and he was like, "This one ain't…it ain't heavy, you know." And I'm like, "Well, is *Second Helping* (Lynyrd Skynyrd) heavy?" No, it's not. I mean, you're going for whatever vibe you're going for on the record. So far, the records we've made, we've gotten what we've gone for. So, I see sometimes that what we're going for might not please everybody. You can't please everybody, you know. There will be some people that don't want to hear a hard-rock song from us. The people that really love "Ain't Got the Blues" or "The Whippoorwill," they want to hear that kind of thing. So, it's a weird thing. And now with social media you see it every day, you know. When we put a record out, I don't go online because I know the first people who say something are the negative people.

Yeah. That's true. That's bad. I hate that.

And it'll hurt your feelings, you know? It's a heartbreaking thing. We just poured our heart and soul into this and the last thing we want to hear… We're proud of it, you know, and the last thing you want to see is somebody go, "I hate it!"

Like you say, it's the first thing you hear because—I mean, I love social media. I use Facebook and Twitter and all that stuff, but there are so many people that I just picture cowering behind a computer at home just waiting for something to bitch about or say something negative about.

Totally.

I just don't get it. My mother—I've quoted this a million times—my mother taught me years ago, when I was a little boy, if you can't say something good, just don't say anything at all.

Exactly.

You know?

That's great advice, yeah. When *The Whippoorwill* came out, I don't even know if we had a Facebook then. Yeah, I guess we did, maybe, but we had a message board on our website that was pretty active. Before Facebook got so widespread. And I remember the week that it came out, it was the day after it came out, because we had signed to Zac Brown's Southern Ground label and there was a whole thread on there about, "Zac Brown has ruined Blackberry Smoke." I wanted to go on there and be like, "Zac was never even in the studio with us. He had nothing to do with it. He was the executive producer of the record."

Right. Exactly.

He hasn't *ruined* anything. We made the record we wanted to make. But those people at the same time turned around six months later and said, "I changed my mind. It's my favorite record that you've made!" (Buffalo laughs.) So I'm like, "Well, thank you! I mean, it sucks to have to see you go through this turmoil, but I appreciate it." (Laughing)

Yeah.

I had a man at a show not long ago come up, and he had a CD and asked me to sign it and I said, "Okay," and signed it. He said, "What's 'The Woman and the Moon' about?" and I said, "It's about being different." He said, "It's not about your mama?" I said, "No, it's not about anybody in particular. It's just about being different." And he goes, "I don't get it." And I said, "Well, I'm sorry!" (Laughs) Don't hurt yourself tryin' to! But, uh, you know, sorry, I guess.

There are a whole of things I don't "get," too. I don't get "In-A-Gadda-Da-Vida's" lyrics, but I still enjoy it. (Laughing) One thing I wanted to tell you… Back in about 2001, I got hired by this record company in England that was called Alice's Records/Z-Rox records to do a *Stars and Bars* CD. I picked the bands, wrote the biographies and everything, and you know, you guys were on it. Did you know about that?

No, I didn't.

Oh, wow, man, I'll have to dig one of those up and get it to you. They wanted me to pick what I felt like were the best "Southern-rock" bands in the world at the time—and that was in 2001, so that was, like, right when you were getting going. And we had Dru Lumbar—he had just regrouped Grinderswitch so they were on there, too—and the Southern Rock Allstars with the guys from Blackfoot and Molly Hatchet. It's a cool little compilation. That's the first time that I'd ever heard of y'all. About that time, y'all also played up at the Handlebar in Greenville and that was the first time I saw you play live. There wasn't a huge audience at all back then, but, you know, I liked it that way. I mean, I felt like, "Man, this is pretty intimate,

you know?" It was great. But I'm so glad that it's gotten so huge. I hope it keeps getting bigger and bigger.

I love it, man. I mean, it's been a lot of enjoyment to be a part of the growth, you know. To watch it. Just a little at a time. And when it happens that way, you feel like you earned it, you know?

Yeah. Definitely. You earned it. You guys didn't go on *America's Got Talent* or something, you know.

Right, and we didn't decide, "Hey, let's change what we do and try and have a commercial hit."

Yeah, I've got friends that I've kind of seen do that and it's like, I'm not faulting them, but…

No. People get frustrated and get tired of riding around in a van and they want to record a "pop-y" song to try and get played on the radio and people do that. But then there are other people who don't care about that. What they care about is feeling good about what they're doing and feeling like they're doing what they want to do or what they should do.

Sure. Yeah. Well, I want to ask you about guitars. I love guitars. But I don't think I love guitars nearly as much as you do.

I bet you don't. (Laughs)

Because every song, it seems like you're playing a different guitar, you know? I wanted to ask you what your favorite guitars in your arsenal are…? I know you play just about everything. I really like the acrylic one that you play sometimes. What is that? Is that a Dan Armstrong?

That's a Dan Armstrong. Yeah.

I always thought those were cool.

For sure. My favorite is this old 1956 Les Paul Junior. It belonged to Rick Richards from the Georgia Satellites for years. I've had it since '93 and I've played it on every record and just about every show. It's been in the shop a couple of times over the years for this and that. I'm always getting guitars so I love 'em all. I just got a '65 Gibson ES330. What happened was, when we were making *Holding All the Roses*, Brandon, he brought a bunch of his guitars down—he's got hundreds of guitars. He had a '64 330 and I played it on "Rock & Roll Again" and "Livin' in the Song," and I think I played the solo on "Holding All the Roses." Anyway, I played a bunch of stuff on the record on it, and I fell in love with it and he would not sell it to me. I mean, I fell in that much love with it! I was like, "I've got to have this. I can't leave here without it. I love it—it's become a part of me now." And he was like, "Ha, nice try. No way." (Both laugh.) So, I started looking and it took me a year to find a good one, because I was very specific with the details. Those guitars, they had some attributes, different attributes for different years. Unfortunately, I've got a good friend that can find just about any guitar I want. (Laughs) And he found me one and I said, "Alright." That's a never-ending thing. I read a post online that said, "My biggest fear when I die is that my wife will sell all the guitars for the prices I told her I paid for them." (Both laugh.)

That's hilarious!

Yeah.

Speaking of guitars, there's one guitar out there that me and you have both played. Can you believe that?

Duane Allman's Goldtop.

Yeah, exactly. Let me ask you, did you…I did—but did you feel any kind of a vibe on that thing at all?

I did. It felt like I was holding a ghost.

Yeah, that's the way I felt.

I kinda got goosebumps and I almost felt, for a second, I was like, "I shouldn't be playing this thing. It's a little bit too holy, you know." But I took a chance. Well, by then, though, it had been played by about 90 people.

I remember back in 2009, it was the 40-year anniversary of the Allman Brothers, and thanks to that Moogus thing that Butch Trucks had, I was watching every show of the Beacon run at night through my computer over the Bose speakers like I was at the concert. They had the Goldtop out there and everybody from Clapton to John Hammond played it—Susan Tedeschi of course, Derek and everybody, and on down the line. Los Lobos—*everybody*—and I was like, "Yeah, man, I'd love to play that thing." Well, then I met Richard down at the Big House and he just pulls this thing out and goes, "Here, play it." Thank you! I was scared.

Oh, yeah.

I was holding it like I was holding an egg, you know?

Right. Well, the first time I played it, it actually came with Richard Brent. We were opening for Zac Brown in Atlanta at the Verizon Amphitheatre and Zac played it. And that was the first night I held it. The man said, "How does it feel to hold a million-dollar guitar?" And I said, "It feels like I oughta put it down!" (Both laughing)

Yeah, that's right. Before I do something with it…make a mistake.

Exactly.

January has been a really sad month for rock and roll. I had a friend…I don't know if you ever heard of Swampdawamp…? But my buddy, Gig Michaels, their lead singer died; and then we lost Lemmy; then David Bowie; then Glenn Frey. Were you friends with or a fan of any of those folks?

All of 'em. A fan, that is. And I met Gig several times on those cruises.

He was a great guy.

My mom actually told me about that because I'm not on Facebook. She said, "Hey, Gig Michaels died," and told me it was pneumonia. Big surprise, too.

It was terrible.

Yeah. I had a friend years ago named Joe; I played in bands with him for a long time and he got—this is about eight years ago—another one of our good friends called me and said, "Joe died yesterday." And I had to sit down. I was like, "What?" And he said, "Yeah, he got swine flu and didn't know it." He got sick and, like most of us, wouldn't go to the doctor. He just kept taking medicine like, "I'll be alright. I've just got the flu." And it killed him. By the time he did go to the hospital, the doctor said, "There's nothing we can do. Your kidneys are shutting down."

Wow, wow…

It's crazy.

Hey, did you guys ever play a David Bowie song?

I used to do "Suffragette City" and "Ziggy Stardust." Back in the days of playing four sets a night, you know.

Of course, you'd play everything then. I remember those days, too. Oh, yeah. I used to do "Rebel Rebel" and "Space Oddity"—of course, everybody did that one.

For sure.

And I'm sure you played a lot of Glenn Frey's songs.

Yeah, the Eagles. Every night. I don't know why a lot of people, like in *The Big Lebowski* movie, people were giving the Eagles a hard time. I love the Eagles.

Yeah, me, too.

There ain't a damn thing wrong with that music. It was pretty much perfect.

Yeah, man. You know the first albums were my favorites, like *Desperado* and all those, when Bernie Leadon was still in there.

Yeah.

I mean, I like 'em all, but the country-ish stuff in the early days, it was really more country back then, I think.

Bernie had played with Gram Parsons in the Flying Burrito Brothers and that's kind of what they were going for, you know—maybe a little slicker version of the Burrito Brothers.

Well, that's about it, man. I appreciate you taking the time for this interview.

Any time, my friend. Take care. •

Les Dudek

2001

Les Dudek is a much sought-after session guitarist due to his talent and versatility of style. Dudek has performed with and written songs for such artists as Stevie Nicks, Steve Miller, Dave Mason, Cher, Boz Scaggs, Maria Muldaur, and the Allman Brothers Band. He co-wrote "Sister Honey," which appeared on Stevie Nicks' Rock a Little *album, and "Blue Eyes" on Steve Miller's* Wide River *album. Les released four critically acclaimed solo albums with CBS Records (1976–1981), collaborated on the* DFK *album with other CBS artists, and appeared on Cher's* Black Rose *album, writing several songs and playing guitar. He also appeared alongside Cher in the movie* Mask.

We spoke to Les by phone back in 2001 from his Florida home.

MBS: I know you reside in Florida now. Where did you come from originally?

Les: From Rhode Island, originally.

Did you come from a musical family?

No, not really.

When did you begin playing the guitar?

I started playing when I was about ten or eleven, and was playing bars by the time I was fourteen. But back in those days, man, it wasn't anything special. It was all about having to sneak me in and out, and hide me in the kitchen during the breaks.

Who were some of your early musical influences?

I had a bunch of them. Obviously the Beatles. But see, my sister was six years older than me, so I always caught up on the trends way ahead of time. When Elvis came in, I was right there for that. In a house where your bedrooms are adjacent and she's always blasting the latest and greatest, you're bound to pick up on it as a kid. I dug Elvis, the Beatles, the Beach Boys—all the stuff that she came up with. And then she just got too mushy for me. She got into Connie Francis and all that stuff. I kind of leaned toward the Beatles. Then I started getting into the blues. I pretty much dug Freddie and

Albert and B.B.—all of the Kings. I got into Mike Bloomfield for a while, that super-session stuff. Early Blood, Sweat & Tears was good; that was kind of a departure from things. I was into Paul Butterfield, Steve Miller, which is ironic, because I ended up playing with Steve Miller.

How did you hook up with the Allman Brothers Band?

I had a band in Florida called Power at the time, and we were doing a lot of shows trying to get a deal in those days. The keyboard player knew Dickey Betts real well, because he had grown up in Venice, Florida, and Dickey was from Sarasota. When Duane died, we heard that Dickey was going to start a band separate from the Allman Brothers. He was auditioning players, and Peter found out about it and said, "Why don't we go up there and see what's going on?" So we went up and hung out with Dickey for a weekend, jammed with him on the back porch there in Macon. We said our goodbyes and went on home and then I got the callback. So, I went back to Macon and was working out with Dickey, and then Gregg caught wind of the fact that Dickey was doing his own band and kind of threw a hissy on that, so Dickey kind of backed out of it. That band with Dickey did some demos for Phil Walden, and we were supposed to be getting something happening but it never came about.

So, they started on the *Brothers and Sisters* album, and I was down there one night when they were cutting "Ramblin' Man," and Dickey would come over and say, "What do you think about this?" And I'd throw a couple of ideas at him. Then he'd go back out and do it again and come back and say, "What about this?" (Laughs) He was talking about the guitar parts. Finally, he said, "To hell with it, why don't you just come out here and play with me?" That's how we ended up doing "Ramblin' Man."

And you played on "Jessica," too.

I co-wrote that one. I never got any credit for it. Dickey says he still feels bad about that. Maybe one of these days he'll write me a check. (Laughs) And put my name alongside his. He was really stumped on that one. We were at his house there in Macon. At the time I was rooming with Joe Dan Petty, who just died recently. He had wanted me to be in Grinderswitch with him. He was starting a band, and that's when I turned him on to Larry Howard and Rick Burnett, cats that were playing with me down in Florida at the time. One night I was over at Dickey's, when they were still doing the *Brothers and Sisters* album. Dickey had the one part of "Jessica" written, the melody on the verse section. He said, "Play this, man. Let's see if we can do something with it." We kicked it around for 45 minutes or so, and my girlfriend and his wife were in there cooking us steaks, so he got frustrated with it and put his guitar down. I kept messing with it and I came up with the bridge. I said, "Dickey, come here a minute, man." (Laughs) I said, "Play this after you play that." He said, "What do we do next?" I said, "Walk it all the way up to the top and stop." He said, "Well what do you do after that?" I said, "Start over!" (Laughs) He was just ecstatic. We ended up not even eating our steaks. We threw the guitars in the back of the pickup; he wanted to go and play it for everybody. Right when we did it, it started snowing in Macon. It was kind of a spiritual moment. How it all came to be. He marched me into Walden's office, and he promised me some points on it and this and that. It took us six nights to cut the thing in the studio. At that time, Phil Walden was trying to get me into the Allman Brothers. He said, "Stick with me. I'm going to make you a star. I'm going to put you in the Allman Brothers." I had already had talks with Dickey, and he kind of felt that he pretty much wanted to take over with the guitar slot. I think for a number of years he was kind of the second guitar player, under Duane. Not taking anything away from Dickey. He was kind of shafted, because if you look back on the early stuff, Dickey wrote it, like "Elizabeth Reed" and a lot of the good tunes, and he played it, too. It's like the quarterback always gets the limelight. But Dickey was always a real contributor to that band, I thought.

Right after *Brothers and Sisters* came out, Bobby Womack was trying to get me to go on the road with him, and Boz Scaggs came into town. Boz had a guitar player that kind of wigged out on him on the road, so he called up David Brown and Phil Walden down in Macon, and they told him about me. It was kind of funny, because the drummer that was gonna be in the band with Dickey and I was going to go with Womack also. We had a cab waiting downstairs and we were gonna fly to L.A. to play with Womack, when I got a call from Phil, who said I should call Boz. He was in Akron, Ohio. It just sounded better to go with Boz. I went downstairs and pulled my bags out of the cab and said, "I gotta get another cab. I'm going to Akron, Ohio!" (Laughs)

How long were you with Boz?

Shoot, I was with Boz for about five years. I did the *Silk Degrees* album with him.

Around that time, didn't you move out to California?

Yeah. When Marshall Tucker came to town, around that time I was working with Boz. Toy Caldwell pulled me over to the side and he wanted me to be in Marshall Tucker. We'd been working for about a year and a half, and towards the end of '74 we did this long tour with Steve Miller and the James Cotton band. This was just after "The Joker," so Steve Miller was huge. And I was popular because of the "Ramblin' Man" thing. At the end of each night, Miller would bring me and Boz and James Cotton out. Finally, at the end of the tour, Miller just invited me to come up to Seattle with them and cut some tracks. He ended up doing one of my tunes, "Sacrifice," on the *Book of Dreams* album. We also cut some of the stuff that was on *Fly Like an Eagle* while we were up there.

Did you tour with Steve Miller, or just record?

Well, we did that four-month tour with Boz and Steve, and for all intents and purposes, I was playing with both of them. After we did the tracks in Seattle, Miller said, "What are you doing now?" I said, "I don't know. I'm going back to Macon. I don't see any future playing with the Allman Brothers, so I don't know." He said, "Well, why don't you come out and play with me?" He got a lawyer for me, because I was signed to Phil Walden, lock, stock, and barrel. So, he got me out of the contract and I flew out to hang out with Miller for a while. We were getting ready to go out and do an acoustic tour, just me and Steve. We were talking about it one morning when Boz called, and he said, "Look, man, I really need you to come out and play this tour with me." He had about three weeks of dates left to do, and he didn't want to break in a new guitar player. I told Miller about it, and he said, "Why don't you do it? I want to take some time off and get ready for the next record." Then I got signed to Columbia Records and did four solo albums, and one band album, *DFK*.

And you recorded with Cher on *Black Rose*.

Yeah. I did a lot of writing on that. I wrote a duet for us that we performed on *The Midnight Special*. We hosted it, Cher and Black Rose.

Tell us a little about Cher.

She has a great work ethic. She's real dedicated to what she does. When I was with her, on a professional level, I went in there to help her do her album. I had heard about it. I was in the Rainbow on Sunset in L.A., and one of my player buddies said, "Hey, did you hear Cher's auditioning some players for a new project?" I went down there and ended up running into Mike Finnigan and Steve Stills. They had come down for the audition, too. (Laughs) We got in there playing and turned it into a big jam session, and Cher stopped it. She said, "Hey! I didn't invite all you people down here for a jam session. This is for my project, dammit!" (Laughs) She invited us all to dinner afterwards at Nick's Fish Market on Sunset Boulevard. After dinner she came up to me and asked, "Are you serious about trying to help me do some stuff with my music?" I wasn't doing anything at the time. I'd just come off of a big tour with DFK and Kansas. I was in between things. I said, "Hell, yeah, I'll help you do it."

She came over to my house, and we were kicking around some tunes. She had one guy producing one thing and another guy producing another. I told her, I said, "Look, man. Let's get one producer for this thing." She said, "Well, I don't really know anybody right now that I'm happy with." I said, "Look, I just did an album with this guy James Newton Howard. He played keyboards with Elton John and has written endless scores for movies." So, we ended up bringing him in. We did the album and went out and did *The Merv Griffin Show*, *The Midnight Special*, *Tom Snyder's Tomorrow* show... We did a little stretch of dates with Hall & Oates, played Central Park, stuff like that. And Neil Bogart, who was president of that label, Casablanca—he had Donna Summer, KISS, and Cher-—he was a sweetheart of a guy, but he had a heart attack and died. So that put that one on hold. It all kind of folded up. Cher was really intent on becoming a rock-and-roll singer again. She was really keeping her name in the background and promoting Black Rose. It could have worked, but it fizzled because the record company fizzled. So, she got real depressed for a while there, trying to decide what to do. And I said, "Your natural progression is staring you right in the face." She said, "What's that?" I said, "You should be a movie star. You've already done the music thing and you can always fall back on that. You've had your two TV shows, one with Sonny and one by yourself." I said, "Go for an Oscar. Go for the gold." So, we got on a plane and flew to New York and met with Robert Altman, who was doing a play in New York called *Come Back to the Five and Dime, Jimmy Dean, Jimmy Dean*. She let him know that she really wanted to get into acting, so she did the play. In the interim she was also doing some of the big Caesar's Palace type of shows.

Was *Mask* done around that time?

No, that was actually after we split up. She did *Come Back to the Five and Dime*, and then she did *Silkwood.* Right after *Silkwood* is when she and I took a split. I started getting back into my thing, and then one day out of the blue I get a call and it was Cher, telling me I should come out to read for a part in this movie called *Mask.* She told me to come over and let her tell me about it. So, I went over. She said, "You are perfect for this script. They need a long-haired guy who plays guitar and rides a Harley." We'd been riding Harleys for a year. We'd been method-acting for a year, man. (Laughs) She said, "Don't think that you already have the part. If you get it, you get it on your own." She gave me the script and I got so inspired that I wrote a song. I demoed it, so when I went down, all I was riding at the time was my Harley, so I went in wearing full leathers to meet Peter Bogdonavich. Peter just sort of had a conversation with me, and said, "Do you see yourself in this movie?" I wanted Sam Elliott's part. (Laughs) But they cast me as Bone, one of her boyfriends. Then I pulled out a cassette and handed it to Peter and said, "Here's a theme song for your movie." The next day I got a call from Peter and he was flipping out over the demo. He wanted to use that song. We actually shot a scene with me playing that song on my dobro, with Cher sitting next to me on a park bench. But they cut that scene from the movie. It was such a cool scene. It pissed off Peter because they took it out, too. Universal cut a lot of the budget and they started cutting up the movie. I was supposed to have budget to go back in the studio and cut the theme song with Cher singing for the beginning credits and in the middle of the movie and in full production at the end. Bogdonavich ended up suing them for $11 million dollars. I don't know what ever became of that. But Peter called me up, because I had Cher come over and sing it on my 4-track. It was just a sketch of the song. It was never meant to be used. She's singing out of tune in places. But he kept calling me, wanting to use that. He wanted to do a director's cut of the movie. I was like, "Peter, give me some money and I'll cut it, but there's no way I'm releasing this demo. She'd kill me!" But I'm going to end up putting this song on my next album.

Are you doing the album now?

Yeah. I had some things already in the can that I wanted to put out. I have two tracks that Jeff Poccaro from Toto played on. Those tracks are smoking! And I have this track called "Boomerang" that will fry your head. And I have a song on there that I co-wrote with Stevie Nicks that Mick

Fleetwood was about to beat me up for because he wanted it for Fleetwood Mac. I tried to get Stevie to do it when I went on the road with her. The song was called "Free Style," and I may even call my album *Free Style.*

What's Stevie like?

Oh, she's a sweetheart. I did the "Whole Lot of Trouble" Tour with her. And that's what it was, man, a whole lot of trouble. (Laughs) Not because of us, but because it seemed like the devil was throwing his pitchfork at us every way we turned. We were in the rehearsals before the tour, and I got in a motorcycle crash on Sunset. The road manager got in a bike crash on the same night. I broke my right arm and wrist, and ended up putting it in a Velcro cast, and I did the whole tour playing with my fingers! I was supposed to be the hot-rod guitar player on that tour, but the roles got switched.

Looking through some of the other stuff that you've done, I see where you played on Bobby Whitlock's *Rock Your Socks Off* album. Did you work with Bobby, or was it just that session?

For some reason I went in to Capricorn to talk to Phil, and I went down to the studios and Whitlock was in there cutting his album. When he found out I was there, he kidnapped me. He handcuffed me and said, "You are gonna cut some stuff on my record with me." (Laughs) I didn't really know him until I got there, but we had a lot of mutual friends. We had some fun doing it.

Let's hit the Internet rumor mill. Do you think you might be doing any work with Dickey Betts anytime soon?

The door is always open. We have been golfing buddies. We do need to do some things together. Last time we did it, we got two hits! (Laughs) •

Joseph "Red Dog" Campbell

2001

He's the most famous "roadie" on the planet, no matter how you slice the pie. Joseph "Red Dog" Campbell, the hardworking, hard-tripping, hard-loving road-crew legend, was there during the glory days of Duane Allman and Berry Oakley, and remained with the band into the 21st century, setting up the drums for Butch, Jaimoe, and Marc's percussion.

Red Dog had long been known for his tales, his road stories shared between brothers and the few select and special friends. In 2001, Red Dog had collected the best of those "tails" into a book called A Book of Tails. *The Legendary Red Dog really was a legend.*

Cameron Crowe, longtime writer for Rolling Stone *and the producer of* Almost Famous, *a movie that drew heavily upon the real-life adventures of the Allman Brothers Band, actually wrote Red Dog into his movie by name. What a tribute to the "world's most famous roadie"! The following is an endorsement Crowe sent to Red Dog for his book, further proof that the Dog has been a legend since time began:*

> I'll admit it right now. I am a big fan of Red Dog, and have been even before he allowed me to interview him back in 1973 for a story in *Rolling Stone*. Hell, he was already legendary back then. But now I just have to say that I am extremely jealous of the Great Dog, because I've just finished reading *A Book of Tails*. True rock, the kind that lasts forever, is about honesty and humor and love and chasing the elusive buzz of greatness.
>
> Red Dog's book captured all this and more. You can't put this thing down, and best of all, it makes you want to listen to music. Not just the Brothers, but all music. Red Dog really caught something with his writing. This book, and a copy of *At Fillmore East*, belong in the time capsule reading—"Kick back and see what you missed." Two centuries from now I doubt anybody will have said it better. As you can tell, I'm still a fan.
>
> Love you, Dog.
> Best, Cameron Crowe
> Vinyl Films, Los Angeles, CA

I spoke with Red Dog via the landline from his home. He was deeply involved in rigging a "squirrel trap" at the time. He had suspended a peanut from a string that hung from the branch of a tree. When the squirrel would move toward the peanut, Campbell's German shepherd would dive for the squirrel. "Evening up the odds," he called it. All in a day's work for the mighty Red Dog. I was extremely grateful to be granted an interview with "the Crimson one," and for his personal insight into the legendary Allman Brothers Band.

MBS: The book is really good. I had a ball reading it. What I like is that you wrote it in much the same way that you talk. It's not over anybody's head. What inspired you to write this book?

Red Dog: I have always wanted to. Duane probably put it in my head when he said I'd be the one to write the book if there ever was one. We were standing in the yellow house one day and Duane walked by me and said, "You'll be the one to write the book, right?" But my gosh, that was thirty years ago. I used to have a real good memory. Duane used to come over and say, "Red Dog, can you tell me the gigs we've played in order?" And I'd tell him. Finally one day he asked me and I said, "No, I can't do that no more," because there were just too many then. But I think that's why he said I'd be the one to write the book.

Do you have one particular band member you work for, or do you just do it all?

Well, in the early days you did it all. Matter of fact, when I started, nobody actually took care of drums. In those days they didn't really have a drum roadie, or technician—whatever they want to call 'em these days. Everybody has got to have a title. That's why in the book it says "roadie" by my name. I was a roadie thirty years ago and I'm a roadie today. It hasn't changed none. In the old days, we used to have to do it all, drive and everything. I'd set up the drums, and if Kim still needed some help with the amp line, I'd just jump over and start setting up the amp line with him. Or I'd help Callahan with the P.A., you know. And vice-versa. If one of them finished before I did, they'd jump right in and help me. In those days, you didn't have to say, "Hey, can you help me?" There was somebody right there. But nowadays everything is what I guess they call specialization. Everybody has their job. I just take care of the two drummers and the percussionist.

(Laughs) Well, it's three-fourths of the truck. We only have a couple of guitar amps and three or four cabinets, and about four bass cabinets. That ain't too much stuff. We have two guys to do all the guitars and one guy to do all the drums. But I still jump in…like if Gregg needs something, I jump in and help. But everybody does their job pretty good. It works.

When you're not on the road, what do you do for fun?

I play golf. I used to play a lot of softball and baseball. I tore my knee up playing basketball about eight years ago. So softball and all that's out of the picture now. I've had a couple of operations on that. And I have a slipped disc in my back, and I've had a couple of operations on that, so my activities are limited to golf now. I'm pretty athletic, though. I like to play a lot of sports when I'm home. Also, I'm in an organization called the I.A. It's a stagehand union all over the country, Broadway and everything. I've been in that over twenty years. Before I got hurt, that's what I'd do when I was at home—work and play ball. Now, I just play golf. Now I can't do my union job because I'm not supposed to lift anything over twenty pounds.

After reading your book, I came to feel that in the beginning you guys in the road crew were pretty much treated as equals by the band. Y'all were like brothers. Do you feel like it's still that way today?

Nah. No, no. It's changed. It's a business thing now. Like the new bands coming out today. Everything is so business-oriented. In the '70s you had freestyle music. You had great music. The visual thing was not the important thing. The important thing was the music. The hippies just stood up there and played. Nowadays everything is just so business-oriented. You audition for the gig, and Disney puts out a band like In Sync or Backstreet Boys, one of them groups. You don't have that camaraderie. Everybody is expendable these days. Let's say the bond is there—it's still business. In my case—with Gregg, Butch, Dickey, and Jaimoe, right?—there's a bond there that has been established over 33 years. So, you can't just push that aside. But yet, it's still business-oriented. You can't just forget it and say, "Let's get rid of him." Like the thing with Dickey.

I was going to ask you about that. What really happened there?

Well, I'll put it this way, in a nutshell… It's just 33 years of being together, right? And things going down. And finally it all just comes to the surface. You couldn't say this happened or that happened. You know what I mean? It's 33 years. And like back in the early '70s, Gregg's thing with Scooter wasn't the most popular thing in the world either. It's just a marriage, man, and somebody's just pissed off. Go live with your mama for a while, bitch—I ain't even talkin' to you. In a nutshell, that's it. I mean, a bad marriage doesn't happen overnight. You started gettin' up wrong six months ago.

So, you are still in touch with Dickey?
Oh, God, yeah. I play golf with him all the time.

I am a real fan of Dickey's. I love the guy.
Oh, yeah. Me, too. Let me tell you, all of this shatters my heart.

What would you say is one of the most memorable shows you ever did?
Oh, man. There were a whole bunch of gigs that were just great. Of course, the Fillmore gigs were unreal. Watkins Glenn was unreal. But the gigs in Piedmont Park that were free—any free gigs—were just a ball. I mean, anytime you set up in the park and play for nothing, that's a gas, man. Now you have to buy $200 million worth of insurance to do that, so you're not playing a free gig anymore. We had some good gigs with Charlie Daniels, too. I could probably write another book just on gigs alone.

I enjoyed the part of the book where you were letting fans sneak in the back door at the gigs. Do you have a real camaraderie with the fans?
Oh, I love the people. If the people don't come, you ain't got nothin.' I feel like this: If I go to a baseball game, I want to get my money's worth. I'm paying enough money for the ticket, so everything ought to be for the audience. But I also like the old days when we used to do free gigs. I used to love that. There was nothing like playing in the park. You were giving something back. It wasn't like giving to a charity so some guy can ride around in a freaking limousine, ya know? You're actually giving something back to the people. But those days are gone, too, I'm afraid.

We all loved Duane Allman. You knew him as well as anybody. Could you give us your take on your friend Duane?
He was my hero. I mean, I would have followed Duane to the end of the earth. I was older than him, but I respected him enough and loved him enough to do it. Duane had a sixth sense—or a seventh sense, man. He just knew what to do at the right time. There's a fork in the road, right? If you go to the left, there's a pot of gold. If you go to the right, you're in a pile of

crap. Duane could walk right up to the fork without thinking and say, "Let's go to the left." And he'd come out smelling like a rose. But he was fair. He was honest. He was upfront and didn't beat around the bush. You didn't have to hear, (drags voice) "Well, you know…I was thinkin'… It ain't really nice for me to say it, but…" You didn't have to hear it. He'd just say, "Red Dog, you messed up bad, man. We're gonna have to let you go." There wouldn't be no beatin' around the bush. I try to live like that myself. I just don't have the tactfulness or the position in life to deal the other way. So, I just hit it—bam-bam-bam! (Laughs) I don't really think you can put it into words, on Duane. He used to say, "You guys do all the work. We just come over and have fun." That's really what it's all about. If these musicians say, "I'm out here working my butt off, something's wrong." I mean, if he ain't out there playing and having fun, something's wrong. It's at the stage of the game now where it's not work. It's, "Hey, let's enjoy ourselves and play." The roadie's the guy who's doing the work to get the thing going.

Tell me a little about the Fillmore auditorium and Bill Graham.

The Fillmore East was unreal, man. Bill Graham had that thing, man. It was the place to play. You'd go in there and set your stuff up on dollies. Nowadays we leave a lot of things in the case trays and all like that. But at the Fillmore they had these dollies. And after you played there one time, they knew what your gear looked like. When you'd come back, them dollies were even better, to go with your gear. They put everything on them 4-wheeled dollies, and rather than having to carry everything out onstage, they just rolled it out there. So, when it came time to change the stage, it was bang-bang-bang—and out of there! Next band! The Fillmore just sounded good, too. Look at that Fillmore East album. That's one of the best live ones ever laid down.

It's always been in my top two albums ever. That and Derek & The Dominos' *Layla* record.

It's amazing to me the Allman Brothers don't get any more recognition than they get. They always come up with some band who had a hit single 30 years ago. You would think that the band that had the best live album to this day would get more airplay, but they just don't for some reason. They play it a little on the classic-rock stations, but you don't ever hear 'em on the tube unless we do something wrong.

MTV covered it when Dickey was fired.

That's what they love, man. It just broke my heart, though. Not to take anything away from Warren. Warren is good, too. But I still say you could take Gregg and Butchie, Jaimoe and Dickey, and have a show. Just the four of them would give you one kickass show. You could sit up there and trip for three or four hours. Them guys are masters.

What did you think of the band during the days of Woody and Haynes?

I liked it. I mean, the difference between Allen and Oteil is, Allen would stay in the pocket more, and his flair-outs had a little more drive to 'em. Allen was more of a driving bass player. Oteil is more of a finesse bass player, and when he comes out of the pocket, sometimes he loses the feel. The tune is pumping—book, boom, book—like a train coming at you. And Oteil will come out of the pocket and play these jazz licks. You lose the pop of the thing. It changes. But he comes right back and it goes again.

Were you close to Allen Woody?

Oh, yeah. You pretty much accept everyone when they come into the band. It's a brotherhood. Unfortunately, the business thing doesn't allow that to go too deep. But there is an acknowledgement of, "Hey, man, we were brothers of the road for a while here." Yeah, I respected Allen a lot. I loved him, man, loved him. It broke my heart that he had to pass away.

Which brings us to Joe Dan Petty.

Oh, man. That's a tough one. Me and Joe Dan were truly the odd couple. It was like people used to say, "They're just like a married couple…leave 'em alone." Joe Dan would want the room cold, I'd want the room hot. He'd want to watch Discovery and I'd want to watch the news. We had all of those things like that, back and forth, but yet we had a big bond between us. We were roommates for 28 years so obviously we had something there. He was just a great person, though. Joe Dan was a little more subdued than I am. He was a little more slow, I'm a little more hyper. We were just a great match. One kept the other in check. Probably more so Joe Dan keeping *me* in check. (Laughs)

It was very cool to see you portrayed by name in Cameron Crowe's movie *Almost Famous*. How did you feel about that?

It felt great! Duane used to say when he'd go out onstage and hear the applause, it was music to his ears. That was music to my ears. Me and Dickey kind of took Cameron under our wing back when he first came out to write about us. I can remember Cameron wanting to go over and talk to Gregg or Dickey—they'd be talking to somebody else—and he'd be wanting to interview them. I'd tell him to wait until the time was right. Then I'd say, "Get on over there. Go on now!" I'd help him pick his spots where he could zip in there and get his interviews, where he'd actually get something. Instead of going over there and something else is on their mind and they just give you little nibbles. My man just paid me back. He threw me a bone. When he called me and told me he was putting me in it, he said, "We're gonna get you in the Rock and Roll Hall of Fame." Man, he blew me away with what he said about my book. I knew I had done something when he said what he did. And I know he wouldn't just blow smoke. I knew I had done something good.

I read in the book that you knew Janis Joplin. What was she like?

I thought that she was a sweetheart. She was like Duane. She was upfront. When you talked to her, you didn't get any bull—you got straight conversation. She was into the people. She was into doing free concerts. She was just a rowdy ol' mama that sang the blues and loved it, and lived it. And the trouble is, she wouldn't make it today. They have disoriented the kids, pumping all that bass and everything. And rap. That ain't singing.

Was Duane the unspoken bandleader of the Allmans?

Without a doubt, he was the leader. What he said went. Everybody respected Duane. If Duane said, "We're leavin' here right now," we were leavin'. That's what made the band so good was that everybody respected his opinion. But Oak was the underlying force. Berry Oakley. Oak did most of the talking. At meetings and stuff Oak did the rapping. When we'd go into a meeting, Berry would bring up the questions. Like I said in the book, one time Phil said to Duane, "Do I have to meet with the roadies?" Duane told him, "This is the band." And in the book I was talking about the gold-record deal, where Dixie said she wanted it and Duane told her, "You didn't earn it." A guy tells you something like that right in front of his old lady, that's something. These days that doesn't happen anymore. Sometimes you wonder if people appreciate what you do. It's all business now. You can be replaced tomorrow. The road crew changes constantly. I'm the only original crewman left.

Back to your book for a minute… The book is as much a must for an Allman fan as the Fillmore East album, I think.

The book and the music go hand in hand. You can almost tell by the drug what the time period was. The first album was a lot of psychedelics. Second album was speed and downers. Of course there was always pot involved. And the Fillmore East, of course, was just pure heroin. On the nod. Here the best, high-energy album recorded is on heroin. That's pretty wild. But of course, when you do heroin, you get kind of pumped up for the first couple of hours before it settles in on you. That is when you're first starting to do it. After a few years that changes. This was during our early heroin use. We weren't really bad junkies at that time. We were just users.

How long were you into heroin?

I gave it up about '73. I'm braindead on that. Sometimes I can remember, sometimes I can't.

When they write the definitive book of Southern rock and roll, how would you like to be remembered?

By my book. (Laughs) Duane had a saying that he wanted to just leave a mark that he had been here. Hopefully with my book I have put a scratch on that tree of life.

Our friend Red Dog passed away on February 21, 2011.

Arthur "Moon" Mullins

1999

Spartanburg, South Carolina's Arthur "Moon" Mullins was almost as popular as the band members of the Marshall Tucker Band during his tenure as road crew chief for them from 1973 until 1985. Along with other roadies like "Puff" and "Blackie," Moon was often talked about in countless press articles, and mentioned time and time again by Toy Caldwell and the other MTB members in radio and TV interviews.

Today, Moon operates MoonLite Cycles in Spartanburg, and back in 1999 he kindly agreed to an interview about those days gone by in which he was traveling the world and setting the stage for America's favorite "hillbilly band."

MBS: You guys all had nicknames. How'd you get the name "Moon"?

Moon: Toy actually tagged the nickname "Moon" on me; it came from a comic strip that ran up into the fifties. A lot of people named Mullins end up being called "Moon." Steve got the nickname "Puff" from a football game at Spartanburg High School years ago, something to do with a powder-puff game. And "Blackie" came from the fact that he always dressed in black, always wore a black t-shirt.

When did you go to work for the Marshall Tucker Band?

I was friends with Tommy after he got out of the service. We were both going to USC-S on the G.I. Bill, to collect that money. During that period of time was when the Marshall Tucker Band formed, and I went to work about 1973.

What was your primary job with the band?

I was responsible for stage right, taking care of Toy's guitars and stuff. You had to learn to tune them and all that stuff. Throughout the years, I basically did every job that was out there. It just happens that way.

But you were the head of the crew, right?

I was the production manager, stage manager—there are a lot of different names for it. I was with the band through 1984. But the job just rolled along. It expanded as the band got bigger and the crews got bigger. Somebody had to take charge and do all that advance work along with all the other. At the time, Puff and Blackie, neither one wanted the job, so it just kind of fell in my hands, quite by accident. After the Tucker Band, it all helped, because when you drop back into the club level, it's good to be able to mix sound or call lights. It all became handy after that. Like I said before, Toy was never hung up on where he played, and I was out with him after the Tucker Band, for about a year and a half or two years.

How did you guys decide who to hire?

The selection of the road crew mostly came about through Tommy. Basically, they picked hometown boys, not because of what they knew, but because of how they fit into the organization. It was important for everybody to get along, a real team effort. Tommy was pretty much the guiding light, as far as making sure you did your job. It went down from there. Me being the crew chief, my ass would get chewed, and it just worked its way on down. That was the best organization I ever worked in, that crew. Those guys were all friends. If a guy was having a bad day, everybody would pull up the slack for him. Same with you—if you were having a bad day, everybody would pitch in and cover for you.

Did you see Tommy Caldwell as the bandleader?

From the formation through his death, Tommy was the leader. Everything was a democratic process and put to a vote, but Tommy had the hands-on control. He was a dreamer, and he had a way of making you believe in his dreams. I think everybody in the band always gave the crew lots of credit. The crew was a necessary and important part of the organization. The promoters would take lots of shows because they knew they were going to have an event with no problems. We were there on time; the show closed down on time. The efficiency of the crew had a lot to do with it.

What do you remember about the European tour?

We'd gotten to the point where we had gotten a little spoiled here. Going over to Europe kind of dropped it back down to a family level, where everybody had to get along. We were traveling in close quarters. It all went well, as far as I remember. Johnny Lawson and I went over first. We were there for about ten days before they came. That was my gig throughout. I did a lot of advance work. Over there, we set up the rehearsal hall and set up transportation, got truck drivers and stuff. I was always involved in all of that.

What would you say was your high point with the band?

I suppose in the late '70s, Madison Square Garden, doing those big shows right before Tommy died. We did some big shows. I remember in Madison Square Garden, when the lights went down and all of those lighters went up, and there were thousands of straw cowboy hats out there. The electricity in the air made the hair on your arms stand up. That left a serious impression on me. The band didn't have that many bad nights. On their worst nights they were good. They were strong onstage.

Tell us a little about Toy Caldwell.

Toy was an absolute clown, with lots of two- or three-line jokes. So funny. But he was such a poet. Many nights I saw him write notes on toilet paper, Gideon Bibles, anywhere he could, just to have something to work off of the next day. His jokes were kind of the same way, you had to kind of just be there. Toy would give you anything. He took care of everybody. He took care of his family, and he wanted to share all his wealth and all his fun with everyone.

What was a typical day like in the life of a roadie or, in your case, the head roadie?

A typical day, as production manager... First, you go in that morning and meet with the union crew, whatever kind of crew is doing the show that day. You organize the union crew, then you go out to the bus and wake up the sound crew, because usually the stage is there on site. You wake up the sound crew, and they take about an hour and a half to two hours to set up. Then you wake up the lighting crew; they move in and set up the lighting stuff. Throughout this, you have to organize breakfast and be prepared for lunch. The band crew are the last ones in, and you finish up about lunchtime. After lunch, you have a soundcheck or a rehearsal, whichever one is appropriate. The band would come in at probably three or four to do a soundcheck. Then dinner, and on to the show at eight. After the show came a two- to three-hour loadout, two hours generally. Then on to the hotel to take a shower. The bus departed every night at three. So, it started for me at nine in the morning and went until three the next morning.

Not a lot of sleep time, huh?

We didn't need sleep; we were young. (Laughs)

How did the band manage to write and arrange songs while touring on a virtually non-stop basis?

Well, I roomed with Toy, so I got to see a lot more of how he went about writing songs. Generally, the way a song would appear was, Toy had a hook line or a riff he'd worked out on his guitar. He'd sit around and play, and come up with these great ideas. That's when you realized how funny he was. He'd be doing this serious song, and go off onto this silly shit, lyric-wise. But as he wrote all this, either me or somebody else would be jotting down notes for him. He'd come in to the show early the next day, usually at the steel guitar, or on his other guitar. He'd start messing around, putting things in order. As soon as that was done, the band would usually take an hour in the dressing room before the show, and that's when songs were usually worked up. It would work into soundchecks, where they'd work them up. They'd usually have songs worked up before studio time, although they could go through some dramatic changes. A country song could become a lot more than a country song. Everybody would come in and record their parts, with Doug and Jerry being the last ones in that process.

As far as your years with the band, any regrets?

Nope. I have no animosities toward anyone. I had twelve years of good work, got paid well, walked away with no problems with anybody. And seeing the world—it's a better education out there than you'd ever get in school.
•

Chris Hicks

1999

To be so young, Macon, Georgia's Chris Hicks has been around the Southern-rock block a few times, and in a big way. As guitarist and singer for the Outlaws and with a stint in the Marshall Tucker Band, and now as a solo artist, Hicks continues to amaze and astound with powerful blues vocals, smoldering-hot guitar work, and great songwriting. We caught up with the well-mannered and cordial Mr. Hicks back in 1999 at his home in Macon for an enlightening conversation.

MBS: Are you originally from Macon?

Chris: I was born in Lizella, Georgia. That's a small town right outside of Macon, about 20 miles or so. A real countrified little place, still is. It's grown up a little bit, but it's still very small compared to Macon. I have a lot of family out there and all. I started playing when I was 8 years old with my grandfather, who's still out there; he's 90 years old. We had a big jam with him a couple of weeks ago. He's a mandolin player. My mom sings and he plays mandolin. He's always played around and had his bluegrass bands. For a while I was playing with them, got a lot of playing time in at a real early age with that stuff. It wasn't really straight bluegrass; it was more like mountain or hillbilly music. There were a lot of the same songs, but more of a country-type arrangement. He's been my master teacher as far as learning how to play. He also plays guitar, and he kinda got me started on it.

Coming up through the teenage years, I started having my garage bands and playing the junior-senior proms. I actually worked a lot while I was in high school doing that, playing homecomings and different little sweetheart dances and things like that. We were always a rock-and-roll band. We were playing Marshall Tucker songs at the junior-senior. Luckily, there were still enough cool people when I was a junior in high school that still got into it. We got in a little trouble by not playing straight Top-40 songs, but we got away with it. You know how that kind of thing goes.

What was your first big break in music?

My first taste of the real thing was a band I had together called Loose Change. That was high school buddies that had a band that had changed faces and names and all that a few times through the years, but really a lot of the same guys played together for a long time. We started doing original music as well as some covers to get into the clubs and all. We started opening for bands like Charlie Daniels, and the Atlanta Rhythm Section, and the Outlaws. We were kind of the hot band in town, so we always got the opening ticket for a few years, as well as killing them in the clubs. We built us a little reputation and went to Muscle Shoals. Alan Walden was our manager then, and we recorded our album. We actually got an album on vinyl before they stopped doing that. It was released regionally and did okay—it didn't break no records, but it did okay. We did a single that was going to be on our second album. By this time we were doing some pretty good shows, playing the Cotton Club in Atlanta and things like that. The song was used in a Jim Varney movie called *Fast Foods.* That gave us a little spark and we got a little airplay. It was called "Love Is on the Line." It wasn't an "Ernest" movie, but he's always the same type of character. It was a college-type movie. And 96 Rock jumped on us and played us because of that.

So, we opened for the Outlaws a bunch at that time. At the time, Alan was also Hughie's (Thomasson) publisher, so I had known Hughie for a few years during this time and we'd get together and jam, and I'd sit in with the Outlaws. And when we'd go down to Muscle Shoals to record, Hughie and them would be down there a lot, too, so I would play on some of their tracks and they'd play on some of mine, mainly Hughie. We got to be big buddies and everything, which eventually led to him asking me to join the Outlaws in 1989.

So, we hooked up, and I still did a few dates that year with my band while playing with the Outlaws, and then we got going real well with the Outlaws and I ended up having to dissolve my band. I stayed with the Outlaws full time right up until the time I joined Marshall Tucker, really. I guess that was 1996, but we had kind of dissolved the Outlaws the year before that when Hughie joined Lynyrd Skynyrd. But we're still going to do a couple of more records.

Who, the Outlaws?

Yeah. We've been working on some demos. But I did a couple of records with them by then. We did *Diablo Canyon* and we did the live record, and I had songs on both of those. My role in the band had expanded to where we were doing some of my material as new Outlaws stuff, and I was getting a lot of freedom in it. I got to play and sing songs during the shows and on the record, so I was a real part of the band. That was a real fruitful time for me; we played about 200 dates a year between '89 and '95. During that time when I'd come off the road, I'd record a song or two with Paul Hornsby, who is a good friend of mine. We ended up with 20 to 25 pretty good tracks. So, I'd start playing around here and there, calling it "the Chris Hicks Band," and I started snooping around and got me a little record deal with Ichiban Records. That actually didn't come about until after we'd shut things down with the Outlaws. I put the band together during that year between Outlaws and Tucker, and we played steadily and did some good stuff, opened for a bunch of bands again. During that time is when Doug (Gray) called me. As a matter of fact, we had a date opening up for Marshall Tucker down in Florida. So, I was sitting at the house and I got a call from Doug. I thought he was probably calling about this date coming up, because I hadn't seen him in 6 to 8 months or so, but what it was, he was calling me to come in and help them out because Stuart (Swanlund) was having hand surgery. So, I said, "Sure, I can do it," and I jumped out there on the road and it ended up being a good situation for both of us, and I joined the Marshall Tucker Band for a year. Doug and all those guys have been real supportive. I kept my band together the whole time, and we opened up a few shows with them in the South. Doug really helped me out with my record deal, too. I was discussing all of these contracts, and Doug's good with those things so he gave me a lot of good advice on those things. I ended up leaving the band when we took the Christmas break, because my album was coming out, and I knew I needed to jump on that or it was just going to go nowhere. So, we talked about it, and I didn't want to leave and I don't think the guys wanted me to leave, but there just wasn't a good way to work it all out. So, we ended up shaking hands and deciding the best thing would be for me to get out and go ahead and get in this thing. As much as we all wanted to stay together, they really supported me in getting out and doing what I had to do. That's one of the things I love about those guys...they were like, "Man, do it! Anything we can do to help." And they have. They've thrown me dates here and there when I wanted to kind of be high-profile, or when they were just coming to town or whatever. That brings us to now. I am working on a second album for Ichiban. We're going to be finishing that up through the holidays and maybe put it out around St. Patrick's Day. That's usually a good time to come out with stuff. So, we are just working real hard with this band, trying to change the world one night at a time. We've been cutting a lot of live stuff, too, in hopes of putting it out either as a part of this album or as a third one. We're that type of band. We inherited a lot from the Allman Brothers and Marshall Tucker; we play them a lot better live.

I'd like to jump back for a minute and get you to share with us your fondest memories of playing with the Outlaws.

I have lots of good memories with them. Those guys were tons of fun. We stayed on the road all the time. We'd come home for a week or two. They were like Tucker—they played all the time. The "Southern Spirit Tour" was a good one, with Tucker and 38 Special and the Fabulous Thunderbirds and the Barefoot Servants. That was a big package tour that hit all the big amphitheaters across the country. That was a lot of fun because we toured with a lot of those bands, but not in a big traveling show like that. It was one big, rolling road show. And we were jamming every night with Tucker, me and Hughie. A lot of people were sitting in and jamming like it used to be. Van Zant was out of 38 a couple of nights and I got up and sang his parts, like on "Wild-Eyed Southern Boys"—and *nobody* sits in with 38, but before it was over they were pulling us out onstage to jam, too!

Same question. Your high points with the Marshall Tucker Band?

I had a lot of fun with them guys, too. I had toured with them and played with them before so much. I knew all the guys real well. A couple of highlights… I did a couple of TV shows with them. We did *Nashville Now*, and we did this Pay-per-View special out in Houston for 65,000 people. It was us and Charlie Daniels and Hank Williams, Jr., in the Astrodome. That was a ton of fun. They do a lot of outdoor stuff in the summertime that evokes memories of the way it used to be. It almost felt like the '70s to me, that same groove.

What are your memories of Toy Caldwell?

Toy was a dear friend of mine. I had cut a lot of tracks with him and was going to be on his second record. I don't know if they'll ever be released or not, but I sang on a couple of the songs. As a matter of fact, I was in the studio with him two nights before he passed away. We did a lot of dates with the Outlaws and Toy, and he'd always get up and jam with us and we'd jam with him. He always loved the way I sang. I used to sing a lot with him, and then after the record came out, I said, "Thanks a lot, man, you got Gregg Allman to sing my part!" (Laughs) I ribbed Toy about it, but he knew I was kidding about it.

Speaking of Volunteer Jam, I rode up there with Lynyrd Skynyrd the first time they played again. We ended up hanging out and partying, and Toy was there. I missed the little shuttle bus that came through to carry you back to the hotel, but a car stopped and picked me up. It was Stevie Ray Vaughn and his people. I sat down right next to Stevie Ray. Him and B.B. King and Toy had just got through jamming. That was far enough back where they still did a lot of jamming, and he had set everything on fire. I never got to know Stevie. That was my only encounter with him, but he was great.

Update: Chris has been back in the Marshall Tucker Band for many years now, writing many of the songs and keeping it real.

Mabron "Wolf" McKinney

2000

As a member of the Hour Glass, Wolf McKinney tasted stardom alongside Duane and Gregg Allman, Paul Hornsby, and Johnny Sandlin. Back at the turn of the century, Wolf kindly agreed to speak with us about his musical career.

MBS: Where are you originally from, Wolf?

Wolf: I am from Birmingham, but I've been living here in Fayette, which is about 35 miles west of Tuscaloosa, for going on 10 years now.

How did you first become interested in music?

We lived way out in the country, and we had a little ol' pearl-green Zenith radio, and the only thing you could pick up on it was country music, and I fell in love with it. I used to live for Saturday night and the Grand Ole Opry. Then when I was 12 years old, a man came 'round selling guitars and teaching lessons. Well, I wanted a steel guitar and Dad bought me a six-string Fender lap steel with a little Champ amp. I took to it like a duck to water; it was a natural instrument for me to play. I eventually got a double-neck 12-string, and eventually a single-neck 12-string with 4 pedals and a knee bar.

How did you come to meet the Five Minutes?

As I said, country music was all I heard, until I was a teenager. I loved Hank Williams, Bob Wills, Flat and Scruggs, Chet Atkins, Hank Snow, Ernest Tubb, people like that. I didn't hear my first blues record until I was about 15 years old. I was in my first band, the Rhythm Rockets, when I was 12 years old. It was basically a country/rock & roll/rockabilly band. By age 15 I joined a blues/rock & roll/rockabilly band called the Checkmates. The guitar player was really into blues and R&B; he even owned his own blues records. In the meantime, I had discovered the bass and fell in love with it. When we broke up, I went looking for a job as a bass player. My first few gigs, I borrowed a friend of mine's ol' cheap bass, till I could get me a Fender Jazz. I eventually got a Precision, too, and a Fender Bassman amp with two 12's. I always wanted a Showman with one 15, but I bought a car instead. I've played all the dives, from the Wig-Wams, the Southern Steak

House, the Hickory Pit, to the Allstate County Line Club. People came from all over the state to hear us play there. Then Jimmy Mitchell lured me to Huntsville to play rockabilly with his trio. His drummer, Ernie Bowman, was playing with Jerry Lee Lewis when they got kicked out of England. Jimmy did a lot of Jerry Lee.

That's where I was playing when Eddie Hinton, Johnny Sandlin, and Paul Hornsby came in looking for a bass player. They introduced themselves and said they had a band called the 5 Minutes. They played me some tapes, and I was sold. I wanted to play with these guys. They were great. Plus, they already had a tour booked. Mind you now, this was Saturday night and they were booked to play Louisville the following Monday night, which only gave me one full day and night to learn an entire new set of music, as I had never really played all R&B before, so it took me a while to get adjusted to that. And just as we were getting really tight, Eddie decided to go into the studio full time, with Marlin Green. I played with Eddie about five months.

How did you first meet Duane and Gregg?

During that time, we were booked to play the Briar Patch following the Allman Joys. They all got excited, because they wanted me to hear "Them" play! We left Paducah, Kentucky, in plenty of time to hear their last night. It was still cold and we were all huddled up in front of the club, waiting for them to get there. Finally, they come drivin' up in an old tan Chevy station-wagon. Duane was drivin', Gregg was in the passenger seat, Bill Connell and Bob Keller were in the back. They piled out and grabbed their instruments, briefcase, and drum bag. We went over to them as they were coming over to us. They exchanged hugs and greetings, and Paul said, "This is our new bass player, Mabron McKinney." Duane was standing right in front of me, in a long black leather coat. He sat his guitar case down and stepped back to get a good look at me. After several seconds he proudly proclaimed, "You're the Wolf!" Seeing as how, with all my hair, I did look like one, everybody thought it was a great name, and it has stuck with me and endured all these years—35, to be exact. Thanks, Duane!

That first night was like taking good mescaline for the first time. They just simply blew my shit away. I can still hear them doing "Spoonful" and "Tobacco Road," and "Walk Away Renee" would make your hair stand up on end. I had never seen such good raw talent before. They raised the use of dynamics to a new level. They were outstandingly great! Little did I know that less than 3 or 4 months later, I would actually be playing with them.

It just so happened that their drummer, Bill Connell, joined the Navy to keep from being drafted into the Army, at the same time we lost Eddie to the studio. We both used the same booking agency, One-Niters, and I suspect our agent, Bill Fennell, got word to Duane that we were available. We had exhausted a statewide search and were sittin' around Johnny's huge fireplace on the verge of abandonment, when the phone rang and it was Duane wanting to know if we would like to get together and jam and see what comes of it. Well, it didn't take Paul long to almost scream, "Hell, yes, man!" So, we got together at Fred Styles' house in Tuscaloosa—he was the Minutes' old bass player who left to go back to college. Afterward, we went back to Johnny's house in Decatur, set up our equipment in his garage, and practiced solid for two weeks.

What happened next?

When we were ready, we didn't know what to call ourselves, so, as I recall, Duane called Peppy's a Go Go in St. Louis and talked to the manager, who suggested that we go ahead and use the name "Allman Joys," seeing as how they already had a big following up there. When anyone ever asked who I played with, I always told them the Allman Joys, and they immediately knew who "They" were. In fact, when I ran into the Nitty Gritty Dirt Band at the airport, and invited them down to the club after their concert, I introduced us as "the Allman Joys."

Very cool.

They were great. During the course of the night, as Bill McEuen was trying to get us to come to Hollywood, he said he wanted to change our name to "the Hour Glass." I spoke with him recently, and he said that was a name that Liberty Records wanted to use, because they had an ad campaign planned around the name. But at the time, we all thought that it was a name Bill had chosen. So, when we got to Hollywood, we changed our name to "the Hour Glass," at the insistence of Bill and Liberty.

What albums did you play on?

I played on the very first Hour Glass album…he one with a collage of upside-down pictures, on a deep blue background, with a big yellow and red hour glass across the top. And the first record in the double white album, which was a re-release of both albums in one.

What do you remember about recording with Duane and Gregg and the guys?

I remember being scared as hell. I had never been in a studio in my life—to record original material, at that. I was very nervous, because of a problem, which I talk about in-depth in the book I've written called *Wolf and the Hour Glass.* Basically, I have a memory problem, brought on by a childhood trauma caused by polio that almost cost me my life, and did brain damage that I wasn't aware of until 30 years later. This caused delays in the studio, which gave me a huge insecurity problem, which exacerbated the problem even more. I just went sort of blank, to be perfectly candid. Think about it. Less than a year before, I was playing in some dives on the county line, where fights, brawls, and gunfights were the norm, to being in one of the absolute finest recording studios in the world, striving for absolute perfection. It was pretty scary, to say the least. I remember wanting to cry a lot, just hovering beneath the surface. I felt like a musically inept spastic on the verge of a nervous breakdown. My wife was asking me for a divorce over the phone, so mentally I wasn't doing so well, plus I was physically very ill, with what I now reflect on as probably being walking pneumonia. I coughed all the time, and blew my nose constantly, too. I honestly don't know why I didn't go to the doctor, but I didn't, and I didn't get any better. The band will back me up on this, as I was very ill in St. Louis, too, and did end up going to Dr. Woo, a bona fide heroin doctor, but that soon wore off, and I was physically, as well as mentally, a very sick puppy.

Wow. That had to be rough.

However, I do remember the day Dr. John played with us on several songs. He didn't even have a name for himself yet—he was just an L.A. side musician—but he seemed to sense that I was having trouble and he deliberately took up time with me, teaching me the bass lines on the piano that he knew I could play. They were simple lines, but were what needed to be there. There were at least 2 or 3 songs that I know he played on, because I remember him teaching me the bass lines. "So Much Love" was one, and at the moment I can't remember the others; but he had a calming effect on me, and gave me reassurance that I could do it, which I eventually did. I enjoyed having him there. He gave me confidence.

"Bells" was recorded using a telephone, and speaking into a grand piano with the sustain peddle held down, and a microphone underneath. We hated that song with a passion, but we were forced to do it anyway. We talked about breaking our contract because of it. In fact, most of those songs we didn't want to do, we were handed a box full of those small reel-to-reel tapes, and told, "Here—pick your new album." And they damn well meant it, too!

I was absolutely and totally surprised at how good Duane's voice was. This first album is the first time Duane's voice was ever recorded professionally, on "I've Been Trying." He did a great job, too. He never sang in the band. We didn't even know he could sing.

What was the high point of your tenure with Hour Glass?

The three months we were in St. Louis at Peppy's were the absolute best playing times of all, when we were the Allman Joys. We were good and tight there. I had a 200-watt silver Kustom amp with two cabinets and four-heavy duty bass speakers, and that baby would punch out notes like chocolate granite. I played a '63 Fender Jazz that was really sweet. I loved my Jazz.

Any other outstanding memories?

There was the time we played with the Doors—that was a blast. Although we were scared shitless, that was a good playing night. In my humble opinion, we blew the Doors off the stage. Duane even had me sing "I Ain't Got You"... "I got a 65 Cadillac, with a spare tire on the back, but I ain't got you, no, I ain't got you." I couldn't believe I pulled it off, but I did. That was the show when Duane flipped his Telecaster over his head and squeezed every drop of feedback out of his Vox amp he could get. When he was through, he just walked off the stage. At this point, I raked all my bass controls wide open, slipped out of my bass strap, and banged my bass as hard as I dared, to make all the strings vibrate, and leaned it against the amp, face first, and raked all of my amp controls wide open so that all of my strings were vibrating at their maximum. It sounded like a B-52 coming in for a landing, until Gooch, our roadie, unplugged them both so the Doors could play. (Laughs)

Cool. Very 1960s!

In the back alley before the show, Jim Morrison walked over to all of us, introduced himself, and stuck a balled-up handkerchief in our noses and said, "Breathe deeply!" It turned out to be animal tranquilizer, which would give you a very deep buzz when inhaled. He kept it over his microphone during their whole show.

We also played with the Grateful Dead, and someone stole Phil Lesh's bass. I loaned him mine to do the show.

We played the Whiskey with Buffalo Springfield and Canned Heat. After we played, I walked over and shook hands with and welcomed Sonny and Cher to the club. That freaked the band out that I actually did that. I think I even got a round of drinks from the band for that little act.

Tell us about the members of Hour Glass.

Johnny Sandlin was the quiet one, although he was very knowledgeable in the studio, as he had worked at Rick Hall's Fame Studio in Florence as a bass player and drummer, and he could engineer some, too. We all had nicknames, and his was "the Duck." He lives in the middle of a wildlife preserve in Decatur. Johnny had a gift for playing the drums and he knew exactly what needed to be played, anywhere in the song.

Paul Hornsby was the opinionated one. If he didn't like something he would tell you, in no uncertain terms, that he hated it—or he loved it. He was very business-minded and meticulous as well. He could play every instrument in the band except drums. His nickname was "the Berry." Go figure! I never really found out why, but it went way back to before I ever played with them.

Gregg was the shy one. He was friendly, yet shy at the same time. Girls fell for him every time. He and Duane had girlfriends out the wazoo! Gregg was a very generous person, too. He once gave me a nice, fur-lined suede-leather coat when it was wintertime and I was cold. I still have that coat. But Gregg was Duane's little bro, and therefore subservient to him. His nickname was "Harlow."

Duane was a stick of dynamite, a virtual powerhouse of energy and drive, that you very rarely ever see in a person. He was ready to go at a moment's notice. What time he wasn't relaxing and listening to some new music, he was constantly practicing his Tele, leaned back on the bed. He would practice for hours on end. When he walked, he tilted forward, put his head in the wind, and just went—even Gregg had to keep up. But for me, having had polio, it was real difficult to keep up with him. He was as likeable a young man as you would ever hope to meet, but he could be ruthless as well, when he had to. He was a no-nonsense guy, although he had a tremendous sense of humor and zest for life. He believed in living every day to the fullest; he tried his best to do just that. He never met a stranger. His nickname was "the Dog," because he reminded you of an Afghan.

Tell us about playing live with the band.

Well, actually, after we became the Hour Glass we weren't allowed to play but a minimum of gigs for fear of overexposure, which was absolutely stupid in my opinion, because we needed to build a loyal following, like we had in St. Louis, in order to sell the records. We did our best songs at Peppy's as the Allman Joys, because after that, the music practically stopped. Plus, I was beginning to completely shut down after we got to Hollywood. I was coming apart at the seams, and there was nothing I could do about it. But to answer your question, I actually don't remember doing any songs off the Hour Glass album onstage. I was asked to leave the band the very day we got our first box of albums, freshly off the press and in their covers. But in St. Louis, we rocked that house to its foundation.

In '71, I went back to St. Louis and Gas Light Square where it really all started, and our music is still reverberating out of that building and across the street at the In-Crowd, where we played a birthday party for a mutual Internet friend of ours, Karen Rocchio.

I could damn near get off on doing those old Allman Joy songs like "Tobacco Road," "Spoonful," "I'm a Man," and "Walk Away Renee." It was hair-raising. The dynamics were dramatic, if not revolutionary. Nobody could touch us at what we were doing. If they would have just left us alone, we could have captured the essence of the Allman Joys in the Hour Glass. What they got was an entirely different band from the one Bill and the Dirt Band fell in love with, and then begged us to come live in their enormous three-story house in Hollywood Hills. They wanted to capture our sound on tape, but it never quite happened that way. But I'm not bitter. In fact, I have a philosophy that I would like to share: "Everything is as it should be; otherwise, it wouldn't be."

Had I never been asked to leave, they might never have formed the Allman Brothers Band. Which is greater? The latter, of course. What a great loss to have never had them at all. Strange, the course of people's lives. Strange indeed. I was only there because of my good luck and the grace of God, beginning with Eddie Hinton and his desperate need for an immediate bass player. Plus, I knew if I was ever going to make it big, I was going to have to go on the road, and this was my big chance to maybe do something with my life—be successful at the only thing I ever wanted to do, and that was play music. I figured I would go to my grave a musician. Little did I know.

Do you have any fun stories you'd like to share about Hour Glass?

Once, when we first got together and were still practicing in Johnny's garage, before we went to St. Louis and Peppy's, Duane got it in his head that he wanted to shoot a B.B. gun. So, we all piled in the car and went down to Johnny's dad's hardware store and bought a couple of B.B. guns, and about 5 lbs. of B.B.'s. We came back home to Johnny's house and were shooting up everything in the backyard, except for one glass-sided birdhouse with a wooden roof on it.

I was standing right next to Duane when he pulled down a bead on that birdhouse and squeezed off a round. Well, that B.B. ricocheted straight back and popped me right in the center of my forehead, right between the eyes. Everybody thought that was very funny, although it could have been dangerous, but we all laughed like hell. I think we put the guns away after that.

What was the biggest show you ever played?

The biggest show I ever played with the Hour Glass was the Hullabaloo, where we played with the Doors, the Grateful Dead, the Dirt Band, and the Sunshine Company. There were probably 3,000 people there. I enjoyed playing the Whiskey, too, but it only holds maybe 300 people. We got to see Cream's debut performance in America there at the Whiskey. That was a real treat. We were sitting dead center about 20 feet back from the stage. Duane never took his eyes off of Clapton for even a second. He now knew he had competition, which drove him even harder to become even better. Duane was like a gunslinger at heart. He wanted to be the best that he knew he could be and, in doing so, become the best guitar player in the world! The only thing I remember him saying was, "Man, that fucker is good!"

Did you ever play the Fillmore with them?

I wasn't with them long enough to play the Fillmore, or Winterland. We only played about five or six gigs as the Hour Glass while I was with them in Hollywood, and they were mostly out-of-the-way clubs in the hills.

One interesting side note…I actually talked to, danced with, and had drinks with Sharon Tate. I remember Manson and some of his followers hanging around the club. He later had the bagpipe player killed, who worked there during our breaks. He and about three of his followers came over to our apartment complex one day, and Gooch (our roadie) called them communists and ran them off.

What kind of music do you like listening to today?

When I'm in my car, I listen to classical and jazz. When I'm home, I enjoy listening to "Bama Bluegrass," "The Grateful Dead Hour," and "Blues Before Sunrise." As far as CDs go, I enjoy listening to the Allman Brothers, of course...Eric Clapton, Bob Dylan, and especially old blues or bluegrass songs.

What caused the Hour Glass to break up?

This is the question that I have feared the most, because the Hour Glass did not end with me. I was asked to leave and Bob Keller was to take my place, but he didn't feel right about it, and simply split town without telling them. And Pete Carr got the job by default, and he didn't even play bass either. I applauded you for having the balls to do that, Pete. That took a hell of a lot of courage, and you have continued to grow and produce and I am very proud of you. You always were a great musician, even when I knew you.

I was with Johnny and Paul for one year, and Gregg and Duane for about seven months. They continued on as a band with Pete for about a year, I suppose.

What did you do after Hour Glass?

In 1975, I was wiped out by a fire that destroyed my home and my instruments. I never did fully recover from that. I lost about 1,000 old albums. I don't even have an Hour Glass album; they were all lost in the fire.

It was just as well, because I have been an alcoholic since my first drink at about age 15. I am also a potential drug abuser. In reality, I didn't need to be playing in or being around clubs. So, I eventually quit playing music altogether.

I have since become a broker for AmeriPlan/Well Point. It is the only company that I can say I truly believe in, and is helping people save money.

What were you telling me about some wrong information about you in the Allman Brothers book?

In Scott Freeman's book *Midnight Riders*, he was interviewing Paul Hornsby, and he forgot and left his pause-button on. When he got home, he had to try and recall the interview from memory, so in chapter 2 he got it all wrong. For one thing, he accused me of deserting the band an hour before a big gig at the Whiskey, quitting the band without telling them, and flying back to Daytona. That simply never happened with me. He was referring to Bob Keller.

Now, Marley Brant has written *Southern Rockers*. In her book, she used Scott's book for some of her reference material, and she repeated the same misstatement about me again. So, in order to correct these misstatements about me, I simply wrote my own book. It is the only book written by a founding member of the Hour Glass. I tell lots of interesting stories that were not in either of their books. I tell the *true* story.

In part 1, I tell how the band was formed, how we evolved, and how I ended up leaving the band. Part 2 tells the story about "Life after the Hour Glass," and how I went to St. Louis and Peppy's and the In-Crowd on a spiritual soul-searching trip down Route 66, and ended up living in several monasteries. For the most part, life after the Hour Glass has been a living hell. But I wouldn't take even one minute away from the entire experience. I will treasure it for the rest of my life. If you want to know the real truth about that period of history, buy my book, *Wolf and the Hour Glass,* when it comes out. I am in the process of trying to find an agent and a publishing company. Part 2 is being edited now, so I'm hoping that maybe it won't be too much longer until it is finally published.

Do you ever see the old band members?

I have seen Gregg several times, when they play the Oak Mountain Amphitheater in Birmingham. I haven't seen Paul but once since I left the band 33 years ago, and that was at Duane's funeral, but I have talked to him on the phone, and we have exchanged e-mails several times.

So, what do you do these days, Wolf?

I am disabled with polio, a bad back, and a rare disease called "Restless Leg Syndrome." I am in a great deal of pain most of the time. I bought this computer to write my book, and to learn how to make money on the Internet. My next project is learning how to design and build websites for myself and other people. It will be called "Medium of Expression" website designs.

My wife is also disabled with brain damage from an auto accident that she had without her seatbelt on. So, we spend 24/7 together. Fortunately, we are soulmates, and after nine years are still very happy together. She is an artist as well, who loves to cross-stitch some of the most difficult patterns of all. I am trying to get her to do freehand cross-stitch. She does some of the most intricate stitches imaginable. Her pen-and-ink drawings are absolutely incredible.

Anything you'd like to say to your fans?

I love you all, and thanks for remembering me. Walk with the Great Spirit. •

Author's Note

Michael Buffalo Smith is a writer and musician from Upstate, South Carolina. He is a Southern music historian and founder of The Southern Rock Hall of Fame & Museum, as well as publisher of *Kudzoo* magazine. This is his fourth book on Southern music for Mercer University Press, and his ninth book overall. His latest album, *Makin' It Back to Macon*, was produced by famed Capricorn Records producer Paul Hornsby, who happens to be the subject of his next book. For more on the author visit his official website at www.michaelbuffalo.net.

Index